STUDENTS WITH BOTH GIFTS AND LEARNING DISABILITIES

Identification, Assessment, and Outcomes

NEUROPSYCHOLOGY AND COGNITION

VOLUME 25

The purpose of the Neuropsychology and Cognition series is to bring out volumes that promote understanding in topics relating brain and behavior. It is intended for use by both clinicians and research scientists in the fields of neuropsychology, cognitive psychology, psycholinguistics, speech and hearing, as well as eduction. Examples of topics to be covered in this series would relate memory, language acquisition and breakdown, reading, attention, developing and aging brain. By addressing the theoretical, empirical, and applied aspects of brain-behavior relationships, this series will try to present the information in the files of neuropsychology and cognition in a coherent manner.

The titles published in this series are listed at the end of this volume.

STUDENTS WITH BOTH GIFTS AND LEARNING DISABILITIES
Identification, Assessment, and Outcomes

Edited by

Tina M. Newman and Robert J. Sternberg

PACE Center, Yale University
New Haven, Connecticut

Kluwer Academic / Plenum Publishers
New York / Boston / Dordrecht / London / Moscow

ISBN 0-306-48379-3

©2004 Kluwer Academic / Plenum Publishers, New York
233 Spring Street, New York, New York 10013

http://www.wkap.nl/

10   9   8   7   6   5   4   3   2   1

A C.I.P. record for this book is available from the Library of Congress.

Permissions for books published in Europe: *permissions@wkap.nl*
Permissions for books published in the United States of America: *permissions@wkap.com*

Printed in the United States of America

9/3/11

CONTRIBUTORS

P. G. Aaron, Department of Educational and School Psychology, School of Education, Indiana State University, Terra Haute, Indiana 47809

Susan M. Baum, College of New Rochelle,1 Castle Place, New Rochelle, New York 10805

Melissa A. Bray, University of Connecticut, Neag School of Education, 2131 Hillside Road, Unit 3007 Storrs, Connecticut, 06269-3007

Linda E. Brody, Johns Hopkins University, Center for Talented Youth, 3400 North Charles Street, Baltimore, Maryland 21218

Elena L. Grigorenko, PACE Center, Department of Psychology, Yale University,PO Box 208358, New Haven, Connecticut 06520-8358

R. Malatesha Joshi, College of Education, Texas A & M University, College Station, Texas 77843-4232

Thomas J. Kehle, University of Connecticut, Neag School of Education, 2131 Hillside Road Unit 3007, Storrs, Connecticut 06269-3007

Carol A. Layton, College of Education, Texas Tech University, Lubbock, Texas 79409

Judy L. Lupart, Faculty of Education, The University of Calgary, 2500 University Drive N.W., Calgary, Alberta, Canada, T2N 1N4

D. Betsy McCoach, University of Connecticut, Neag School of Education, 2131 Hillside Road, Unit 3007, Storrs, Connecticut, 06269-3007

Carol J. Mills, Johns Hopkins University, Center for Talented Youth, 3400 North Charles Street, Baltimore, Maryland 21218

Kate Nation, Department of Experimental Psychology, St. John's College, Oxford University,St. Giles, Oxford, England OX1 3JP

Tia M. Newman, PACE Center, Department of Psychology, Yale University Box 208358, New Haven, Connecticut 06520-8358

Emily S. Ocker, College of Education, Texas A & M University, College Station, Texas 77843-4232

Sally M. Reis, NEAG School of Education, University of Connecticut, 249 Glenbrook Road, Storrs, Connecticut, 06269-2064

Lilia M. Ruban, College of Education, Department of Curriculum and Instruction, University of Houston, 256 Farish Hall, Houston, Texas 77204-5023

Del Siegle, University of Connecticut, Neag School of Education, 2131 Hillside Road Unit 3007, Storrs, Connecticut 06269-3007

Robert J. Sternberg, PACE Center, Department of Psychology, Yale University, PO Box 208358, New Haven, Connecticut 06520-8358

Mary K. Tallent-Runnels, College of Education, Texas Tech University, Lubbock, Texas 79409

Catya von Károlyi, Department of Psychology, University of Wisconsin-Eau Claire, Eau Claire WI 54702-4004

Ellen Winner, Department of Psychology, Boston College, Chestnut Hill, Massachusetts 02167-3807

PREFACE

We were motivated to edit this book when we began to hear stories of exceptional students who were struggling with reading, writing, or math, but who could solve seemingly any problem with computers, or build the most intricate structures with Legos, or could draw beautiful pictures, or could tell the most creative stories but ended up in tears when asked to write it out. How is it possible to have so much talent in some areas and yet to appear to have a disability in another? What resources are available for these students? How can we ensure that these students' abilities are nurtured and developed? Our goal in this book is to provide ideas and possibly even tentative answers for educators and to stimulate more questions to be answered by researchers.

We have ourselves been addressing related questions for some time. Our group at the PACE Center at Yale has explored the development of abilities, competencies and expertise that allow people to be successful in life. Through this work, we have collaborated with school districts and other educators and researchers across the country to expand the notion of what is traditionally thought of as intelligence. We use the concept of successful intelligence to allow for the possibility that the skills traditionally taught in school are not the only ones, and often not even the most important ones, that allow people to be successful in the world. This notion has excited educators who see children in their classrooms who have enormous talent or potential for great ability in a domain that is less valued within the constraints of the traditional curriculum. In particular, this concept leads many teachers and parents to think of the children who struggle in the classroom, but who shine in creative tasks or show leadership skills or wisdom beyond their years.

While the past 25 years has seen a growing interest in students with both gifts and learning disabilities, the published literature has focused predominantly on students who have only one area of gifts—high IQ. Through this volume we have tried to provide the reader with a broader conceptualization of the gifted/LD learner to include students who have gifts in other domains and who would benefit from being identified and having their talents nurtured.

In compiling this volume, we realized the potential it had to inform educators at the elementary, secondary, and college levels, including preservice teachers, special and regular education teachers, gifted coordinators, college resource centers, and educational administrators who may have seen students with unusual learning profiles, and who are looking to have a better understanding of their learning. In addition, this volume holds resources for both education and psychology researchers to inform the state of research in this area and to provide the impetus for future work. Finally, we feel that this volume offers information for families, including parents and students who have differential learning profiles and who are looking for a better understanding of what this means for them.

We would like to thank the contributors to this volume who have devoted their time and abilities to this important issue. The chapter authors have provided a range of expertise that makes this volume both interesting and informative for educators, parents, students, and researchers. In addition, many people at the PACE Center contributed to the successful completion of this book, especially Robyn Rissman, Sara Bozzuto, and Brad Walters, who spent considerable time editing and formatting the contents of this volume. Finally, we would like to thank Elena Grigorenko, who first suggested that this volume be compiled.

Preparation of this book was supported by a grant under the Javits Act Program (Grant No. R206R000001) as administered by the Institute of Educational Sciences, formerly the Office of Educational Research and Improvement, U.S. Department of Education. Grantees undertaking such projects are encouraged to express freely their professional judgment. This volume, therefore, does not necessarily represent the position or policies of the Institute of Educational Sciences, or the U.S. Department of Education, and no official endorsement should be inferred.

We hope you will find this volume both enjoyable and stimulating.

Tina M. Newman and Robert J. Sternberg

CONTENTS

INTRODUCTION

Susan M. Baum
College of New Rochelle

Can students be both gifted and learning disabled? What are their characteristics and how can we meet their needs? These questions have haunted the field for over 30 years. Professionals concerned with the plight of these youngsters have written extensively supporting the idea of bright children who simultaneously struggle with school (Baum, Cooper, & Neu, 2001; Baum, Owen & Dixon, 1991; Fox, Brody, & Tobin, 1983; Maker, 1977; Reis et al; 1995; Whitmore, 1980; Whitmore & Maker, 1985). While this work has made a difference for many youngsters, others remain underserved and misunderstood. The following excerpt describes the frustration faced by many families who live with youngsters who are doubly different—exhibiting intellectual prowess on the one hand and struggling with academic tasks on the other.

"I was appalled to hear the principal discourage one of my twice-exceptional sons from taking honors math in 7th grade next year because of his attention and organizational difficulties. I was told that his special education services do not apply to this honors class "because it's an accelerated class" even though the team agreed that my son could easily handle the curriculum content and the pace of the concept introduction. The principal argued that he will probably have some difficulty with the 45 minutes of nightly homework and it will tax his weak organizational skills.

"I suggested that we come up with creative supports for him, i.e. e-mailing or faxing homework so that it doesn't get lost. I was told that if he needs accommodations, that he doesn't belong in the accelerated class. Can they deny him gifted and talented services on the basis of a disability? Are they misinformed, ignorant, or arrogant?

"We are losing our minds trying to work within the system but our children, especially the twice-exceptional ones, are truly suffering. "I love to learn but I hate school" has been my older son's battle cry, and it breaks my heart. I am a pediatrician with a strong background in child development and behavior, yet they won't listen to me about my boys' needs or anyone else's for that matter... I advocate for hundreds of students in my practice...anyway thanks for your time."

Geralyn Szuba, MD

This ongoing struggle to recognize and serve twice-exceptional students may be the result of looking at the two populations of students—gifted and talented and students with special needs separately. It was not until about 25 years ago, with the publication of *Providing Programs for the Gifted Handicapped* (Maker, 1977) that we were first introduced to the seemingly paradoxical notion of twice-exceptional children. This seminal work appeared at a time when both special education and education of the gifted and talented were priorities in the educational theater. Major legislation during the 1970s forever changed the landscape of who was eligible to receive a free and appropriate education, especially for students with unique learning needs. The 1975 Public Law 94-142, *The Education of All Handicapped Children Act,* mandated an appropriate education for students with disabilities. This legislation provided criteria for identifying students with disabilities and required teams of professionals to design individual educational plans for each identified student. These plans would be carefully monitored, and schools would be held accountable for reaching the educational goals and objectives stated in the plans. The act assured parents' rights of due process and their active participation in developing the educational plans for their children.

Students with gifts and talents, however, were not included under this legislation. Instead, Public Law 95-561 was passed in 1971 and revised in 1978 to address the need for education of gifted and talented students. Unlike the special education law, this law did not provide a mandate. It provided a definition of "gifted and talented" and indicated that identified students require additional services to develop their unique gifts and talents. Parents, however, were not afforded legal rights to assure gifted education for their youngsters. In fact, under this legislation, gifted students receive services at the discretion of state or local policies.

Cursory understandings of these separate educational policies as well as stereotypical views of students with disabilities and students with gifts and talents seemed to obscure the reality that some students could indeed fall under both regulations. For some, the notion of being gifted and disabled was impossible. It appeared unorthodox and careless to label someone gifted and talented if they could not read or write. Furthermore, because gifted education is not a mandate, identifying such children would only assure their special education needs were met with no accommodations for their superior abilities and talents.

Maker's book drew attention to the idea that students could indeed be twice exceptional—gifted and talented in specific areas, while disabled in others—and therefore require attention to both areas of exceptionality. Researchers and professionals, mainly from gifted education, found this idea appealing and followed this line of inquiry, which resulted in a growing number of publications on this topic. Special programs to meet the dual needs of these youngsters began to appear (Baldwin & Gargiulo, 1983; Baum, Cooper, & Neu, 2001; Baum, Owen, & Dixon, 1991; Neilson, Higgins,

Wilkenson, & Webb, 1994; Weinfeld, Barnes-Robinson, Jeweler, & Shevitz, 2002).

Although the field is amassing a well-researched knowledge base outlining the needs of these youngsters, many are not identified, and if they are, it is for one or the other exceptionality. (Baum, Cooper, & Neu, 2001; Brody & Mills, 1997;Reis et al, 1995; Richart, 1997; Yewchuk & Lupart, 1996). Even worse, the lack of knowledge about the consequences of the coincidence of gifts and disabilities has resulted in misidentification and inappropriate services for far too many youngsters, leading to serious emotional and behavioral problems among gifted/learning-disabled youngsters. (Baum & Olenchak, 2002).

A CASE IN POINT: MARK'S STORY

Consider the case of Mark, an extremely bright 11-year-old who thinks deeply and can express his ideas poetically. His full-scale IQ measures 137; his Verbal IQ 128 and Performance IQ 140. Mark has extraordinary spatial abilities. He has been an expert at building structures and putting together complex puzzles since toddlerhood. However, he has never been able to memorize his multiplication tables and still counts on his fingers. He has poor organizational skills and difficulty with handwriting. As a result he often resists putting his ideas down in writing. The poem below is a recent example of his abstract understanding and gift with words.

TIME

Time runs at its own speed,
Never stopping, never waiting.
It goes like the wind on a stormy day,
Like old friends when they pass away.
Time is a killer,
But still it gives life,
It comes and it goes,
Be it the day or the night.
It does not appeal to the average person,
But they do not think as I do.
For me time goes by like I first learned to walk just yesterday,
An eternity of life slipping through my grasp,
Like I could have done more with my life.
Like it wasted away,
Like the time I had,
Was just another day.
So I want you to think,
Before your day is over,

To remember it only comes once.
So, What will you do with your time?

−Anonymous 5th Grader, 2003

Mark is now in the fifth grade in a regular classroom, succeeding relatively well after years of erroneous diagnoses, harmful medications, and inappropriate learning environments and interventions. Sadly, even though he is succeeding, his parents claim that he has lost his love of learning.

How sad it is to me that Mark seems to have lost so much of his motivation to learn. When he was four and five years old he used to get into bed with workbooks at night doing story problems and things like that. Now all he cares about is not being different. He has become so tired of adult intervention, being pulled out, treated differently He doesn't want to hear the words "gifted" or "twice-exceptional." He just wants to be left alone and be a regular kid. He's been overworked by a system that wants him to fit in and be like everyone else to the point that the majority of his day is spent singling him out, pulling him out, and pointing out what is wrong.

The Early Years

Mark's disabilities were never noted by the professionals. It was his behavior that became the focus of diagnoses and interventions. In preschool he was often frustrated by the rules and the readiness curriculum. He wanted to be in charge when playing with his classmates—typical behavior for many bright preschoolers. He would cry easily when he did not get his way. The teacher suspected that he had ADHD. His parents had him tested when he was barely four. He was not cooperative, as he wanted to give different answers to the questions in more creative ways. The psychologist reported that the results of the test were inconclusive and not what he believed to be an accurate assessment of his intelligence "It is unclear as to whether his style is a result of an oppositional test-taking attitude or a sign of creativity. It is recommended that Mark's behavior both at home and in the classroom be monitored to decide if this behavior is based upon a low frustration tolerance, creativity, or boredom."

The Impact of School

When Mark began kindergarten things worsened. He refused to do the work requested, and he had tantrums in the classroom. His teacher reported that he was bright and participated eagerly in group discussions, but he did not want to do his work: math packets and other readiness worksheets. He was disruptive, controlling, made noises annoying the other students, and was frustrated easily. Mark's parents took him to a social worker, whose opinion was that these behaviors may be due, in part, to boredom. His teacher viewed this with great disbelief: "How can he be bored, he never does anything?" The social worker suggested that with Mark's personality, giving him choices might improve the climate for learning and his willingness to comply. Even this suggestion was misinterpreted for, when Mark refused to do his work, the teacher provided the choice but as a threat: "You can do the math packet, or you can go sit in the principal's office." Behavior modification strategies were not successful in controlling Mark's inappropriate behavior. His superior academic ability was ignored in favor of his disruptive behavior. "We don't have to talk about how Mark is doing academically. We do need to talk about his behavior" was the typical comment at parent conferences.

As the situation became more volatile, Mark's parents consulted a psychiatrist. Even his superior score of on the WPPSI of 148 was considered depressed due to his anxiety during testing. The psychologist felt Mark had emotional issues interfering with his performance. She described him "as having a Ferrari parked in his driveway but he was still riding a tricycle." She was concerned that some of his difficulty may have been related to epilepsy and placed him on medication.

Ongoing school problems and the increasing occurrence of destructive behaviors caused the psychiatrist to alter the diagnosis; in addition to the diagnosis of epilepsy she now added, ADHD, OCD, ODD, tic and bi-polar disorders, and psychosis (added to the Tegretol, she prescribed a cocktail of micro-doses of the following: Neurontin, Seroquel, Risperdal, Eskalith and Thorazine.) Mark's behavior worsened and he was placed on Dexedrine and Clonodine. His parents felt that the medication regimen was actually harming Mark, and questioned the diagnosis. They wondered if his frustration, noncompliance, and outbursts were severe anxiety attacks, not seizures or psychotic episodes, and told his doctor that they no longer wanted him on all the medication. Most of the medication was removed and things appeared stable.

The school had identified Mark as having other health impairments (OHI) and placed him in a special school setting for children who were lower functioning and had severe emotional problems. The small class size was helpful, however, with no intellectual peers or positive role models, social and behavioral issues remained a challenge. One teacher did notice that when Mark was academically accelerated he had no difficulty staying on task and completing work. But that observation did not encourage the school to find opportunities where Mark could interact with his intellectual or even "normal" peers. In fact, because he often read ahead when his classmates were struggling with decoding and comprehension, the teacher stapled the pages together leaving accessible only the ones that the group was discussing. His teacher interpreted this practice as another example of his defiant behavior and unwillingness to follow rules. It is apparent that the teacher had little understanding of the needs of gifted students and felt her major role in Mark's life was to help him to become more compliant.

In addition, Mark's Individual Educational Plan (IEP) reflected little sensitivity to his high level of academic potential and performance. For instance, many objectives focused on the mastery of below and on-grade level skill and the preparation of materials and assignments, even though testing indicated higher levels of functioning and written documentation by his teacher attested to the fact that he was well prepared in class.

A Change for the Better

Finally, in fourth grade, Mark's family sought out an educational psychologist who was familiar with students who were both gifted and learning disabled. She did find discrepancies between high abilities in some areas and problematic weaknesses in others, such as discerning orthographic patterns, handwriting difficulties, and his inability to memorize math facts and algorithms, especially when presented without conceptual meaning. She found the restrictiveness of the environment harmful to Mark. Among her comprehensive list of recommendations was the need for Mark to attend to his gifts and talents and receive specific strategies to overcome his learning difficulties.

"Above all else, Mark needs a rich curriculum with the opportunity to explore and use his intellectual resources to understand. Teaching by rote has impeded Mark's ability to use his high abilities to problem solve and synthesize information." The psychologist suggested that most of his resistance resulted from being forced to do things that had no meaning for him. "A crucial part of an appropriate curriculum for him should be intentionally planned opportunities for him to develop his interests. This is essential to his regaining enough trust in his school environment to be willing to abide by school rules without viewing compliance as a defeat for him."

In essence, for students like Mark, education too often becomes a battle for control and compliance. In Mark's case no one recognized or chose to focus on his gifts or understood the needs of a gifted student. The team used strategies typical of more disabled students who don't also "suffer" from extraordinary gifts and talents. For these professionals medication and behavioral strategies are typical and often successful interventions. In truth, Mark's disruptive behavior and his ability to compensate for some of his academic difficulties obscured the reality of his learning difficulties. If the team expanded its perspective by considering the information that is available, Mark's journey may have avoided the potholes, detours, and hazards along the way.

IDENTIFICATION OF ISSUES, ESSENTIAL QUESTIONS, AND KNOWLEDGE

Over the past 20 years, my colleagues and I have gained much information about the major issues facing this special population of students (Baum, 1985; Baum, Cooper, & Neu, 2001; Baum, Dixon, Emerick, & Herman, 1989; Baum & Olenchak; 2002; Baum, Olenchak, & Owen, 1998; Baum & Owen, 2003; Baum, Owen, & Dixon, 1991). The outline below provides an overview of the issues, essential questions, and what we have learned in response to the questions. Many of these ideas are revisited, explored, extended, and elaborated upon in the collection of chapters assembled in this volume.

Issue: Appropriate Identification

Essential Questions:

• How do we discover gifts and talents among students who are severely learning disabled and unable to read or write?
• How can we identify learning disabilities among gifted students, especially when they may be achieving at grade level and there is no evidence of a significant discrepancy between achievement and potential?

What We Have Learned:

• Multiple sources must be used to identify students' disabilities and gifts. The use of both quantitative and qualitative information to document performance provides information about product and process that relates to characteristics of this special population of students. (See Reis et al., 1995, for an extensive list of synthesis of characteristics.) It is necessary to document how students are achieving, strategies used to compensate, time it takes to complete classroom tasks, and assistance needed in school and at home to measure the discrepancy between ability and performance compared to intellectual peers.
• Authentic identification of specific gifts and talents using performance and product assessments can provide evidence of extraordinary abilities. Looking for talents in specific domains is preferable to assessing general intellectual abilities; and subtest analyses of individual intelligence tests are helpful in understanding learning patterns of twice-exceptional youngsters.
• Using assessment techniques based on theories of multiple intelligences (Sternberg, 1981; Gardner, 1999) can underscore the

discrepancies between cognitive strengths and weaknesses as well as identify gifts and talents.

Issue: The Need for Talent Development

Essential Questions:

* Why is talent development important?
* How can students' gifts be addressed especially if there is no mandate for providing gifted services in most states?

What We Have Learned:

* Focused attention to students' gifts builds self-efficacy, self-regulation, and a positive sense of self. It provides an opportunity to see how these students learn naturally. During talent-development opportunities, students are more receptive to learning new self-regulation strategies.
* Talent development provides a creative outlet to cope with the emotional concomitants of being doubly different.
* Improvement in overall achievement most often results when students are producing in an area of talent.
* Developing the students' talents will best prepare them for adult success. Talent-development opportunities can be provided in advanced classes, special programs, mentorships, internships, and independent studies.

Issue: Providing Least Restrictive Environments

Essential Questions:

* Where are these students best served?
* What are the elements of a supportive environments?

What We Have Learned:

* A least restrictive environment for gifted/learning-disabled students is one where they can learn with their intellectual peers, especially in areas of talent. Opportunities may include honors classes, enrichment programs, AP classes, online courses, and college courses.

• These students can achieve in regular classrooms where teachers are sensitive to and honor individual differences, and applaud and encourage diversity in how students learn and communicate knowledge.

• For some students, the best settings are full-time special programs where all students have talents and experience learning challenges.

• The best environments include small class settings where teacher talk is minimized, and experiential learning is encouraged.

• The best instruction includes project learning, problem-based learning, lively discussions, and simulations. Arts integration is especially suitable for students talented in nonverbal areas.

Issue: The Provision of Remediation and Compensation Strategies

Essential Questions:

• Which kinds of remediation are required?
• What are appropriate accommodations that allow students to compensate for problematic weaknesses?

What We Have Learned:

• Students need specific remedial instruction in basic skills in areas of their disability—reading, writing, spelling, and mathematics. Programs chosen should align to students' learning strengths.

• Teachers must offer students accommodations to counteract problems caused by the disability. These may include more time on tests, books on tape, use of technology (especially for writing). Students who achieve despite their learning disabilities have developed compensation strategies to confront problematic weaknesses. These strategies are unique for each student and seem to align to their strengths and personalities.

Issue : The Need for Social and Emotional Support

Essential Questions:

• How does the cross-pollination of being gifted and learning disabled impact the social and emotional development of these students?
• What kinds of supports are needed?

What We Have Learned:

• Gifted/learning-disabled students must often function and survive in an unfriendly world where they are judged and judge themselves according to what they can't do.

• Feelings of inferiority and poor academic self-efficacy may result in behavioral responses that divert attention away from their lack of academic prowess or lack of self-confidence.

• Exhibiting appropriate social skills within a hostile milieu is an unreasonable expectation. In fact, poor social skills and negative behaviors may be protecting gifted/learning-disabled students from their academic and emotional vulnerabilities.

• These same students seem completely transformed in situations when they are performing in an area of strength. Under these circumstances, they become considerate, confident, and caring. Parents and counselors must provide emotional support for these youngsters. Parents must advocate for their children in order to assure appropriate services in school as well as to help their children deal with their frustrations. Counselors must work with the students to develop strategies to help them overcome or cope with their issues and assist them in setting goals that accentuate their gifts and talents.

CHALLENGES

The question becomes, then, why, with the knowledge we have, do we still find students underserved and, in some cases, harmed by professionals who mean well? Why was the mother mentioned above thwarted in and frustrated by her attempts to assure her children appropriate services? Why was Mark's story fraught with disaster at every turn? To understand this, we must consider philosophical, practical, and legal policies that impede appropriate services for these students. Professionals still challenge the research behind the idea that students can be simultaneously gifted and learning disabled and need different services (Vaughn, 1989). Worse, with the *"No Child Left Behind"* mentality, services will tend to focus on remediation of basic skills when we know that gifted/learning-disabled students thrive in programs based on a strength-based philosophy. An educational approach based on singular attention to remediation for gifted/learning-disabled students will negatively impact their development.

Even if this construct is viable, professionals often question the practicality of providing educational support for students who are not achieving below grade level. Many gifted/learning-disabled students do not fall below grade level for many years because they can compensate for their weaknesses when the curriculum is simple; others struggle to maintain their grade level or above grade level performance, often at great social and emotional costs. Testing may not reveal significant discrepancies between potential and achievement until these youngsters advance to middle or high school, when their compensation strategies begin to fail them (Baum & Owen, in press). By this time, these youngsters' academic self-efficacy is greatly compromised and positive aspirations about a productive future have dimmed.

Coupled with the under-identification of the disability is the reluctance to provide a challenging curriculum for high-ability students who have academic challenges. Legally, as mentioned previously, most schools are not mandated to provide gifted services and parents remain frustrated in their attempts to have schools meet their children's talent development needs. The more information that we can provide, in as many different ways and venues as possible, is our primary weapon to fight the ignorance and provincial attitudes that hinder the chances that these students will be served. This scholarly anthology highlights and extends many of the major themes and issues mentioned above. The chapters reflect core issues that express our efforts to understand conceptual and theoretical challenges, our attempts to clarify and sort out areas of confusion and concern, and to undertake the challenges to provide research-based practice aimed at serving the needs of this special population. The issues under investigation involve identification and assessment, cognitive profiles that characterize the population of students, and successful interventions that enhance development of the individuals on their journey from novice to expert

LOOKING AHEAD: BOOK OVERVIEW

This volume addresses three main issues:

Issue 1, *Identification & Assessment*, explores the critical issues surrounding identification and assessment.

Issue 2, *Different Cognitive Profiles of G/LD (Beyond High IQ Giftedness)*, explores the characteristics and possible connections that exist between the gift and the disability.

Issue 3, *Successful Outcomes*, provides great detail about the kinds of compensation strategies these students use to be successful.

The first four chapters discuss issues of *Identification & Assessment*, examining issues relating to labeling individuals, identification issues, and assessment procedures. The authors suggest new approaches to identifying learning disabilities and argue that appropriate assessment should inform intervention strategies. The first chapter, written by Sternberg and Grigorenko and titled *Learning Disabilities, Giftedness, and Gifted/LD*, explores the issue of labeling anyone as either gifted or learning disabled. These authors make a compelling case for the fact that everyone has multiple strengths and weaknesses and being labeled depends on how severe or unusual the characteristics are. Because we all have a profile of strengths and weaknesses, it is more than likely some individuals will be rightly diagnosed as gifted/learning disabled. The probability of being labeled for the strength as gifted or the weakness as disabled, however, is also contextual and contingent upon the values of one's culture. The authors describe the benefits and cautions of labels. While labels may assure intervention services, they do not always align to the individual needs of the students. All services should be tailored to the individual's specific gifts or deficits. To provide the best education would be to assure that gifts, talents, and strengths be nurtured and deficits remediated for all individuals, regardless of any label.

In the next chapter, *The Identification of Gifted Students with Learning Disabilities: Challenges, Controversies, and Promising Practices*, McCoach, Kehle, Bray, and Siegle critique the current practices in identifying gifted/learning-disabled students. The authors focus on identifying learning disabilities among those students who have been identified as intellectually gifted as evidenced by superior performance on an intelligence test. They describe the complex issue of masking among these students where the disability obscures the gift, and the gift allows students to compensate for weaknesses. They provide cautions about using profile analysis to identify a learning disability and make fine suggestions about using longitudinal data to trace the students' achievement patterns over time.

In Chapter 3, Lupart extends these ideas in her chapter, *Unraveling the Mysteries of GLD: Toward the Application of Cognitive Theory to Assessment.* She argues for assessment procedures that offer an in-depth analysis of how these students think and learn in real-world contexts and offers the results of case study research to explore the issue. She, too, dismisses relying on the analysis of test scores to identify gifted/learning-disabled students. She explains that these scores are insufficient in uncovering learning disabilities and provide inadequate information for successful interventions. Her approach is two-fold: First, she uses both qualitative and quantitative assessment procedures based on cognitive theories to diagnose the problem. Next, the results are tied to strategies for helping these students succeed. She insists that intervention should align to the cognitive patterns uncovered during in-depth observations and assessments of how these students learn.

The fourth chapter, *Linking Assessment and Diagnosis to Interventions for Gifted Students with Learning Disabilities* by Brody and Mills, offers three case studies applying many of the principles described in earlier chapters. The authors claim that comprehensive assessment must include documentation of the gift or talent, evidence of a processing problem and discrepancy between potential and achievement, and supporting information about the social and emotional concomitants to the problem. Once a diagnosis is made, the team must develop a comprehensive program that includes challenge in the areas of strength, grade-level instruction where needed, remediation of weaknesses, accommodation strategies, and social and emotional support. The authors apply these ideas to three diverse gifted/learning-disabled students. As was the case in the earlier chapters, the authors validate the need for looking at these youngsters uniquely, as each individual's needs dictate different intervention strategies.

The next two chapters discuss issues related to *Different Cognitive Profiles of G/LD (Beyond High IQ Giftedness)*, extending the idea of assessment to looking for distinct cognitive patterns in individuals with gifts and learning disabilities. We have seen that many gifted individuals with learning disabilities seem to have unique talents in the arts and sciences—areas that rely on spatial abilities and unique creative talents (Baum, Cooper, & Neu, 2001; Whitmore & Maker, 1986). These chapters examine the unique combinations of specific talents and cognitive patterns beyond IQ.

In Chapter 5, *Dyslexia and Visual Spatial Talents: Are they Connected?*, Karolyi and Winner discuss the relationship between dyslexia and spatial ability. There have been many claims based on case studies that dyslexia and spatial talents are highly associated with one another. The authors present empirical evidence supporting this notion. Karily and Winner describe the relationship they have found between dyslexia and a particular kind of spatial talent—global spatial ability. They claim that this kind of spatial ability may underlie real world talents such as mechanical skill, carpentry, invention, visual artistry, surgery and even the ability to interpret x-rays or MRIs.

In Chapter 6, *To Read But Not to Read: Identifying the Nature of Poor Reading Comprehension in Children,* Nation builds on the theme of reading problems described in the preceding chapters. Her interest is in examining students who demonstrate a significant discrepancy between their at least average-for-age decoding and their impaired reading comprehension. This chapter is particularly intriguing as many twice-exceptional students have difficulty with aspects of reading. Nation distinguishes between students who have difficulty with decoding and those who struggle with comprehension. Many seemingly gifted students master decoding at early ages and can decipher passages written for advanced readers. These same students, however, have little idea of meaning. This pattern is particularly true for gifted students with Asperger's syndrome (Neihart, 2000). Nation presents four cases, each of which represents a unique cause for the discrepancy—weak language skills, weak cognitive ability, nonverbal learning disabilities, and autism-spectrum disorder. This chapter is especially helpful in explaining the peaks and valleys we see in students who are gifted and learning disabled.

The final chapters examine *Successful Outcomes*, describing how gifted students with learning disabilities succeed in postsecondary settings and beyond and how we can foster these successes. Chapter 7, *Gifted Students with Learning Disabilities in Postsecondary Settings,* focuses on the ways talented and disabled students survive beyond high school. Talent-Runnels and Layton provide three case studies of talented adults at different stages who describe how they succeeded during their college years. The sample includes an assistant professor, a presidential appointee who had just received his bachelor's degree and a college junior still in the process. The authors focused on these questions: How did the individual grow and change? Did their disability diminish as they grew older, and what were the keys to their survival in and beyond school? As discussed previously, their findings confirm that these students need to be given a challenging curriculum that taps their intellectual strengths, be provided with a variety of strategies to compensate for weaknesses due to their disability and possess willingness to work hard and cleverly if they are to be successful.

In Chapter 8, *Compensation Strategies Used by High Ability Students with Learning Disabilities,* Reis and Ruban describe strategies that bright, learning-disabled young adults used to succeed in challenging environments. Findings from their extensive research indicate that students need a variety of compensation techniques over the course of their journeys. In short, these students must have strategies to assist them to address academic, legal, and career-related issues. They need to develop self-regulation strategies and learn how to compensate for problematic weaknesses and social and emotional difficulties. These bright youngsters should also seek out opportunities and environments where they can develop and apply their talents. The authors include two extensive tables identifying strategies for each of these areas. They call for the need for collaboration among the adults in the lives of these students, including teachers, LD specialists, G/T specialists, counselors, parents, and the students themselves to help with planning, goal setting and transitions.

Chapter 9, *Summoning up the Spirits from the Vast Deep: LD and Giftedness in Historic Persons*, reinforces the notion that people with learning difficulties can demonstrate extraordinary gifts. Aaron, Joshi, & Ocker analyze the cognitive profiles of gifted historical figures: Thomas Edison, Leonardo da Vinci, Auguste Rodin, Charles Marion Russell, Hans Christian Anderson, and Agatha Christie. Each of these individuals had talent in spatial areas and also had difficulty reading. Using their Component Model of reading, the authors offer evidence of the cognitive plausibility of the coincidence of learning disabilities and giftedness. They use a comprehensive set of information-gathering techniques to present evidence of difficulty in some area of language including reading and spelling. They also document the superior ability the sample possessed in simultaneous processing of information. This kind of processing can be seen in spatial reasoning and creativity.

The volume concludes with a chapter by Newman that discusses the current state of the intervention literature for students with gifts and learning disabilities. The author discusses the consensus in the literature on the importance of capitalizing and developing the strengths these students possess and finding ways to assist them in compensating for their weaknesses. In addition, intervention strategies are discussed and an argument is made for adopting a broader view of giftedness beyond the traditional IQ-based definition to insure that students with diverse gifts receive appropriate intervention services.

CONCLUSION

As you read through the many chapters of this intriguing and thought-provoking volume, I am sure that you will gain an appreciation for the many talented youngsters who are faced with academic challenges. Their road to success will be hard and filled with challenges. Hopefully, the knowledge gained through the many ideas contained in each chapter can help you make their journey a bit easier.

REFERENCES

Baldwin, L., & Gargiulo, D. (1983). A model program for elementary-age learning disabled gifted youngsters. In L. Fox., L. Brody, & D.Tobin (Eds.) (1983). *Learning-disabled gifted: Identification and programming*. Baltimore: University Park Press.

Baum, S. (1988). An enrichment program for gifted learning disabled students. *Gifted Child Quarterly. 32*, 226–230.

Baum, S., Cooper, C., & Neu, T. (2001). Dual Differentiation: An approach for meeting the curricular needs of gifted students with learning disabilities. *Psychology in the Schools, 38*, 477–490.

Baum, S., Emerick. L., Herman, G., and Dixon, J. (1989). Identification, programs, and enrichment strategies for gifted learning disabled youth. *Roeper Review. 12*, 48-53.

Baum, S., & Olenchak, F., (2002). The Alphabet Children: GT, ADHD and more. *Exceptionality 10*(2), 77–91.

Baum, S. M., Olenchak, F.R., and Owen, S.V. (1998). Gifted students with attention deficits: Fact and/or fiction? Or, can we see the forest for the trees? *Gifted Child Quarterly, 42* (2), 96–104.

Baum, S. & Owen, S. V. (in press). *Alphabet Children: Gifted students with learning disabilities and more*. Mansfield Center, CT: Creative Learning Press.

Baum, S. & Owen, S. V., & Dixon, J. (1991). *To be gifted and learning disabled: From identification to practical intervention strategies*. Mansfield Center, CT: Creative Learning Press.

Brody, L., & Mills, C. (1997). Gifted children with learning disabilities. *Journal of Learning Disabilities, 30*, 282–296.

Fox L., Brody, L. & Tobin, D. (Eds.) (1983). *Learning-disabled gifted: Identification and programming*. Baltimore: University Park Press.

Gardner, H. (1999). *Intelligences reframed*. New York: Basic Books. Maker, J. (1977). Providing programs for the gifted handicapped. Reston, VA: Council for Exceptional Children.

Neilson, Higgins, Wilkenson, & Webb, (1994). Helping twice-exceptional students to succeed in high school. *The Journal of Secondary Gifted Education, V*, 35–39.

Reis, S. M., Neu, T. W. & McGuire, J. (1995). Talent in two places: Case studies of high-ability students with learning disabilities who have achieved. Research Monograph No. 95114. Storrs, CT: The University of Connecticut.

Chapter 1

LEARNING DISABILITIES, GIFTEDNESS, AND GIFTED/LD

Robert J. Sternberg
PACE CENTER, Yale University

Elena L. Grigorenko
PACE CENTER, Yale University
Moscow State University

INTRODUCTION

Ellen is a superb musician but has trouble reading the newspaper. Mario can read the newspaper easily, but has difficulties with even the simplest mathematical problems. Ernest, a marvelous poet, can read and do mathematical-computation problems, but he has great difficulty with simple mathematical-reasoning problems. These hypothetical individuals, like many others, are gifted and yet have a learning disability. To understand the nature of such individuals, sometimes referred to as characterized by being "gifted/LD," one must understand both the nature of giftedness and the nature of learning disabilities separately, and then in combination.

Various theories characterize gifted children in different ways (Sternberg & Davidson, 1986, in press). We view giftedness and learning disabilities in terms of excellent in various forms of developing competencies and, ultimately, expertise (Sternberg, 2001).

The model of developing expertise has five key elements (although certainly they do not constitute an exhaustive list of elements in the development of expertise): metacognitive skills, learning skills, thinking skills, knowledge, and motivation. Gifted individuals excel in the development of expertise in some combination of these elements, and, at high levels of giftedness, in all of them. Although it is convenient to separate these five elements, they are fully interactive. They influence each other, both directly and indirectly. For example, learning leads to knowledge, but knowledge facilitates further learning.

These elements are, to a large extent, domain-specific. The development of expertise in one area does not necessarily lead to the development of expertise in another area, although there may be some transfer, depending upon the relationship of the areas, a point that has been made with regard to intelligence by others as well (e.g., Gardner, 1983, 1999, 2000; Sternberg, 1997, 1999b).

In the theory of successful intelligence (Sternberg, 1985, 1997, 1999), intelligence is viewed as having three aspects: analytical, creative, and practical. Our research suggests that the development of expertise in one creative domain (Sternberg & Lubart, 1995) or in one practical domain (Sternberg et al., 2000; Sternberg, Wagner, Williams, & Horvath, 1995) shows modest correlations with the development of expertise in other such domains. Psychometric research suggests more domain-generality for the analytical domain (Jensen, 1998). Moreover, people can show analytical, creative, or practical expertise in one domain without showing all three of these kinds of expertise, or even two of the three.

ELEMENTS OF THE EXPERTISE MODEL

We consider the following six elements to be the key elements of our model of developing expertise.

1. Metacognitive skills. Metacognitive skills (or metacomponents, Sternberg, 1985) refer to people's understanding and control of their own cognition. For example, such skills would encompass what an individual knows about writing papers or solving arithmetic word problems, both with regard to the steps that are involved and with regard to how these steps can be executed effectively. Seven metacognitive skills are particularly important: problem recognition, problem definition, problem representation, strategy formulation, resource allocation, monitoring of problem solving, and evaluation of problem solving (Sternberg, 1985, 1986). All of these skills are modifiable (Sternberg, 1986, 1988; Sternberg & Grigorenko, 2000; Sternberg & Spear-Swerling, 1996). Gifted individuals excel in metacognitive skills (Borkowski, 1986; Butterfield, 1986; Shore, 2000). Gifted/LD students tend to be high in general metacognitive processes.

2. Learning skills. Learning skills (knowledge-acquisition components) are essential to the model (Sternberg, 1985, 1986), although they are certainly not the only learning skills that individuals use. Learning skills are sometimes divided into explicit and implicit ones. Explicit learning is what occurs when we make an effort to learn; implicit learning is what occurs when we pick up information incidentally, without any systematic effort.

Examples of learning skills are selective encoding, which involves distinguishing relevant from irrelevant information; selective combination, which involves putting together the relevant information; and selective comparison, which involves relating new information to information already stored in memory (Sternberg, 1985). Learning skills are not necessarily equally distributed across content domains. An individual might function very well in one content domain but poorly in another. For example, an individual might learn well in the verbal domain but not the mathematical one, or vice versa. Gifted/LD students tend to excel in the use of learning skills in many domains, but to have one or more domains in which they exhibit a clear weakness.

3. Thinking skills. There are three main kinds of thinking skills (or performance components) that individuals need to master (Sternberg, 1985, 1986, 1994a). It is important to note that these are sets of, rather than individual, thinking skills. Critical (analytical) thinking skills include analyzing, critiquing, judging, evaluating, comparing and contrasting, and assessing. Creative thinking skills include creating, discovering, inventing, imagining, supposing, and hypothesizing. Practical thinking skills include applying, using, utilizing, and practicing (Sternberg, 1997; Sternberg & Grigorenko, 2000). They are the first step in the translation of thought into real-world action. Gifted/LD students have strong general thinking skills, but often have difficulties in applying them to their domain of weakness because they have not learned well in this domain. One needs to have learned about an area in order to think well about it.

4. Knowledge. There are two main kinds of knowledge that are relevant in academic situations. Declarative knowledge is of facts, concepts, principles, laws, and the like. It is "knowing that." Procedural knowledge is of procedures and strategies. It is "knowing how." Of particular importance is procedural tacit knowledge, which involves knowing how the system functions in which one is operating (Sternberg et al., 2000; Sternberg, Wagner, Williams & Horvath, 1995). Gifted/LD children tend to have a strong knowledge base, except in the area or areas of weakness, because their reduced learning skills in that area have reduced their chances of acquiring knowledge in that area.

5. Motivation. One can distinguish among several different kinds of motivation. A first kind of motivation is achievement motivation (McClelland, 1985; McClelland, Atkinson, Clark, & Lowell, 1976). People who are high in achievement motivation seek moderate challenges and risks. They are attracted to tasks that are neither very easy nor very hard. They are strivers—constantly trying to better themselves and their accomplishments.

A second kind of motivation is competence (self-efficacy) motivation, which refers to people's beliefs in their own ability to solve the problem at hand (Bandura, 1977, 1996). Experts need to develop a sense of their own efficacy to solve difficult tasks in their domain of expertise. This kind of self-efficacy can result both from intrinsic and extrinsic rewards (Amabile, 1996;

Sternberg & Lubart, 1996). Of course, other kinds of motivation are important too. Indeed, motivation is perhaps the indispensable element needed for school success. Without it, the student never even tries to learn.

A third kind of motivation is motivation to develop one's own intellectual skills. Dweck (1999) has distinguished between "entity" and "incremental" theorists among children. The former believe intelligence largely to be fixed; the latter believe it to be modifiable. Those who believe that intelligence is modifiable are more likely to make the effort to improve their skills simply because they believe that these skills are subject to improvement.

Gifted/LD children tend, on average, to be highly motivated. But they may be only poorly motivated in their area of weakness because it is the one thing, or one of the few things, that frustrates them. When they can do so many things well, why dwell on what they do poorly? They may also find ways of compensating for their weakness so that they can get by without correcting the weakness, a strategy that may cost them in later life if they later need the skill for which they have compensated.

6. Context. All of the elements discussed above are characteristics of the learner. Returning to the issues raised at the beginning of this document, a problem with conventional tests is that they assume that individuals operate in a more or less decontextualized environment. A test score is interpreted largely in terms of the individual's internal attributes. But a test measures much more, and the assumption of a fixed or uniform context across test-takers is not realistic. Contextual factors that can affect test performance include native language, emphasis of test on speedy performance, importance to the test taker of success on the test, and familiarity with the kinds of material on the test (Ceci, 1996; Sternberg, 1997). Ultimately, who is labeled as *gifted/LD* is highly contextually determined, as it depends on what the society considers to be appropriate domains both for gifts and for learning disabilities.

Interactions of Elements

The novice works toward expertise through deliberate practice. But this practice requires an interaction of all six of the key elements. At the center, driving the elements, is motivation. Without it, the elements remain inert. Eventually, one reaches a kind of expertise, at which one becomes a reflective practitioner of a certain set of skills. But expertise occurs at many levels. The expert first-year graduate or law student, for example, is still a far cry from the expert professional. People thus cycle through many times on the way to successively higher levels of expertise. They do so through the elements in the figure. Those who are able to combine the elements in a particularly effective way so as to advance more quickly to expertise, or to a quantitatively higher level of expertise, or to a qualitatively superior kind of expertise, are called gifted. Those who merely show up as gifted on tests when they are young, but not in more consequential kinds of performance when they are older, often are viewed as gifted individuals who failed to fulfill their potential. This explanation may be correct, or it may simply be that the main expertise of these individuals was in taking tests of the kinds used to label young people as gifted.

Motivation drives metacognitive skills, which in turn activate learning and thinking skills, which then provide feedback to the metacognitive skills, enabling one's level of expertise to increase (see also Sternberg, 1985). The declarative and procedural knowledge acquired through the extension of the thinking and learning skills also results in these skills being used more effectively in the future.

All of these processes are affected by, and can in turn affect, the context in which they operate. For example, if a learning experience is in English but the learner has only limited English proficiency, his or her learning will be inferior to that of someone with more advanced English-language skills. Or if material is presented orally to someone who is a better visual learner, that individual's performance will be reduced.

UNDERSTANDING GIFTEDNESS, LEARNING DISABILITIES, AND GIFTED/LD IN TERMS OF THE MODEL

Gifted individuals excel in the elements of the model of developing expertise. They may not excel in all elements, but they excel in at least some combination—in some way that renders them able to produce exceptional work. Many gifted individuals excel in all of the elements of the model, but they need not.

Individuals with learning disabilities fall short, at least relatively speaking, in at least one element of the model. Their learning skills in one domain are likely to be impaired, with the result that their achievement suffers in that domain as well. Their gifts may actually, in some ways, put them at a disadvantage, because they may be able to use these gifts to mask their learning disability. For example, someone who performs very poorly in the spatial domain may nevertheless get by through solving spatial problems verbally, to the extent he or she can.

Our views of giftedness and learning disability diverge somewhat from the standard views. Consider each in turn.

Although many different definitions of intelligence have been proposed over the years (see, e.g., "Intelligence and its measurement," 1921; Sternberg & Detterman, 1986), the conventional notion of intelligence and intellectual giftedness is built around a loosely consensual definition of intelligence in terms of generalized adaptation to the environment. Some theories of intelligence extend this definition by suggesting that there is a general factor of intelligence, often labeled *g*, which underlies all adaptive behavior (Brand, 1996; Jensen, 1998; see essays in Sternberg & Grigorenko, 2002). In many theories, including the theories most widely accepted today (e.g., Carroll, 1993; Gustafsson, 1994; Horn, 1994), other mental abilities are hierarchically nested under this general factor at successively greater levels of specificity. For example, Carroll suggested that three levels could nicely capture the hierarchy of abilities, whereas Cattell (1971) and Vernon (1971) suggested two levels were especially important. In the case of Cattell, nested under general ability are fluid abilities of the kind needed to solve abstract reasoning problems such as figural matrices or series completions and crystallized abilities of the kind needed to solve problems of vocabulary and general information. In the case of Vernon, the two levels corresponded to verbal: educational and practical: mechanical abilities. These theories and others like them are described in more detail elsewhere (Brody, 2000; Carroll, 1993; Embretson & McCollam, 2000; Herrnstein & Murray, 1994; Jensen, 1998; Sternberg, 2000). Most tests used to identify gifted children are based on tests of general intellectual abilities. Tests of creativity and of motivation, as well as school performance and other variables, also may be taken into account.

The situation with learning disabilities is more complex. Although specific learning disabilities can be and have been defined in a number of different ways, a consensus view has emerged that is based loosely on the point of view represented in the *Diagnostic and Statistical Manual* (4th ed., 1995) of the American Psychiatric Association. According to this consensus view, learning disabilities are marked impairments in the development of specific skills, such as reading skills, mathematical skills, or writing skills, relative to the level of skills expected on the basis of an individual's education and intelligence. These impairments interfere with daily life and academic achievement. However, they are not due to physical deficits, such as visual or hearing deficits, or acquired neurological conditions such as those caused by brain trauma. Learning disabilities seldom can be diagnosed before the end of kindergarten or the beginning of first grade.

We view learning disabilities in a way that goes beyond this kind of standard definition. The thesis of this chapter is that *virtually everyone has a learning disability in something but that society chooses to recognize only some individuals as having an LD. Whether someone is labeled as having a learning disability in many respects resembles the result of a lottery* (Sternberg & Grigorenko, 1999). This means that many gifted students have some kind of "LD."

Many theorists of abilities agree that abilities are multiple—that there are many of them (see Sternberg, 2000), although they may be correlated. These theorists may disagree as to exactly what the abilities are or how they are structured, but they agree that the abilities are distinguishable from each other. For example, the skills that constitute reading ability are different from the skills that constitute artistic ability, which are in turn different from the skills that constitute musical ability. Thus, someone could be an able reader but a poor musician, or vice versa.

If one were to make a list of the many abilities people can have, one would find that virtually no one is proficient in all the skills constituting all of these abilities, and virtually no one is hopelessly inept at all these skills. Rather, almost everyone is more proficient in some skills and less proficient in others. Some people may be proficient in more skills, or more proficient in particular skills, but virtually everyone shows a pattern of multiple strengths and multiple weaknesses.

Put another way, virtually everyone shows a complex pattern of abilities and disabilities. For example, even the straight-A student in school may be inept in certain aspects of interpersonal relations. Even the straight-F student in school may be able in many aspects of dealing with other people. This intuition is captured in modern theories of intelligence, which argue on the basis of plentiful and diverse data that interpersonal and practical skills actually are distinct from traditional academic skills (Gardner, 1999; Sternberg, 1999, 2003). High and even gifted levels of these different kinds of skills may or may not be found in the same persons.

Given that everyone has a pattern of abilities and disabilities, how does it happen that some people get labeled as a gifted learner, or as having learning disabilities, whereas other people do not? The reason is that learning abilities and disabilities reside neither totally in the individual nor totally in the society. *Labeling someone as having gifted or as having a learning disability is the result of an interaction between the individual and the society.* Labeling is a function of the contextual variable in the model described above. On the basis of many factors to be discussed, the society selects some people to label as being gifted or as having learning disabilities, and does not select others.

How does the society make this selection? It selects on the basis of the set of skills that it values in school and on the job. If the society views a certain set of skills (such as reading skills) as essential, and views them as constituting a "specific" rather than a general ability, then individuals with low levels of proficiency in these skills are labeled as having a specific disability. People with high levels of proficiency are labeled as gifted, often whether the abilities are general or specific. One has a set of abilities and disabilities and metaphorically enters a lottery that determines whether the particular pattern will result in a label of *giftedness* or *learning disability* being assigned. We are not saying that the labeling process is arbitrary. Rather, we are saying that there are many different possible labeling processes that can yield totally different results.

Our society currently defines seven areas of learning disabilities: (1) listening, (2) speaking, (3) basic reading skills, (4) reading comprehension skills, (5) written expression, (6) arithmetic calculation skills, and (7) mathematics reasoning skills. These disabilities are viewed as specific. But in fact, there are no completely general abilities or disabilities. For example, IQ tests are sometimes seen as measuring "general ability," but in fact, a high score on an IQ test is no guarantee of a high level of creative ability, practical (common-sense) ability, athletic ability, musical ability, or any of a number of other abilities. So all abilities and disabilities are specific in greater or lesser degree. The society invests much less in the gifted and does not have a corresponding societal (i.e., federally legislated) definition of giftedness. The most frequently used bases for assessing giftedness, at least in school children, are IQ and school achievement. Someone who has societally recognized gifts and who also has recognized deficits may be labeled as gifted/LD.

Where and when an individual is born has a tremendous impact on whether that individual will be labeled as being gifted, as having a learning disability, or as gifted/LD. In a preliterate society, for example, there are no individuals labeled as having a reading disability. There are no gifted readers either. One society might label someone with minimal musical skills as having a musical disability, whereas another society might not, just as whether musical precocity counts as a gift depends on whether the society values music. In effect, each individual becomes a mandatory participant in a lottery that determines whether the particular pattern of abilities and disabilities he or she has will lead to the individual's being labeled as having a learning disability. But the lottery applies only to the labeling process. Everyone has a pattern of both abilities and disabilities. The lottery represents how society chooses to label that pattern.

Given that all individuals have both strengths and weaknesses, individuals labeled as having learning disabilities have many strengths to offer society. Individuals who are labeled as gifted also have strengths, but may also have weaknesses. Our society often inadvertently positions individuals with learning disabilities to view themselves as potential victims rather than as potential victors, and does the reverse for the gifted. In this regard, we have three main contentions:

1. Individuals with specific learning disabilities often have considerable strengths in other abilities. Individuals with gifts often have weaknesses that need to be dealt with rather than ignored.

2. All these individuals should be encouraged to be successes who capitalize on strengths and compensate for or correct weaknesses.

3. Modifications of curriculum that excuse individuals with learning disabilities from learning important skills or from the normal experiences of schooling may be well-intentioned, but they often (but certainly not always) end up hurting these individuals more than helping them. The reason is that for the society to have labeled the individuals as having a learning disability in the first place, the ability for which they were labeled as lacking (i.e., as having a disability) must be one that the society views as important for adaptive living in that society. Modifications of curriculum that leave gifted

children *only* to capitalize on strengths, without addressing weaknesses (such as specialized schools for young children) also are nonoptimal. For example, overlooking the social weaknesses of students gifted in academic areas may seem defensible when the children are in school, but will prepare them poorly for life.

We challenge a system that, in meaning to do well, is often doing the opposite. We believe that society can do better, and that science can play a role. Here are some crucial points toward doing better.

1. *The "LD" and "giftedness" labels can be and often are misunderstood.* Virtually everyone has a learning disability of some kind. Many people have gifts of one kind or another. What differs is whether the society chooses to label that way or those ways as recognized "gifts" or "learning disabilities." For example, U.S. society labels certain poor readers as having a learning disability but does not label certain people who are poor in shooting a bow and arrow as having a learning disability. Similarly, in today's developed world, an expert archer would be labeled as gifted only by a narrow segment of the population. Another society might choose the opposite path, labeling only the poor archers (who are unable to feed themselves or their families) as having a learning disability and the gifted archers as very valuable because of their superior hunting skills.

2. *The "LD" label can be costly both to the individual and to society.* Once children are labeled as "LD," a complex set of mechanisms is put into effect that renders it likely that the label will become a self-fulfilling prophecy, whether it was originally correct or not. A well-intentioned labeling procedure thus can become harmful to our young people.

3. *Genuine LD and giftedness are interactions between the individual and the environment.* Certain biological predispositions can render an individual susceptible to the development of specific kinds of learning disabilities or gifts. These biological predispositions do not determine whether or not the individual will actually have a learning disability or gift. For example, as we mentioned, in a preliterate society, no one manifests reading disabilities or precocious reading. Even among literate societies, some orthographic (writing) systems impose challenges that others do not impose, challenges that affect the probability of individuals manifesting reading disabilities or reading gifts. For instance, Spanish is pronounced exactly the same way it is written; English is not. Chinese uses a logographic (picture-based) writing system, whereas Indo-European languages such as English, French, German, and Russian use alphabetic writing systems. Whether a child will have a reading disability or excel will be affected not only by that child's biological makeup, but also by where and when the child grows up.

4. *Biological does NOT imply immutable.* Even to the extent that the origins of learning disabilities are biological, these biological origins have nothing at all to do with whether the symptoms of learning disabilities are modifiable. Put another way, the partially biological origins of learning

disabilities in no way preclude successful educational interventions. Contrary to a popular misconception, "biological" is in no way synonymous with "fixed."

The remedies used to improve performance of individuals with learning disabilities should always depend on the specific deficits that individual people experience, not on how these people are labeled. Similarly, instruction for gifted children should reflect the kinds of gifts they have. Lumping together all of the labeled children into one global category such as "LD" or "gifted," and then giving them what usually amounts to a single form of remediation or enrichment, may harm more students than it helps.

To sum up, these labels produce many effects. But we need to remember that the label is only a label. Everyone has learning abilities and disabilities. The label is not only about whether people have unusual abilities or disabilities, but about whether the disabilities they have are ones the society chooses, for reasons of its own, to label as such. Whether one is labeled is the result of a lottery into which one is automatically entered, like it or not.

In the recent past, more and more children have been labeled every successive year as having a learning disability. Although there are many motivations to label children as having a learning disability, it is important to remember that the LD label in the United States means different things to different populations. For children of parents who are of high socioeconomic status, the label can provide a means to maintain for the children the benefits of the society that the parents have enjoyed. To such parents, the thought that their children may be downwardly mobile, for whatever reason, may be distressing.

For children of parents of low socioeconomic status, the LD label also may help to insure that the children stay where they are. Ironically, when these children are identified, they too may end up being assured a stable socioeconomic environment for the rest of their lives. What happens to these children is that they, too, often get special attention, but it often comes in the form of a warehousing phenomenon where the children are given ineffective educational gruel labeled as "interventions." These interventions sometimes insure only that the children will fall further and further behind.

For children with rich parents, a label of giftedness accelerates the benefits they may have gotten anyway, or enhances their already existing advantages. For children with poor parents, a label of giftedness may be one of the few ways of saving the child from an inferior education or placement in unchallenging classes that will poorly serve the child.

There has been an increase in labeling of children in a positive way, but it is subtler than the increase in the labeling of children with LDs. It has occurred in several ways. First is grade inflation. A "C" was once a respectable grade. It is no longer. Today there are not so many students who are not A or B students. A second way is in letters of recommendation, which educators find to be highly inflated and, as a result, difficult to interpret. Third, the re-centering of SAT scores (to re-place the means at 500) has even raised SAT scores, which previously had been declining. Finally, people are afraid to label anyone as "below average." Garrison Keillor suggested that the Lake Wobegon dream is for everyone to be above the 50th percentile. In our society, we actively seek to realize this impossible dream.

The *gifted/LD* label is, in some ways, a potentially risky one. We believe that it is often appropriate. But it may be misused. It could become a way for affluent parents to get the best of both worlds—to have their child labeled as gifted, which is advantageous in our society, and labeled as having an LD as well, which has also come to be advantageous. We think that this "game" is not at the present time being widely played. That could change as parents and those who do assessments realize that the label is not strange, that it is not pejorative, and that it may benefit children in their school careers. The solution is to have a clear notion of what gifted/LD is, and apply it assiduously. In this chapter, we have proposed such a notion based on the model of abilities as developing into competencies, and competencies, into expertise.

NOTES

Preparation of this chapter was supported under the Javits Act Program (Grant No. R206R00001) as administered by the Office of Educational Research and Improvement, U.S. Department of Education. Grantees undertaking such projects are encouraged to express freely their professional judgment. This chapter, therefore, does not necessarily represent the position or policies of the Office of Educational Research and Improvement or the U.S. Department of Education, and no official endorsement should be inferred.

Requests for reprints should be sent to Robert J. Sternberg, Director, PACE Center, Yale University, P.O. Box 208358, New Haven, CT 06520-8358.

REFERENCES

Adams. M. J. (1990). *Beginning to read: Thinking and learning about print.* Cambridge, MA: MIT Press.

Christensen, C. A. (1999). Learning disability: Issues of representation, power, and the medicalization of school failure. In R. J. Sternberg & E. L. Grigorenko (Eds.), *Perspectives on learning disabilities* (pp. 227–249). Boulder, CO: Westview.

Coles, G. S. (1987). *The learning mystique: A critical look at "learning disabilities."* New York: Pantheon.

Cummins, J. (1976). The influence of bilingualism on cognitive growth: A synthesis of research findings and explanatory hypotheses. *Working Papers on Bilingualism*, 9, 1–43.

Diagnostic and Statistical Manual (1995, 4th ed.). Washington, DC: American Psychiatric Association.

Finucci, J. M., Gottfredson, L. S., & Childs, B. (1985). A follow-up study of dyslexic boys. *Annals of Dyslexia*, 35, 117–136.

Galaburda, A. M., Sherman, G. F., Rosen, G. D., Aboitiz, F., & Geschwind, N. (1985). Developmental dyslexia: Four consecutive cases with cortical anomalies. *Annals of Neurology*, 18, 94–100.

Gardner, H. (1999). *Intelligence reframed*. New York: Basic Books.

Grigorenko, E. L. (in press). Developmental dyslexia: an update on genes, brains, and environments. *Journal of Child Psychology and Child Psychiatry and Applied Disciplines*.

Hallgren, G. (1950). Specific dyslexia ('congenital word blindness'): A clinical and genetic study. *Acta Psychiatrica et Neurologica*, 65, 2–289.

Hermann, K. (1959). *Reading disability: A medical study of word blindness and related handicaps*. Springfield, IL: Charles C. Thomas.

Hinshelwood, J. (1917). *Congenital word-blindness*. London: Lewis & Company.

Humphreys, P., Kaufman, W. E., & Galaburda, A. M. (1990). Developmental dyslexia in women: Neuropsychological findings in three cases. *Annals of Neurology*, 28, 727–738.

Kelman, M., & Lester, G. (1997). *Jumping the queue: An inquiry into the legal treatment of students with learning disabilities*. Cambridge, MA: Harvard University Press.

Leonard, C. M., Voeller, K. K. S., Lombardion, L. J., Morris, M. K., Hynd, G. W., Alexander, A. W., Andersen, H. G., Garofalakis, M., Honeyman, J. C., Mao, J., Agee, O. F., & Staab, E. V. (1993). Anomalous cerebral structure in dyslexia revealed with magnetic resonance imaging. *Archives of Neurology*, 50, 461–469.

Liberman, I. Y., & Liberman, A. M. (1990). Whole language versus code emphasis: Underlying assumptions and their implication for reading instruction. *Annals of Dyslexia*, 40, 51–76.

Lyon, G. R., Fletcher, J. M., Shaywitz, S. E., Shaywitz, B. A., Wood, F. B., Schulte, A., & Olson, R. (2000). *Learning disabilities: An evidence-based conceptualization*. Unpublished manuscript.

Morgan, W. P. (1896). A case of congenital word-blindness. *British Medical Journal*, 11, 1378.

Morgan, A. E., & Hynd, G. W. (1998). Dyslexia, neurolinguistic ability, and anatomical variation of the planum temporale. *Neuropsychology Review*, 8, 79–93.

Olson, R. K. (1999). Genes, environment, and reading disabilities. In R. J. Sternberg & L. Spear-Swerling (Eds.), *Perspectives on learning disabilities* (pp. 3–21). Boulder, CO: Westview.

Orton, S. T. (1928). Specific reading disability—strephyosymbolia. *Journal of the American Medical Association*, 90, 1095–1099.

Perfetti, C. A. (1985). *Reading ability*. New York: Oxford University Press.

Samuels, S. J. (1999). Developing reading fluency in learning-disabled students. In R. J. Sternberg & L. Spear-Swerling (Eds.), *Perspectives on learning disabilities* (pp. 176–189). Boulder, CO: Westview.

Shaywitz, S. E., Shaywitz, B. A., Fletcher, J. M., & Escobar, M. D. (1990). Prevalence of reading disability in boys and girls. *Journal of the American Medical Association*, 264, 998–1002.

Siegel, L. S. (1999). Learning disabilities: The roads we have traveled and the path to the future. In R. J. Sternberg & L. Spear-Swerling (Eds.), *Perspectives on learning disabilities* (pp. 159–175). Boulder, CO: Westview.

Skrtic, T. M. (1999). Learning disabilities as organizational pathologies. In R. J. Sternberg & L. Spear-Swerling (Eds.), *Perspectives on learning disabilities* (pp. 193–226). Boulder, CO: Westview.

Spear-Swerling, L., & Sternberg, R. J. (1996). *Off-track: When poor readers become learning disabled*. Boulder, CO: Westview.

Stanovich, K. E. (1986). Matthew effects in reading: Some consequences of individual differences in the acquisition of literacy. *Reading Research Quarterly*, 21, 360–407.

Stanovich, K. E. (1991). Word recognition: Changing perspectives. In R. Barr, M. L. Kamil, P. Mosenthal, & P. D. Pearson (Eds.), *Handbook of reading research* (Vol. 2, pp. 418–452). New York: Longman.

Sternberg, R. J. (1997). *Successful intelligence.* New York: Plume.

Sternberg, R. J. (1999). The theory of successful intelligence. *Review of General Psychology,* 3, 292–316.

Sternberg, R. J. (Ed.) (2000). *andbook of intelligence.* New York: Cambridge University Press.

Sternberg, R. J., & Grigorenko, E. L. (1999). *Our labeled children: What every parent and teacher needs to know about learning disabilities.* Cambridge, MA: Perseus.

Sternberg, R. J., & Spear-Swerling, L. (Eds.) (1999). *Perspectives on learning disabilities.* Boulder, CO: Westview.

Sternberg, R. J., & Wagner, R. K. (1982, July). Automatization failure in learning disabilities. *Topics in learning and learning disabilities,* 2, 1–11.

Torgesen, J. K. (1999). Phonologically based reading disabilities: Toward a coherent theory of one kind of learning disability. In R. J. Sternberg & L. Spear-Swerling (Eds.), *Perspectives on learning disabilities* (pp. 106–135). Boulder, CO: Westview.

Wagner, R. K., Torgesen, J. K., & Rashotte, C. A. (1994). The development of reading-related phonological processing abilities: New evidence of bi-directional causality from a latent variable longitudinal study. *Developmental Psychology,* 30, 73–87.

Wong, B. Y. L. (1996). *The ABCs of learning disabilities.* San Diego, CA: Academic Press.

Chapter 2

The Identification of Gifted Students with Learning Disabilities: Challenges, Controversies, and Promising Practices

D. Betsy McCoach
Thomas J. Kehle
Melissa A. Bray
Del Siegle
University of Connecticut

INTRODUCTION

What does a gifted student with learning disabilities look like? How can school psychologists and teachers recognize gifted students with learning disabilities? Consider the case of Ronald, a fourth grade boy with a 145 IQ. In kindergarten, before students are expected to read, Ronald was at the top of his class. Teachers raved about Ronald's verbal skills and his clever responses in class. He was inquisitive and he loved books. He had memorized several of his favorite picture books, and could "read" them verbatim to the delight of his family and friends. In first grade, Ronald struggled with phonics, but had a fairly large sight-word vocabulary for a student his age. He was in the top reading group. By second grade, Ronald had slipped into the middle reading group, and he no longer seemed to enjoy books and reading. By fourth grade, Ronald was a very average-looking student. Ronald seemed to daydream in class. Teachers began to notice that Ronald had some difficulty reading textbooks in the content areas. Ronald's mother reported that at home, Ronald was inquisitive and curious, that he enjoyed building models and playing with Legos. However, Ronald's teachers only rarely saw such a spark in school. Occasionally, he would contribute something clever to the classroom discussion, but mostly he seemed disengaged.

Ronald could be a gifted learning-disabled student. In this chapter, we will discuss best practices for identifying students as intellectually gifted and learning disabled.

After reviewing definitions and identification criteria for learning disabilities and giftedness, we present current best practices in the identification of students with learning disabilities. We also explore several controversial or unresolved issues in the identification of gifted students with learning disabilities: How does a learning disability manifest itself in a student who is intellectually gifted? Do gifted students with learning disabilities experience masking effects? How can we effectively identify intellectually gifted students with learning disabilities? We discuss the possible implications of the elimination of the discrepancy formula for identifying students with learning disabilities for the identification of gifted students with learning disabilities within public educational systems. In addition, we provide an argument against using profile analysis to identify gifted students with learning disabilities, and suggest alternative criteria for their identification. Finally, we propose guidelines for school psychologists to identify students with intellectual gifts and learning disabilities.

DEFINITION OF LEARNING DISABILITY

Although the recognition of children with average or above average intelligence who have learning problems began over a century ago, the field of special education has still been unable to reach a consensus on a completely acceptable definition of learning disabilities (Silver & Hagin, 2002).

The United States Office of Education (USOE, 1977) defines a specific learning disability as

> ...a disorder in one or more of the basic psychological processes involved in understanding or in using language, spoken or written, which may manifest itself in an imperfect ability to listen, speak, read, write, spell, or do mathematical calculations. The term includes such conditions as perceptual handicaps, brain injury, minimal brain dysfunction, dyslexia, and developmental aphasia. Such terms do not include children who have learning difficulties that are primarily the result of visual, hearing, or motor handicaps, of mental retardation, of emotional disturbance, or of environmental, cultural, or economic disadvantage. (p. 65083)

Although the federal definition of learning disability does not include the concept of a discrepancy, the U.S. Office of Education (1976) published an operational definition of learning disability (LD) that specified that

> A specific learning disability may be found if a child has a severe discrepancy between achievement and intellectual ability in one or more of several areas: oral expression, written expression, listening

comprehension or reading comprehension, basic reading skills, mathematics reasoning, or spelling. A severe discrepancy is defined to exist when achievement in one or more of the areas falls at or below 50% of the child's expected achievement level, when age and previous educational experiences are taken into consideration. (p. 52405)

The interpretation of this operational definition impacts the identification of students as learning disabled. This operational definition specifies that an individual with a learning disability must exhibit a significant discrepancy between his or her level of performance in a particular academic area and his or her general intellectual ability (or expected achievement). This discrepancy cannot be explained by lack of educational opportunity in that academic area or other health impairment. Further, learning disabilities may differentially affect all areas of knowledge acquisition. Finally, there are variable degrees of severity of learning disabilities, and learning disabilities can exist in children of all ability levels. The conflict between the formal definition and the operational definition of a specific learning disability has resulted in confusion about the nature, definition, and identification of students as learning disabled (Kavale & Forness, 2000). Kavale and Forness assert "the lack of correspondence between the formal and the operational definition of LD means that two distinct and independent views of LD are being presented" (p. 247–248).

Because in most states students diagnosed with a specific learning disability must demonstrate evidence of a discrepancy between their intellectual ability and academic achievement in one or more particular areas, the diagnostic procedure includes assessment of both intellectual and academic functioning.

Most states include some mention of "processing deficits" in their definition or identification criteria (Mercer, Jordan, Allsop, & Mercer, 1996). However, exactly what qualifies as a processing deficit remains vaguely defined. Usually, processing deficits include problems in the areas of perceptual–motor, psycholinguistic, and executive functioning (Mercer et al.). "Although a myriad number of processes are available, a limited number have received substantial research support, and thus, represent validated deficits associated with LD" (Kavale & Forness, 2000, p. 251). Nonetheless, assessments typically attempt to document aspects of perceptual–motor, psycholinguistic, and/or executive functioning using tests of processing ability or neuropsychological batteries (Mercer et al.).

The National Joint Committee on Learning Disabilities reported a series of proposed policy changes relative to the reauthorization of IDEA (retrieved from www.nasponline.org/advocacy/IDEAinfromation.html, 2002). Most noted that the statutory definition of LD should be retained, the IQ–achievement discrepancy formula should be eliminated in the diagnosis of LD, and that all preschoolers should be screened for language deficits as they relate to future reading problems and LD. Most significant for gifted students with LD is the proposal to eliminate the IQ–achievement discrepancy. If the discrepancy formula is eliminated, it will be difficult to identify a gifted student with a learning disability. Gifted students with learning disabilities may indeed exhibit relative discrepancies between their potential and performance, but they may not exhibit academic deficits when compared to their peers. Therefore gifted students who achieve average levels or slightly below average levels academically would be difficult to diagnose as gifted/LD without inspecting the discrepancy between their superior potential and their average academic performance. Consistent with this line of reasoning, Beitchman and Young (1997) suggest that if a student is not functioning below age or grade-level norms, he or she should not be labeled learning disabled even if there is a significant discrepancy between his or her IQ and achievement scores.

DEFINITION OF INTELLECTUAL GIFTEDNESS

The continuing evolution of the definition of giftedness encompasses an increasingly more diverse set of capabilities, and consequently includes a greater number of children (Borland, 1989; Renzulli, 1978; Renzulli & Reis, 1985; Sternberg, 1988). Many contemporary definitions of giftedness argue against the use of the unitary full-scale IQ score in favor of more specific attributes. These include Gardner's (1993) multiple intelligences, the three-ring conception of giftedness (Renzulli, 1978), and Sternberg's triarchic theory of intelligence (1988). Other definitions perceive giftedness as a developmental process, rather than an inherent ability or a set of abilities. For example, the Columbus Group defined giftedness as "asynchronous development in which advanced cognitive abilities and heightened intensity combine to create inner experiences and awareness that are qualitatively different from the norm"(The Columbus Group, 1991, as cited in Morelock, 1996, p. 8).

Perhaps one of the most inclusive definitions of giftedness is the most recent version of the federal definition of giftedness, which states

> Children and youth with outstanding talent perform or show the potential for performing at remarkably high levels of accomplishment when compared with others of their age, experience, or environment. These children and youth exhibit high capability in intellectual, creative, and/or artistic areas, possess an unusual leadership capacity, or excel in specific academic fields. They require services or activities not ordinarily provided by the schools. Outstanding talents are present in children and youth from all cultural groups, across all economic strata, and in all areas of human endeavor (U.S. Department of Education 1993, p. 26).

Unfortunately, the federal definition is so exhaustive and inclusive that it becomes difficult to operationalize and utilize in schools. Furthermore, the federal government fails to provide specific guidelines to identify particular students as gifted. Therefore, the interpretation and application of these definitions is left to states and local school districts. Fewer than half of the states have adopted the federal definition of giftedness (Reis, 1989).

While giftedness may encompass a wide variety of talent areas, a fundamental function of schools is to develop students' academic potential. In addition, we find most paradoxical the intellectually gifted student who is simultaneously learning disabled. Identifying these students is complex and confusing. Providing appropriate educational programming for these students can be equally complicated. Therefore, in the remainder of this chapter, we consider only one form of giftedness: intellectual giftedness. However, we acknowledge the existence and importance of other theories of giftedness.

Because there is no universally agreed upon definition of intellectual giftedness (Davis & Rimm, 1994), it is the school district's implicit or explicit definition that determines eligibility for specialized services. Therefore, criteria needed to identify intellectual giftedness vary as a function of the state or school district, thus preventing comparisons. This phenomenon is sometimes called "geographic giftedness" (Borland, 1989). Many school districts choose to define giftedness as general intellectual ability, or the potential for exceptionally high performance on academic tasks. A common method of doing so involves the use of an IQ test such as the Wechsler scales (Wechsler, 1991). Some states (e.g., Pennsylvania) require the use of an IQ test in combination with other criteria to determine giftedness. As Gagné (1997) points out, the widespread use of IQ tests to identify students as "gifted" in most school districts and in most empirical studies "confirms that a high IQ is THE operational definition of giftedness" (p.78) in the United States, Canada, and throughout the world.

In this chapter, we define intellectual giftedness as an outstanding ability to grapple with complexity. Further, this general cognitive ability should be assessed using the most psychometrically sound indices available, such as individually administered IQ tests (e.g., Wechsler scales). Arbitrarily determining the rarity of "gifted" ability is controversial and debatable. For instance, Terman's (1925) children evidenced a mean full-scale IQ of 150. Historically, the 98th percentile, two standard deviations above the mean, or a full-scale IQ of 130 or above, has been employed to designate students as intellectually gifted. However, some states and districts consider IQ scores in the 120s to be indicative of intellectual giftedness. However, educators should be aware that the special educational needs of highly intellectually gifted students (IQs of 145 and above) might be very different from the educational needs of moderately intellectually gifted students (IQs of 120–130).

Furthermore, many contemporary views of intellectual giftedness posit that these abilities represent more than quantitative differences in general cognitive ability. Some scholars in the field of gifted education have suggested that intellectually gifted children appear to be qualitatively different from other children (Columbus Group, 1991; Winner, 2000). These qualitative differences suggest that gifted children possess an intense drive to master new concepts, require little explicit instruction, and often pose deep philosophical questions (Winner). However, the concept of qualitative differences is also controversial (see Gagné, 1997 for a fuller discussion of qualitative versus quantitative differences), and currently, no infallible methods to identify gifted students based on these qualitative differences exist.

DEFINITION OF GIFTED/LEARNING DISABLED

Gifted/LD students are students of superior intellectual ability who exhibit a significant discrepancy in their level of performance in a particular academic area such as reading, mathematics, spelling, or written expression. Their academic performance is substantially below what would be expected based on their general intellectual ability. As with other children exhibiting learning disabilities, this discrepancy is not due to the lack of educational opportunity in that academic area or other health impairment. Because academically gifted students with learning disabilities demonstrate such high academic potential, their academic achievement may not be as low as that of students with learning disabilities who demonstrate average academic potential. Consequently, these students may be less likely to be referred for special education testing (Brody & Mills, 1997).

Three Types of Gifted/Learning-Disabled Students

The literature in this area suggests that there are three different types of gifted/LD students (Baum, Owen, & Dixon, 1991; Brody & Mills, 1997; Gunderson, Maesch, & Rees, 1987). The first type, gifted students with subtle learning disabilities, often do well in elementary school and participate in gifted programs. However, as work becomes more demanding and reliant upon skills that are impacted by the students' area of disability, gifted/LD students may begin to experience learning problems and periods of underachievement. Because these students exhibit above average achievement in elementary school, they are rarely identified as learning disabled (Baum et al., 1991; Brody & Mills, 1997). The second type of student is identified as learning disabled, but is also gifted. These students have severe learning disabilities, but they may also have superior aptitudes in one or more academic or intellectual areas, although they are rarely formally identified as gifted (Baum et al, 1991, Brody & Mills, 1997). The third type of gifted/LD student remains unidentified as either learning disabled or gifted. These students have disabilities that conceal their gifts and gifts that camouflage their disabilities. These students appear average to their teachers. They are probably not referred for psycho-educational evaluation; therefore, the discrepancy between their IQs and academic performance is not noted. They perform at grade level on most academic tasks, but their learning disability hinders them from reaching the superior range of performance (Baum et al., 1991, Brody & Mills, 1997). This typology of gifted/LD students is philosophically appealing; however, it leads to pragmatic difficulties in the identification of gifted students with learning disabilities.

THE CONCEPT OF MASKING

Masking refers to the principle that many gifted students with learning disabilities have patterns of strengths and weaknesses that make them appear to have average abilities and achievement. Masking hinders the identification of these students as both gifted and learning disabled. The concept that intellectual giftedness masks learning disabilities and that learning disabilities mask giftedness is a central tenet within the current literature in the field of gifted education. Proponents of masking would argue that, to a certain extent, all three types of gifted/LD students experience masking; however, the masking is most severe for the third type of gifted student, the child who is identified as neither gifted nor learning disabled. Some proponents of masking believe that even intelligence test scores will be depressed for students who are gifted and learning disabled, thereby hindering their identification as either gifted or learning disabled. For instance, Waldron and Saphire (1990) state that "the primary problem with the use of an intelligence test to identify gifted students with LD is that the disability may lower their IQ score so dramatically that the students do not qualify for inclusion in the school district's criteria for gifted, even though they demonstrate strong abilities in some areas" (p. 491).

Problems with the Concept of Masking

The notion of masking is fraught with theoretical and pragmatic problems. First, a central theoretical question is whether or not students who are performing at an average level should qualify for services as learning disabled (Gordon, Lewandowski, & Keiser, 1999). Although "high functioning/LD" students may exhibit relative discrepancies between their potential and their performance, they do not exhibit performance deficits when compared to same age peers. Some educators in the field of learning disabilities worry that identifying average or nearly average achieving students as learning disabled will decrease the resources that are available to serve more severely disabled students, will discriminate against average students with flatter aptitude/achievement profiles, and will weaken public support for the "truly" learning disabled (Gordon et al., 1999).

For example, consider again Ronald, a student who scores 145 on the WISC-III, but who is performing at the 50th percentile when compared to same age peers. Ronald does show a significant discrepancy between ability and achievement, even if his achievement seems average for students his age. Gordon et al. (1999) would argue that a student like Ronald should not qualify for services as learning disabled. They assert that individuals should qualify "as disabled only if they suffer from 'substantial impairment' in a major life function." They take exception to the application of the LD label to bright students. They assert that, "In fact, a bright, unmotivated student will qualify for LD classification more easily than a hard working student with generally below average capabilities" (p. 487).

In contrast, we believe that students like Ronald who achieve at average levels should be considered for the diagnosis of gifted/LD if they show evidence of superior potential and evidence of processing deficits. However, there are many other plausible alternative hypotheses for Ronald's ability/achievement discrepancy. Therefore, diagnosticians should exert caution when making an LD diagnosis. Students with high measured ability who achieve at an average level may or may not be learning disabled. Cognitive ability is an imperfect predictor of academic achievement in that it accounts for approximately 50% of the variance in achievement (Brody, 1992). Many factors other than ability influence students' academic achievement, and there are many reasons that a student does not perform at the level of his or her estimated ability. Motivation level, interest, academic self-efficacy, self-regulation skills, goals and values, perceived environmental control, and other non-cognitive factors also to contribute to academic success (Bandura, 1997; Gordon et al., 1999, Reis & McCoach, 2000; Siegle, 2000). "If achievement depends on other normally distributed factors in addition to ability, such as motivation, interest, energy, and persistence, and if all these factors act multiplicatively, then theoretically, we should expect achievement to show a positively skewed distribution" (Jensen, 1980, p. 97). Jensen concludes, "it is probably more correct to say that a person's achievements are a *product*, rather than a summation, of his or her abilities, disposition, and training" (p. 98, emphasis in the original). Therefore, rather than expecting exceptional achievement from all students of exceptional ability, Jensen suggests that far fewer people will achieve at exceptional levels than have the potential for such achievement.

Regression to the Mean and Masking

There are also statistical reasons for disparities between ability and achievement at the highest ability levels. The phenomenon of regression to the mean posits that extreme scores will tend to shift toward the middle of the distribution (Campbell & Kenny, 1999). Given regression toward the mean, we would expect the achievement scores of students who scored in the top 2% of the ability distribution to be lower than their ability scores would indicate. Therefore, at the highest levels of measured ability, we would not necessarily expect all students to demonstrate equally high levels of achievement. In part, the masking argument relies upon the primacy of ability in determining consequent educational achievement. In reality, students of high ability who perform at average levels may or may not exhibit learning disabilities (Reis & McCoach, 2000).

Practical Problems with Masking

There are practical problems with the concept of masking as well. If this masking of students' potential does occur, what signs should teachers look for to identify these students? How should school psychologists identify this phenomenon? The concept of masking, although intuitively appealing, creates pragmatic problems for school psychologists. Realistically, we cannot screen all children who are performing at average levels to assess for the possibility of hidden learning disabilities. At the present time, no substantive suggestions exist for identifying these hidden LD students within the school population until their academic achievement becomes an area of concern. Future research should focus on documenting the existence of these students and identifying their distinguishing characteristics so that practitioners may effectively identify students who are at risk for hidden learning disabilities. However, currently, there is very little empirical research to guide the identification of these masked gifted/LD students.

Some advocates of the masking concept argue that a gifted student's learning disability attenuates his or her true IQ score (Fox & Brody, 1983; Tannenbaum & Baldwin, 1983; Waldron & Saphire, 1990), thus preventing the student from obtaining scores in the superior range on an individually administered IQ test. These authors suggest that variability within the subtests may indicate the presence of a learning disability, and that if one or more of the subtests is in the superior range, the student may be gifted and learning disabled. Fox and Brody further state that on the WISC-R, "high scores on parts of the test may suggest giftedness, while poor performance in other areas suggests disability" (p. 105). Again, although this idea may be intuitively appealing, it becomes problematic for practitioners who work with the child. In reality, intraindividual discrepancies are very common, and are not necessarily indicative of a disability or disorder (Gordon et al., 1999). Although the highest scores on an assessment could be considered an indication of innate aptitude, and any average scores could be regarded as deficit areas, one could reinterpret these results in the opposite direction. One could consider average results an indication of natural aptitude and the highest scores as areas of strength (Gordon et al., 1999). It is inappropriate to assume that any intraindividual variability in IQ is indicative of a disability. Furthermore, IQ tests lack treatment validity. They do not provide any information about how to best serve a student within an educational setting. Using an IQ test to provide the only indication of a student's masked learning disability does not provide educators with any practical suggestions for how to best meet the student's educational needs. In addition, school psychologists should never use the results of only one assessment instrument to determine whether a student has a learning disability (Baum et al., 1991).

THE CASE AGAINST USING PROFILE ANALYSIS WITH GIFTED/LEARNING-DISABLED STUDENTS

Profile analysis is defined as inspecting the individual subtest scores on a test of cognitive ability and interpreting differences as evidence for distinct patterns of intellectual functioning. The notion of subtest analysis is reinforced by the composition of the Wechsler Scales. These subtests appear to assess different content, which leads many educators to intuitively come to believe that students can exhibit unique patterns of strengths and weaknesses. Although the overwhelming majority of the research mitigates against the use of profile analysis, numerous practitioners continue its practice (e.g., Watkins & Kush, 1994; Truscott, Narrett, & Smith, 1994). The major reasons against the practice of profile analysis include: a) individual subtests are not as reliable as deviation IQs; b) statistically significant differences among subtests may also be quite common occurrences in student's patterns of subtest scores, c) ipsative scores are used and therefore generalized variance is removed.

The arguments presented by Bray, Kehle, and Hintze (1998) against the use of profile analysis in psycho-educational diagnoses are also applied here as arguments against the diagnosis as gifted/LD using similar procedures. They suggest that profile analysis should not be employed because "individual subtests are not as reliable as deviation IQs and/or factor scores as indicated by their corresponding reliability and stability coefficients, standard error of measurement (SE_m), and confidence intervals..." (p. 211).

Further, as stated by Bray et al. (1998), even with the use of the most rigorous .01 level of significance to lower the probability of a Type I error, any statistically significant differences among subtests may be quite common occurrences in children's patterns of scores, and consequently of little practical significance. For example, Bray et al. noted that "a difference of 11 points between the verbal and performance scales is significant at the .05 level for all ages, but it occurs in 40.5 percent of the standardization sample on the WISC III (Wechsler, 1991)" (p. 212).

Also, Jensen (1992) argued that profile analysis uses ipsative scores and therefore removes generalized variance; consequently, the general factor of intellectual or cognitive ability (*g*) is substantially diminished. According to Watkins and Kush (1994), the use of ipsative score analysis is simply an inappropriate method to interpret test results. Although the full-scale IQ score is remarkably stable, there is variability in the profile as a result of the lower reliabilities of the individual subtests. Consequently, a particular profile does not represent a particular disorder such as a learning disability (Truscott et al., 1993; Watkins & Kush, 1994).

The substantial discrepancy between research and practice prompted a special issue of *School Psychology Quarterly* published in 2000. Although this issue was consistent with the voluminous research confirming the lack of efficacy in the use of profile analysis, it did contain articles that suggested, given further research development, methods that may eventually justify the utility of profile analysis. Simply, it was suggested that if neurological evidence for the validity of the verbal-performance discrepancy could be confirmed (Riccio & Hynd, 2000), or the employment of configural frequency (Stanton & Reynolds, 2000), or modal profile analysis (Pritchard, Livingston, Reynolds, & Moses) could be accurately conducted, or finally, that refinement of the Cognitive Assessment System could be accomplished (Nagleri, 2000), then profile analysis may become a worthwhile assessment tool. These methods may eventually prove to be beneficial in diminishing the gap between research and practice. However, Watkins (2000), within the same issue, provided strong caution for using profile analysis at this time.

Using profile analysis to identify students as both gifted and learning disabled can be especially problematic. Some research suggests that the scaled score range among subtests increases as the full-scale IQ score increases (Patchett & Stansfield, 1992) and that subtest scatter increases as the value of the highest subtest score rises (Schinka, Vanderploeg, & Curtiss, 1997). If these findings are true, then we should expect intellectually gifted children to exhibit more atypical and scattered profiles than other students. Since profile analysis capitalizes on chance variability, it would be especially inappropriate for students of superior ability. Waldron and Saphire (1990) found that both gifted students and gifted/LD students showed strengths in the similarities subtest, and deficits in digit span. They also noted that neither examining verbal/performance discrepancies nor rank-ordering the WISC-R subtests proved an effective method of identifying or documenting the existence of a learning disability. The evidence refuting the use of profile analysis is even stronger for gifted or gifted/LD students than for the general school population.

RECOMMENDED BEST PRACTICES FOR IDENTIFYING GIFTED STUDENTS WITH LEARNING DISABILITIES

In previous sections of this chapter, we have outlined problems inherent in the current methods used to identify students as both gifted and learning disabled. Based on this research and our personal experiences, we propose several guidelines for identifying gifted students who exhibit learning disabilities. First, the identification of gifted students with learning disabilities should parallel the identification of all other students with learning disabilities. Naturally, the process must be in compliance with both federal and state special education regulations. In addition, practitioners must utilize valid and reliable indices of both ability and achievement, and they must employ appropriate methods to document a discrepancy between measured ability and achievement. To assess academic achievement, we recommend that school psychologists collect information documenting a child's current level of functioning within the classroom environment as well as standardized measures of achievement. Measures of achievement within the classroom could include, but are not limited to, curriculum-based assessments, informal reading inventories, permanent product reviews of a student's written work, and portfolio reviews. We discourage the use of profile analysis to detect the presence of learning disabilities in students under any circumstances. Currently, there is little empirical evidence to support the concept of masking. However, to conduct empirical research on students with hidden gifts and/or learning disabilities, we must find a defensible way to identify such students.

How should gifted students with learning disabilities be identified? Using a complete assessment battery to identify and plan interventions for gifted students with learning disabilities is critical. This assessment should consist of behavioral observations, an individual intelligence test, measures of cognitive processing, and a full achievement battery (Brody & Mills, 1997). It is also very important to assess the student's level of functioning within the regular classroom environment. Is the student having difficulty completing assignments and keeping up with the other students in the class? In addition, evaluations should include curriculum-based assessments or other measures of the student's functional level within the district's curriculum in any areas of suspected disability. Finally, the evaluator should conduct an interview with the student to assess the student's perceptions of and attitudes toward academics, especially in the suspected area of disability.

Examining Achievement Longitudinally

Furthermore, to assist in the screening and identification of gifted students with learning disabilities, we suggest that evaluators should examine the student's patterns of achievement and academic performance longitudinally. The standardized achievement test scores of gifted students with learning disabilities may decline over time as the specific learning disability exerts an increasingly greater influence on their academic achievement. For example, gifted students who exhibit specific reading disabilities may demonstrate exceptional academic achievement during the primary grades; however, they may experience greater and greater difficulty in school as assignments become more reading-intensive (Reis, Neu, & McGuire, 1997; Rosner & Seymour, 1983). Therefore, gifted students with learning disabilities may show a pattern of declining achievement test scores and classroom grades coupled with indicators of superior cognitive abilities. Educators should screen for this pattern of declining achievement by reviewing the standardized achievement test scores of students in a longitudinal manner. Larger than expected declines in academic achievement in one or more subject areas across grade levels could be cause for concern. Screening students who exhibit declining achievement test scores over the first three to five years of formal schooling may be an effective way to identify students with above average to superior cognitive abilities who also exhibit learning disabilities. Any children who appear to exhibit patterns of declining achievement would be referred for further assessment. This screening process could lead to earlier intervention for such students, and might result in better long-term educational outcomes for these bright students with learning disabilities. Empirical research is needed to ascertain whether this longitudinal screening method aids in the early detection of gifted students with hidden learning disabilities. However, we believe that this approach is more justifiable than using profile analysis to identify gifted students with masked learning disabilities. Table 1 provides guidelines for identifying students as gifted/LD.

Let's return to the example of Ronald, the boy with average academic grades and a 145 IQ. In all likelihood, we would not be aware of Ronald's high IQ, since it would be unlikely that he would receive an individual IQ test prior to his LD referral. However, imagine that we examine Ronald's file and discover that his standardized achievement scores in reading have dropped from scores in the 85th percentile in first grade to the 40th percentile by fourth grade. Such scores would be a sign that, relative to his peers, Ronald's academic achievement has declined significantly over the first four years of school, and we would consider him a candidate for further evaluation.

Using this system will certainly also produce false positive referrals. Therefore, it is important to try to identify the cause of a student's underachievement using a formal psycho-educational assessment, which includes IQ and achievement tests, and classroom interviews and observations. Otherwise, "diagnoses separating gifted students who exhibit learning difficulties into subgroups of those with learning disabilities, those with normal variation in cognitive development, and those who are unmotivated for a variety of reasons can be problematic" (Brody & Mills, 1997, p. 287).

Table 1. Steps for Identifying Gifted Students as Learning Disabled

----

1.   Examine student's school records longitudinally. Examine both classroom grades and standardized measures of achievement. Is there a pattern of decreasing academic achievement over time? Have scores on standardized measures of achievement decreased over time?

2.   Conduct observations of the student within the classroom environment. Evaluate the student's level of difficulty within the classroom environment as well as any observable compensation strategies that he or she uses to cope with academic demands.

3.   Conduct an individual intellectual assessment using an individually administered IQ test.

4.   Conduct an academic assessment using both individually administered standardized achievement tests and curriculum-based assessments.

5.   Assess processing using standardized tests/scales that you have not used to assess intellectual functioning or academic achievement.

6.   Collect and evaluate work samples from the student's teachers.

7.   Conduct a short interview with the student to assess his or perceptions of any academic difficulties.

8.   Solicit input from teachers and parents.

CONCLUSION

The identification of gifted students as learning disabled has received increasing attention in recent years. Most of the recommendations for identification of gifted/LD are based on clinical practice and professional judgment rather than empirical research because very little research has been done in this area. In addition, federal laws mandate using certain procedures to identify students with disabilities. Therefore, we recommend using the already established federal and state identification criteria to identify gifted/LD students until sufficient evidence exists to create differential identification procedures for these students. The use of profile analysis to identify a student as either gifted, learning disabled, or gifted/LD is not warranted based on current research. Utilizing longitudinal data collection to identify declines in achievement across the primary and elementary years may help educators to identify high-ability students with learning disabilities. Finally, more empirical research is needed to determine whether different subsets of gifted students with learning disabilities exist, and how to best identify and serve this unique population of students with learning disabilities.

NOTES

1. A previous version of this paper was published as McCoach, D. B., Kehle, T. J., Bray, M. A., & Siegle, D. (2001). Best Practices in the identification of gifted students with disabilities. *Psychology in the Schools, 38,* 403–411. The present chapter represents an adaptation, an update, and an expansion of the aforementioned article.

REFERENCES

Bandura, A. (1997). *The exercise of control.* New York: W. H. Freeman and Company.

Baum, S. M., Owen, S. V., & Dixon, J. (1991). *To be gifted and learning disabled.* Mansfield, CT: Creative Learning Press.

Beitchman, J. H., & Young, A. R. (1997). Learning disorders with a special emphasis on reading disorders: A review of the past 10 years. *Journal of the American Academy of Child and Adolescent Psychiatry, 36,* 1020–1033.

Borland, J. H. (1989). *Planning and implementing programs for the gifted.* New York: Teachers College Press.

Bray, M. A., Kehle, T. J., & Hintze, J. M. (1998). Profile analysis with the Wechsler Scales: Why does it persist? *School Psychology International, 19,* 209–220.

Brody, L. E., & Mills, C. J. (1997). Gifted children with learning disabilities: A review of the issues. *Journal of Learning Disabilities, 30,* 282–296.

Brody, N. (1992). *Intelligence* (2nd ed.). San Diego, CA: Academic Press, Inc.

Campbell, D. T., & Kenny, D. A. (1999). *A primer on regression artifacts.* New York: The Guilford Press.

Columbus Group (1991, July). *Unpublished transcript of the meeting of the Columbus Group.* Columbus, OH.

Davis, G. B., & Rimm, S. B. (1994). *Education of the gifted and talented.* (3rd ed.). Boston: Allyn & Bacon.

Fox, L. H., & Brody, L. (1983). Models for identifying giftedness: Issues related to the learning disabled child. In L. H. Fox, L. Brody, & D. Tobin (Eds.), *Learning disabled/gifted children: Identification and programming* (pp. 101–116). Baltimore, MD: University Park.

Gardner, H. (1993). *Multiple intelligences: The theory in practice.* New York: Basic.

Gagné, F. (1997). Critique of Morelock's (1996) definition of giftedness and talent. *Roeper Review, 20,* 76–85.

Gordon, M., Lewandowski, L., & Keiser, S. (1999). The LD label for relative functioning students: A critical analysis. *Journal of Learning Disabilities, 32,* 485–490.

Gunderson, C. W., Maesch, C., & Rees, J. W. (1987). The gifted learning disabled student. *Gifted Child Quarterly, 31,* 158–160.

Jensen, A. R. (1980). *Bias in mental testing.* New York: The Free Press.

Jensen, A. R. (1992). Commentary: Vehicles of g. *Psychological Science, 3,* 275–278.

Kavale, K. A., & Forness, S. R. (2000). What definitions of learning disability say and don't say: A critical analysis. *Journal of Learning Disabilities, 33,* 239–256.

Mercer, C. D., Jordan, L., Allsop, D. H., & Mercer, A. R. (1996). Learning disabilities definitions and criteria used by state education agencies. *Learning Disability Quarterly, 19,* 217–232.

Morelock, M. J. (1996). On the nature of giftedness and talent: Imposing order on chaos. *Roeper Review, 19,* 4–12.

Naglieri, J. A. (2000). Can profile analysis of ability test scores work? An illustration using the PASS theory and CAS with an unselected cohort. *School Psychology Quarterly, 15,* 419–433.

National Joint Committee on Learning Disabilities (2002). *The Learning Disabilities Roundtable*. Retrieved December 9, 2002 from nasponline.org/ advocacy/ IDEA information.html

Patchett, R. F., & Stansfield, M. (1992). Subtest scatter on the WISC-R with children of superior intelligence. *Psychology in the Schools, 29*, 5–11.

Pritchard, D. A., Livingston, R. B., Reynolds, C., & Moses, J. A. (2000). Modal profiles for the WISC-III. *School Psychology Quarterly, 15*, 400–418.

Reis, S. M. (1989). Reflections on policy affecting the education of gifted and talented student. *American Psychologist, 44*, 399–408.

Reis, S. M., & McCoach, D. B. (2000). The underachievement of gifted students: What do we know and where do we go? *Gifted Child Quarterly, 44*, 152–170.

Reis, S. M., Neu, T. W., & McGuire, J. M. (1997). Case studies of high ability students with learning disabilities who have achieved. *Exceptional Children, 63*, 463–479.

Renzulli, J. (1978). What makes giftedness? Reexamining a definition. *Phi Delta Kappan, 60*, 180–184.

Renzulli, J. S., & Reis, S. M. (1985). *The schoolwide enrichment model: A comprehensive plan for educational excellence*. Mansfield, CT: Creative Learning Press.

Riccio, C. A., & Hynd, G. W. (2000). Measurable biological substrates to verbal–performance differences in Wechsler scores. *School Psychology Quarterly, 15*, 386–399.

Rosner, S. L., & Seymour, J. (1983). The gifted child with a learning disability: Clinical evidence. In L. H. Fox, L. Brody, & D. Tobin (Eds.), *Learning disabled/gifted children: Identification and programming.* (pp. 77–97). Baltimore, MD: University Park Press.

Schinka, J. A., Vanderploeg, R. D., & Curtiss, G. (1997). WISC-III subtest scatter as a function of the highest subtest score. *Psychological Assessment, 9*, 83–88.

Siegle, D. (2000, December). Parenting achievement oriented children. *Parenting for High Potential*, pp. 6–7, 29–30.

Silver, A. A., & Hagin, R. A. (2002). *Disorders of learning in childhood* (2nd ed.). New York: John Wiley & Sons, Inc.

Stanton, H. C., & Reynolds, C. (2000). Configural frequency analysis as a method of determining wechsler profile types. *School Psychology Quarterly, 15*, 434–448.

Sternberg, R. J. (1988). *The triarchic mind: A new theory of human intelligence*. New York: Viking Penguin, Inc.

Tannenbaum, A. J., & Baldwin, L. J. (1983). Giftedness and learning disability: A paradoxical combination. In L. H. Fox, L. Brody, & D. Tobin (Eds.), *Learning disabled/gifted children: Identification and programming.* (pp. 11–36). Baltimore, MD: University Park Press.

Terman, L. M. (1925). *Genetic studies of genius: Vol. 1. Mental and physical traits of a thousand gifted children*. Stanford, CA: Stanford University Press.

Truscott, S. D., Narrett, C. M., & Smith, S. E. (1993). WISC-R subtest reliability over time: Implications for practice and research. *Psychological Reports, 74, 147–156.*

United States Office of Education. (1977). Assistance to states for education for handicapped children: Procedures for evaluating specific learning disabilities. *Federal Register, 42*, 62082–62085. Washington, DC: U.S. Government Printing Office.

United States Office of Education. (1976). Proposed rulemaking. *Federal Register, 41*, 52404–52407. Washington, DC: U.S. Government Printing Office.

U.S. Department of Education. (1993). *National excellence: A case for developing America's talent*. Washington DC: Author.

Waldron, K. A., & Saphire, D. G. (1990). An analysis of factors for gifted students with learning disabilities. *Journal of Learning Disabilities, 23*, 491–498.

Watkins, M. W. (2000). Cognitive profile analysis: A shared professional myth. *School Psychology Quarterly, 15*, 465–479.

Watkins, M. W., & Kush, J. C. (1994). Wechsler subtest analysis: The right way, the wrong way, or no way?" *School Psychology Review, 23*, 640–651.

Wechsler, D. (1991). *Manual for the Wechsler Intelligence Scale for Children-III*. San Antonio, TX: The Psychological Corporation.

Winner, E. (2000). Giftedness: Current theory and research. *Current Directions in Psychological Science, 9*, 153–156.

Chapter 3

UNRAVELING THE MYSTERIES OF GLD: TOWARD THE APPLICATION OF COGNITIVE THEORY TO ASSESSMENT

Judy L. Lupart
University of Alberta

INTRODUCTION

Traditional special education systems in our schools have been configured primarily to deal with students who present symptoms or characteristics associated with one category or condition, such as *behavior disorder* or *visual impairment*. These traditional systems have been highly instrumental in defining the type and extent of service provided for students who are gifted and students who are learning disabled. In fact these two classifications have been central to the mushrooming numbers of identified special-needs students in the schools over the past 40 years (Andrews & Lupart, 2000; Mercer, 1997).

Unfortunately, when traditional special and regular education systems are presented with students having dual or multiple exceptionalities, there is often confusion about how the combination of needs could best be identified and served. As Baum and Owen (1988) describe it, special education programs are designed either to remediate weaknesses or to develop superior abilities. Indeed, it is very likely that students with dual or multiple exceptionalities will be overlooked (Baum, Cooper, & Neu, 2001; Lupart, 1992; Lupart & Pyryt, 1996; Richert, 1997), and in the case of students who are gifted and learning disabled (GLD), they will most likely be underserved (Whitmore, 1986). Since the early 1970s there has been an increased professional awareness of the rapidly growing number of students who have been identified as gifted and learning disabled (Yewchuk & Lupart, 2000), however, this awareness has not translated into the actual provision of an appropriate educational program for such students (Brody & Mills, 1997).

There has been considerable discussion concerning why this subpopulation continues to be underserved (Brody & Mills, 1997; Whitmore, 1989; Yewchuk & Lupart, 2000). Johnson, Karnes and Carr (1997) have proposed several reasons: (1) inappropriate procedures used in identification; (2) stereotypical attitudes; (3) limited information concerning the nature and impact of developmental delays; (4) inadequate training of professionals; (5) lack of appropriate program models, research and dissemination strategies; (6) limited access to supportive technology; (7) limited and inappropriate career counseling; and (8) inadequate funding. In addition, Yewchuk and Lupart (2000) have suggested that the traditional separation of special and regular education systems and the conflicting values of excellence and equity may be major factors to consider. At a time when schools are under enormous pressure to meet the ever-increasing expectations of society, they are being asked to support the values and the practice of inclusive education. For gifted students who are learning disabled, the paradox may be so profound that educators may dismiss entirely the possibility of such students being in their classrooms. In answer to these seemingly contradictory trends of promoting excellence and equity, Yewchuk and Lupart (2000) have noted that "many reform leaders are now promoting a merged or unified system of educational provision for all students, in the belief that all children, particularly those with exceptional learning needs, stand to reap significant, positive benefit" (Goodlad & Lovitt, 1993; Lupart & Webber, 1996; Lupart, 1998; Skrtic, 1995; 1996). Although the scope of the problem is well beyond the parameters of the current chapter, many of these factors have direct impact on the identification and assessment of students who are gifted and learning disabled and thus are raised here as general problems. The following section addresses issues that specifically impact on GLD identification and assessment.

APPROACHES AND ISSUES ASSOCIATED WITH GLD IDENTIFICATION AND ASSESSMENT

A review of the research literature concerning individuals with high potential and learning disability (GLD) over the past three decades reveals a preponderance of articles dealing with identification as opposed to assessment concerns. Practices associated with the identification of GLD students typically involve a combination of procedures, borrowing from both the gifted and learning disability fields. Despite the fact that there is no real consensus as to the best means for GLD identification, there is widespread agreement concerning the futility of schools and school boards trying to operate within the guidelines for identification of students who are either gifted or learning disabled (Baum, 1994; Brody & Mills, 1997; Whitmore, 1986; Yewchuk & Lupart, 2000). Apparently, in most school systems, whatever identification program is pursued, neither will be likely to have adequate flexibility to allow for the recognition of the other condition or characteristics of gifted learning disability. Worse yet, if a student is successfully identified, intervention tends to favor the tradition of the associated area and consequently is not.likely to address unique learning needs in the other area of exceptionality (Baum, Owen & Dixon, 1991; Reis, McGuire & Neu, 2000).

In an attempt to resolve the issues surrounding GLD identification, several alternate approaches have been advanced. Most widely recommended in the literature is an approach often referred to as "profile analysis" (Baum, Emerick, Herman, & Dixon, 1989; Schiff, Kaufman & Kaufman, 1981; Silverman, 1989). In this approach, patterns of ability and difficulty as indicated by IQ test analysis are posited as being distinctly associated with individuals who are GLD. More recently, however, this approach has been effectively challenged in the literature (McCoach, Kehle, Bray & Siegle, 2001; Bray, Kehle, & Hintze, 1998), mainly because of concerns about using a single test to determine classification.

A second common alternative approach is the search for identifying characteristics of gifted students with learning disabilities (Fox, Brody & Tobin, 1983; Silverman, 1989; Vespi & Yewchuk, 1992). Combinations of characteristics identified, such as perfectionism, distractibility, super sensitivity, chronic inattention, illegible handwriting, high creativity, and unrealistic expectations are just a few of the constellation of findings that have been attributed to the GLD subpopulation of students. Though this tradition has been very helpful to educators responsible for instructional interventions, concern has been expressed regarding making an accurate distinction between students who are truly gifted and learning disabled, versus those gifted students who may lack academic motivation and as a result may simply be underachieving (Jeon, 1992; Yewchuk, 1986). Such distinctions, however, may not be viable. Lupart and Pyryt's (1996) research revealed that students who are underachieving gifted and special population gifted (i.e., GLD, culture minority, and visually impaired) may indeed have shared characteristics that are circuitous and indistinguishable.

A third approach, reported by Barton and Starnes (1989), calls for the taxonomic classification of subgroups of GLD students into categories of mild, moderate, and severe, using a process of case cluster analysis. The approach capitalizes on using a combination of approaches and represents one of the few attempts to venture beyond identification to the comparison of profiles of gifted and GLD samples to identify a distinguishing pattern of characteristics unique to the latter group from several information sources (i.e., WISC-R subtest profiles, standardized achievement test scores). Their findings, however, led them to conclude that the GLD population is notably heterogeneous and that more comprehensive assessment measures may be required to inform adequate instructional programming.

Other relevant research can be found in general surveys and studies of GLD identification practices in different schools, districts, and states

(Boodoo, Bradley, Frontera, Pitts & Wright, 1989; Coleman & Gallagher, 1995; Tallent-Runnels & Sigler, 1995). Overall, collective results have confirmed that the GLD student is most likely to slip through the cracks, mainly due to existing practices and policies that are best suited for single, not dual, exceptionalities. It is, however, of interest to note that based on their analysis of state identification policies for gifted students from special populations from all 50 U.S. states and a follow-up examination of policy implementation in three states, Coleman and Gallagher (1995) concluded that it was not the actual policy in most cases but rather the interpretation and implementation of policy that could be attributed to the under-representation of gifted students from special populations. Indeed, their findings from a follow-up study revealed that a broader, more flexible and comprehensive program with greater discretionary power at the local school level was most conducive to the identification of gifted students from special populations.

Even though researchers and practitioners are still struggling with these and other issues relating primarily to identification, the reality of the situation is that teachers in many school programs are finding that once the GLD student has been identified, this typically marks the end of the assessment process. In fact, this should be the point where in-depth assessment begins. Identification measures provide only limited information with respect to individual learning needs and appropriate instructional accommodations. For the most part, the primary purpose of identification assessment within the schools is to confirm the student's exceptional learning needs, remove them from the regular classroom, and place them in a specialized setting with others who are similarly labeled for instructional purposes. Since most schools do not have special classes or programs that are appropriate for the unique learning needs of GLD students, and typical identification procedures are ineffective, chances are that these students remain in regular classrooms. Accordingly, teachers are left on their own to work out any accommodations for GLD students within their classrooms. Most teachers will not have any knowledge about the unique learning needs of these students, and given the complexity of the learning needs these students have, the onus will be on the student to cope with the regular instructional program as best as possible. Consequently, it is highly likely that the high potential of these students will not be actualized and the learning difficulties will become more pronounced. This reality is far a-field from what current theory and research in special education and learning suggest (Bransford, Brown & Cocking, 2000; Trent, Artiles & Englert, 1998).

MOVING TOWARD IN-DEPTH ASSESSMENT OF GLD STUDENTS

Recent trends that have stimulated a radical paradigm shift in traditional educational approaches to student assessment over the past two decades (Gipps, 1999; Hoy & Gregg, 1994; McMillan, 2001). For example, Gipps (1999) describes the shift from traditional standardized tests toward "a broader assessment of learning, enhancement of learning for the individual, engagement with the student during assessment, and involvement of teachers in the assessment process" (p. 367). This change is directly linked to recent theory and development in our understanding of how learning takes place (Bransford, Brown, & Cocking, 2000). Cognitive learning theories have been highly influential in catapulting prevailing views in educational assessment and instructional planning to more authentic and contextualized approaches (Gipps, 1999; Lupart, 1991; McMillan, 2001).

Drawing broadly from contemporary information processing, Piagetian, and socio-cultural theories, some of the more prominent features of this alternate approach to assessment can be identified. The process: (a) is student-centered and reflects the quality of students' thinking and understanding; (b) engages the student in meaningful, dynamic activities that are similar and relevant to everyday classroom learning; (c) focuses on the match between the learner's abilities and self- and other regulation of learning within the social context of the school classroom; (d) captures student competence in "high road" (intentional, conceptually oriented) and "low road" (practice and automaticity-oriented) learning; (e) offers the student opportunities to demonstrate new learning and transfer of learning; (f) promotes the central involvement and ongoing monitoring of the classroom teacher; and (g) attempts to factor in key contextual features of learning at school and home (Bransford, Brown, & Cocking, 2000; Bransford & Schwartz,1999; Case, 1985; Lupart, 1990,1991, 1995; Salomon & Perkins, 1998; Sternberg, 1986, 2003; Zimmerman & Schunk, 1989; Vygotsky, 1963; 1978).

Given the degree and extent of influence contemporary cognitive learning theories have had on current educational assessment practice, it is surprising that there are so few publications incorporating these notions in the GLD literature (Barton & Starnes, 1989; Hansford, Whitmore, Kraynak, & Wingenbach, 1987; Lupart, 1990; Starnes, Ginevan, Stokes, & Barton, 1988; Svec, 1985). In fact, since it has been aptly demonstrated that there is a high risk in schools for GLD students to be under-identified and under-served, it seems reasonable to suggest that more effort and resources need to be put into helping teachers to become partners in assessing the unique learning needs of GLD students and to encourage teachers to use this knowledge in their ongoing instructional planning. The present study focuses on the bridging of identification approaches traditionally implemented in the schools with the development and implementation of a contextualized, theory-based approach for the in-depth assessment of GLD students as a means of informing instructional practice.

METHOD

The purpose of this study was to consolidate and enrich existing assessment records of high-ability Grade 7 students with learning disabilities and to investigate learner perceptions and experiences about school and learning to inform instructional programming. In-depth structured interview questions that focused on "how" GLD students view their particular learning abilities and disabilities, how this view affects their school performance, their explanations of why they feel and act the way they do, and their experiences, were developed, implemented and analyzed using qualitative case-study methods. Patton (1990) has noted that case studies

> ...become particularly useful where one needs to understand some special people, particular problems, or unique situation in great depth, and where one can identify cases rich in information—rich in the sense that a great deal can be learned from a few exemplars of the phenomenon in question (p. 54).

Within the field of education, case-study research is used as a method to influence the development of knowledge and improve educational practice. Research that is based on the perceptions, insights, and experiences of the participants offers great potential to the contemporary understanding of the unique learning needs of high-ability students with learning disabilities. For the purposes of this investigation, an *instrumental* case-study approach is used to examine the effectiveness of a theory-based, in-depth assessment process (Stake, 1995). Instrumental means that the study "will have a research question, a puzzlement, a need for general understanding, and feel that we may get insight into the question"(p. 3). In order to gain a proper understanding of the *puzzle* under study, it is recommended that data collection involve multiple sources of information rich in context (Cresswell, 1997; Stake, 1995; Yin, 1994). The in-depth assessment approach adopted in this study included classroom observation and interviews with students, teacher, and parents as a means of depicting the unique characteristics and perceptions of GLD learners in their school context.

Sample

Three male junior high school students identified as having high ability and a learning disability attending a mid-size urban junior high school participated in this study. The students had been identified as special students in elementary school based on their disabilities, and they were all age 13 at the time of the data collection. The students were enrolled in a self-contained GLD class, newly implemented during that school year, and they received their academic subject instruction from a female teacher with expertise in gifted education. Students were included in regular Grade 7 classes for their optional courses.

Data Collection

This study relies on the combination of data-collection techniques in an attempt to develop what Yin (1989) described as "converging lines of inquiry, a process of triangulation..." (p. 97). Data collection consisted of the researcher's observation notes, student records and testing information, videotaped structured interviews, student's texts, scribblers, free reading books, school materials, and writing samples. The parent(s) of each of the three students were interviewed and filled out a questionnaire prior to meeting with the research team. The classroom teacher was interviewed on a number of occasions to confirm or extend observations and interpretations of the data analysis (Tomlinson, 1995). In addition, she was asked to complete two questionnaires about each student to capture teacher perceptions of the student within the classroom context. By combining several sources of information in the context of the students' classroom and home life, a more accurate account of the student's learning profile and perceptions of the individual's abilities and limitations at school was obtained.

Stage One: Summary Profile. *This phase of the assessment approach was modeled after several studies in the GLD literature utilizing multiple-source approaches to determine unique learning characteristics and patterns (Barton & Starnes, 1989; Baum & Owen, 1988; Baum, Cooper, & Neu, 2001; Crawford & Snart, 1994; Lupart, 1990; Reis, Neu, & McGuire, 1997; Reis, McGuire, & Neu, 2000). The first step in the data-gathering process involved the specification of relevant assessment domains and the syntheses of existing information. Drawing from the available literature and typical practice in the local school district, the six domains examined consisted of intelligence, achievement, creativity, self-concept, teacher evaluation, and family support.*

Like many of the youngsters in special classes, these three students had huge cumulative records files documenting long histories of referral and assessment. Once all available information was documented and organized, further assessment measures were implemented to create a comprehensive, comparative summary profile for each of the three students. Recent intelligence test results (WISC-R) and achievement scores (Canadian Abilities Test) were already available for each of the students. Further assessment in the areas of creativity, self-concept, teacher evaluation, and family support was carried out to complete the summary profile. Performance scores obtained in the six domains, as well as the relevant subcategories or subtests for each of the three GLD students, are presented in Figures 1, 2 and 3. The graphic representation of each of the domains is important in targeting the major areas of strength and weakness of the GLD student.

The inclusion of a creativity measure in the student profile was seen to be important, especially in GLD assessment, since this domain is one in which GLD students often excel in compensation for poor performance in certain academic areas (Baum, 1994; Baum & Kirschenbaum, 1984; LaFrance, 1994). Moreover, this area offers a positive balance in the overall assessment of learning strengths and weaknesses (Howard, 1994). For this assessment project, the William (1980) instrument *Exercise in Divergent Thinking* was used.

The importance of self-concept in relation to a student's learning ability has long been recognized in the learning disability literature (Chapman, 1988; Lerner, 1981; Russell, 1974). Lerner (1981) notes that a student who has a history of failure in school is liable to fall victim to a continuous cycle, "the failure to learn leads to adverse emotional responses—feelings of self-derision, poor ego perception, and anxiety, which augment the failure to learn syndrome" (p. 404). Researchers in the GLD area have similarly noted the destructive effects of poor self-concept (Maker, 1977; Senf, 1983; Whitmore, 1980). A study of the relationships among academic achievement, self-concept, and behavior of GLD students revealed significant relationships between self-concept and hyperactive/asocial behaviors (Waldron, Saphire, & Rosenblum, 1987). On the positive side, other research has demonstrated that exposure to a long-term enrichment program can have a significant positive impact on self-concept (Olenchak, 1995). Self-concept measures were included within the in-depth assessment procedure to assess how each GLD student viewed himself in general and, more importantly, how he viewed himself within the learning context. For this assessment, two measures were utilized: the William (1980) *Exercise in Divergent Feeling* and the Weber and Battaglia (1982) *Spend Your Dollar*.

An area often overlooked in GLD assessment is the area of parent and family perception and support of the learner. For example, Starnes, Ginevan, Stokes, and Barton (1988) used parent checklists in their study of GLD students and noted that this information was particularly useful for determining student frustration levels and the time spent compensating. In addition, parent information revealed that these students had highly developed interests, often outside school. In further support, a more recent study of high-ability students with learning disabilities who were successful at the college level (Reis, Neu, & McGuire, 1997) revealed the consistent, pervasive support of parents, particularly mothers. In school-based efforts to develop instructional programming for the GLD student, the level of parent support may be highly informative to the overall assessment procedure. For this component of the GLD summary profile, data collection included the administration of the Weber and Battaglia (1982) *Parent Appraisal of Out-of-School Production* measure and an individual interview with the parent(s).

The final area, important in piecing together a comprehensive summary profile of the GLD student, has to do with the teacher's perceptions of the student within the classroom context. It has been argued that teachers can be valuable, active participants in the systematic investigation of professional practice and classroom application (Tomlinson, 1995). An overview of how the student typically presents in comparison to other students in the classroom, from the teacher's perspective, can provide useful information in formulating instructional recommendations. Moreover, socio-cultural theory asserts there must be a close association between assessment and instruction; hence, ideally it should be the teacher who makes these important connections since s/he has multiple opportunities to support student learning potential over the course of the school year (Vygotsky, 1963). Two instruments were used in the current project, including the Weber and Battaglia (1982) *Personal Characteristics Appraisal* and the Treffinger (1986) *IPPM Referral Form*.

The six assessment domains in Stage One were intended to provide a comprehensive summary profile of the strengths and weaknesses, in addition to the socializer (i.e., parent and teacher) perception and support of the GLD learner. Each domain represents an area that has been shown to have primary impact on the learning ability and potential of GLD students. Specific published instruments were used in this particular project to provide data for each of the six domain areas. However, assessment measure selection can be left to the discretion of the person carrying out the assessment. What is important at this stage is that multiple sources of input are necessary in creating a comprehensive overview. As Starnes et al. (1988) describe it, "the whole picture came from putting all the pieces of the puzzle regarding an individual child together, and no one piece could give the whole picture" (p. 5).

Stage Two: Learner in Context. *Stage Two of the in-depth assessment of GLD learners was based on a structured interview procedure that incorporated the theoretical concepts and cognitive-psychology framework described earlier. In particular, this stage of the assessment approach attempted to delve into the unique patterns of cognitive and metacognitive functioning of the three students. Emphasis was given to probing student self-perceptions about their learning abilities and challenges, and how these were orchestrated in their day-to-day classroom learning activities (Hannah & Shore, 1995; Howard, 1994; Miller, 1991; Reis, Neu, & McGuire, 1997; Reis, McGuire, & Neu, 2000).*

The three GLD students were instructed to essentially empty their school lockers and bring to the assessment sessions all materials used within the classroom as well as current reading and writing materials. Each student was seen individually in a university lab/classroom equipped with a one-way mirror and videotaping equipment, and the length of sessions ranged from 2–2.5 hours. The format and sequencing of the structured interview session varied with each student.

Since all three students had specific learning difficulties in the language arts area, writing and reading as well as the typical organizational and school program awareness difficulties were examined (Baum, Cooper, & Neu, 2001). A shared writing/response activity as well as a silent reading activity was carried out with each student. In addition, student notebooks, previous writing samples, their current subject texts, and recreational reading books and magazines were used as core assessment materials in these sessions. Examples of questions that framed the **writing** structured interview are: (1) Are you a good writer? What do these teacher comments tell you about your writing? (2) What would you like to change about your writing? How could you improve your writing? (3) What has to be in a good story? In a good essay? In your notes? And (4) If you knew someone was having difficulty writing a story how would you help him/her?

Examples of questions that were included in the **reading** structured interview are: (1) What is reading? (2) I am going to have you read a story out loud, and when you are finished, I am going to have you retell me the story. Is there anything else you would like to know? (3) How do you think you can improve your reading? And (4) What do you do if you don't understand?

Examples of questions included in the structured interview for **organization and program awareness** are: (1) How do you organize your schoolwork? Is there anything you could do to improve in this area? (2) What kind of a class is this? What is the purpose of this class? (3) If you could change the way things are at school, what would you like to see? (4) Why do you go to this class? How will being in this class help you?

The Stage Two assessment sessions were video recorded and transcribed, and the field notes and observations made by the researcher during the sessions were added to the transcriptions. In addition, after reviewing the entire set of videotapes, the researcher carried out three sessions of classroom observation along with subsequent individual meetings with the GLD classroom teacher. The latter activities were undertaken to ascertain the strength and credibility of emergent themes within the classroom context and through discussion and verification of these themes with the classroom teacher. As a central participant in this practical inquiry, the teacher was encouraged to assist the researcher in tracing out relevant themes in the learning and classroom behavior of each of the GLD students.

Data Analysis

Data analysis was conducted using techniques designed by Bassey (1999) and Yin (1994). Both support the notion that theory plays an important role in the analysis and generalization of case-study research. Yin (1994) explicitly described the process by which "a previously developed theory is used as a template with which to compare the empirical results of the case study. If two or more cases are shown to support the same theory, replication may be claimed" (p. 31). In the present study, cognitive theory is the theoretical template used to examine the unique abilities and limitations, perceptions and learning experiences of adolescent GLD students. The overall goal of the research is to assess both products (i.e., test scores, surveys, interviews) as well as processes (i.e., individual and interactive) that contribute to the GLD student's learning potential (Bransford, Brown, & Cocking, 2000; Gipps, 1999). Accordingly, the in-depth assessment procedure utilized in this study included traditional static measures of learning accomplishment as well as dynamic interactive procedures.

For Stage One, data analysis consisted of the recording and graphic representation of existing assessment information from each student's cumulative file and other common self-perception and creativity measures, along with measures of parent and teacher perceptions and support compiled into a summary profile of the individual learner. Verbatim transcriptions of the Stage Two assessment sessions were produced to accompany the analytic review of the videotapes, and relevant field notes and observations were included in the transcripts. As Bassey (1999) suggested, all aspects of the data were studied to generate the initial draft of analytical statements and then tested against the data within a cognitive-psychological theoretical perspective. This iterative process of analysis and testing the analytic statements eventually led to the compilation of a final set of analytical statements that were deemed to be trustworthy by the researcher. Additional indicators of trustworthiness included classroom observations and discussions with the GLD classroom teacher undertaken prior to the formulation of the final set of analytical statements or emergent themes.

RESULTS AND DISCUSSION

As is typical of case-study research, the data collection resulted in several volumes of transcriptions and notes and produced an average of three one-hour videotapes for each GLD student. Space limitations for this chapter preclude a full, detailed analysis of the findings, and therefore, this section will be limited to a few examples of the most salient results and their connection to contemporary cognitive theory.

One Label: Multiple Manifestations

A comparison across summary profiles reveals that even within the restricted high IQ range there was considerable heterogeneity. Each student demonstrated some discrepancy in the comparison across Verbal IQ and Performance IQ, with Cole (see Figure 1) scoring a 30–point discrepancy favoring Performance IQ and Craig (see Figure 3) scoring a 19–point discrepancy favoring Verbal IQ. Similar scatter was evident in the breakdown of achievement scores. At the time of data collection, students were in the eighth month of Grade 7. Ken's (see Figure 2) academic achievement was approximately three grade levels above average in reading, language, and math, whereas both Craig and Cole were performing below grade level in at least two of the four subject areas. An extreme achievement discrepancy is noted in Craig's profile, showing a grade level score of 2.5 in spelling.

Measures of creativity and self-concept were similarly variable. For the creativity measure used in this study, students had to sketch an interesting object or picture starting with incomplete line drawings and then provide a title for the completed drawing. Not surprisingly, all three students excelled in the originality subcategory. For example, one of the 12 frames featured a line drawing of a circle. Craig drew in three eyes, two noses and a crooked smile and titled the completed frame *"Have a not so great day!"* Another feature evident in the student responses was the extensive use of humor. It is of interest to note that self-concept was consistently low for all three students, and extremely low for two of the three. Moreover, this self-rating did not appear to be consistent with their actual profiles. This area is examined further in the Stage Two data analysis.

Perhaps the most interesting comparisons come from the ratings of parents and the teacher. In the case of Ken, whom the teacher rates most poorly, his school achievement scores are the highest of the three boys. In contrast, Craig received consistent, positive ratings, particularly in the Social–Emotional subcategory. There are wide discrepancies noted in the teacher's assessments of individual Social–Emotional behavior, Work Study habits, and overall Productivity. How the teacher perceives an individual student will have implications for the day-to-day classroom dynamics, and this type of profiling was seen to be especially effective in terms of helping to heighten teacher sensitivity to unique student characteristics and to plan instructional activities to help improve student performance in areas of particular challenge.

It is important to note that for two of the three students, parent responses to the Weber and Battaglia (1982) questionnaire indicated a limited acknowledgment of the student's giftedness. Generally, these parents did not see their child as being particularly self-motivated or outstanding in his accomplishments. In contrast, Craig's parents seemed to be quite accurate in describing the talents and unusual abilities of their child, and in response to the question "What do you consider the most outstanding accomplishment of your child to date?" stated: "He has accomplished the ability to go and talk with people of all ages and have a conversation with them (probably from age 2 on). He also has a great vocabulary and excellent comprehension."

In general, the results of the profile analysis indicated the importance of treating each student as a unique learner and findings are consistent with previous research noting the extreme heterogeneity of GLD students (Barton & Starnes, 1989; Crawford & Snart, 1994). Traditional special education approaches that focus on instructional programming based of the defining characteristics of a particular category of exceptional children should be avoided as a strategy for GLD students. This conclusion is similarly affirmed in the analysis of the Stage Two data.

Self-Regulation

Even though cognitive theory and research have repeatedly demonstrated the central importance of self-regulating one's learning to achieve full development of potential (Bransford, Brown, & Cocking, 2000; Zimmerman & Schunk, 1989), especially for exceptional learners (Borkowski & Day, 1987; Borkowski, Schneider & Pressley, 1989; Lupart, 1995), this ability appeared to be substantially immature in two of the three GLD readers in this study. Cole, for example, found the organizational aspects of his learning to be particularly challenging. He arrived at the assessment session with two large paper bags of school materials and other items such as leftover lunches, an old winter hat, a miniature toy airplane, and a toothbrush. A considerable amount of time was spent initially sorting out notes, binders, crumpled up papers, returned assignments, school texts, and garbage. Cole seemed to think his disorganization was somewhat humorous and did not give any indication of any concern when he was asked about it. During a discussion about his dad, an accountant, and Cole's understanding that "his work is organized a lot better than mine," Cole was asked how he would go about getting organized at school.

Cole: I'd just organize it. I'd take it out and put it back in until it was organized.
Researcher: So what would you do? Take all your math?
Cole: Like, I'd probably take all this junk here and take it out and organize it into the binder somewhere, just organize all the dividers and everything.

Cole did not appear to have many ideas for improving his organization of school materials, and more importantly, he did not seem to be concerned about the problem and the need for him to take responsibility for the self-regulation of his learning environment and materials.

Another example of self-regulation avoidance in everyday learning habits was observed with Ken. As part of a pre-reading procedure to stimulate self-questioning and interest, Ken was asked, "If you were going to check your knowledge about earthquakes, ...How would you go about doing that?" Ken's response revealed his tendency to choose the least demanding solution when confronted with a learning task. In this instance he replied, "Well, I'd find someone who knew more about earthquakes and then ask them is this right, is this wrong, or whatever." Not only does Ken avoid the learning challenge by opting for outside or other regulation of the task, he also chooses a strategy that is unrealistic, not to mention unlikely to be carried out.

Habitual deference of learning responsibility and lack of engagement in everyday learning activities is akin to a learning disability and unfortunately yields similar results in negatively affecting one's learning and learning potential. These tendencies to avoid self-regulation and to over-rely on others in everyday learning pursuits, left unattended, could have major negative cumulative effects on academic achievement in junior high, and particularly high school subjects.

Metacognition: Awareness of Learning Strengths and Limitations

Cognitive theory and research has advanced the very powerful notion of metacognition (i.e., self-awareness of one's learning abilities and limitations and the effective deployment and orchestration of these abilities in learning situations) and its importance in the development of learning competency (Bransford, Brown, & Cocking, 2000). Though research on metacognition and GLD children is very limited, one study by Hannah and Shore (1995) has indicated that GLD students may be more like their gifted peers in comparison with average performing and average performing students in demonstrating high levels of metacognitive abilities. Findings of the present study, however, are equivocal, in that only one of the three students, Craig, demonstrated advanced metacognitive skills. For example, Craig was quite forthright in his acknowledgment of his spelling disability:

Researcher:	So you're in Grade 7 right now.
Craig:	Ya, should be in Grade 8 though but I failed Grade 2.
Researcher:	You failed Grade 2. Do you know why you failed Grade 2?
Craig:	Language Arts. My spelling is what didn't get me past Grade 2...My spelling is really terrible.
Researcher:	Is it really? How do you know it's really terrible?
Craig:	5 out of 50. 5 right out of 50. I mean I usually sound the words out as best I can but then you go to, I mean

they make this great set of rules for words. Then you have a mile long [list] of exceptions. I mean if you are going to make a rule, make it stick, so as not to confuse other people.

Researcher: Now I recall looking at all your stories, I didn't see many, were there many spelling mistakes in there?

Craig: No. Because I usually have my mom proofread them and help me go through them and we take all the spelling mistakes before and then we print them.

Unlike Cole, described in the previous section, not only does Craig have a good awareness of his particular learning problems, his comments reveal that he has developed a number of strategies to overcome or at least compensate for the problem; in the above example he talks about having his mother proofread his written assignments.

Quality of Student Thinking and Understanding

Recent research in cognitive psychology has shown that learning can be either incidentally or intentionally achieved or designed (Salomon & Perkins, 1998; Vygotsky, 1978). A key concept of cognitive socio-cultural theory is the notion that learning is first observed and practiced in social situations, such as the school classroom, where guidance and assistance accompany the introduction of a new learning task, and ideally, eventually the learner can independently accomplish the demands of the task and ultimately transfer what has been learned to new learning situations. Much of one's learning is achieved incidentally as day-to-day experiences and contexts unfold. However, formal school learning most often requires the active, conscious engagement and motivation of the learner, a notion that Salomon and Perkins refer to as "high road" learning. Competent learners demonstrate a tendency, early on, to rely upon numerous intentional and conceptually oriented learning strategies and habits to maximize their learning experiences, and teachers can vary in their ability to foster and utilize intentional learning activities in the classroom (Pressley, Harris, & Guthrie, 1992; Salomon & Perkins).

One particular reading task, a passage about earthquakes, revealed marked differences for Ken and Craig in the way they used prior knowledge and how they posed questions to guide their reading understanding.

Researcher: What I have here, I have a really interesting passage for you on earthquakes. Now I was wondering, could you give me, tell me a little bit about earthquakes, what do you know about earthquakes before we start?

Ken: They shake the earth.

Researcher:	They shake the earth, O.K.
Ken:	Actually, I saw a program on them once. Only supposed to happen along the edges of huge pieces of rock and the rock moves and causes a big earthquake and that's really about all I know.
Researcher:	O.K. If you were going to check your knowledge about earthquakes, check to see what you knew about earthquakes. How would you go about doing that?
Ken:	Well, I'd find someone who knew more about earthquakes and then ask them is this right, is this wrong, or whatever.
Researcher:	O.K. What kinds of questions could you ask yourself about earthquakes to see what you knew about earthquakes?
Ken:	Well, why they happen, when they happen, where they happen, who they happen *(laughs)*.

It is obvious from the above conversation that Ken was only moderately prepared for his reading of the earthquake passage and his self-questioning indicated minimal interest in finding out more information. His posing of generic why, when, where questions prior to reading the earthquake passage would do little to further his understanding of the topic, and his low level of interest was predictive of an observed low level of engagement with the task, and a poor rating on his answering of follow-up comprehension questions. Salomon and Perkins (1998) would categorize Ken's efforts, in this instance at least, as low-road learning because the response to the pre-reading task is automaticity-oriented and shallow.

Faced with the identical task, Craig's responses reveal an entirely different quality of learning preparedness.

Researcher:	But now, before you start, tell me what are some things you know about earthquakes?
Craig:	I know they are measured on a meter called the Richter Scale. I think it's the lower they go—the lighter they are; or the higher they go—the more damaging it is. Caused by plates of the earth moving together in a fault. What else? Earthquakes usually send shock waves through the earth, which can be felt at the exact opposite side of the earth. Like if it was a *(points)* here you could feel it *(points)* there by going straight through. Earthquakes are generally caused, or have caused I'm not sure, well they do a lot of damage. I forget what other parts were though—fault, hmm, I know that several of them

	have happened in L.A. I thought they were related to volcanoes in some way, I'm not sure.
Researcher:	So that's something you would like to learn further about?
Craig:	Ya.
Researcher:	So you know a fair amount about earthquakes or rather you think. What more would you like to know about earthquakes?
Craig:	What more?
Researcher:	Like what are some of the questions that you have about earthquakes?
Craig:	Can they be prevented? Can they be artificially created? Like, can the waves be reproduced by a machine so [they] actually move the earth? We should generate it someplace else without the plates. What else? What's it like to be at the fault when an earthquake occurs? I wonder what that would be like? Like make a grinding noise or is it more violent there or less? Be interesting.

The qualitative contrasts in the responses of Craig and Ken toward the same task are quite striking, and tend to support Salomon and Perkins' (1998) contention that two seemingly similar students may derive significantly different individual and social learning benefits, even though the two students are participants in the same learning context. In the case of Craig, it would also seem that his advanced individual and social learning tendencies might have been interacting over several years to strengthen one another in what Salomon and Perkins describe as a "reciprocal spiral relationship." Recall the earlier mention by Craig's parents that Craig was able to effectively engage in conversation with people of all ages from as early as age two.

Transfer of Learning

Cognitive psychologists have studied the effects of initial learning and how they transfer across a variety of similar learning conditions in educational contexts (Bransford & Schwartz, 1999; McKeough, Lupart, Marini, 1995). Moreover, it has been consistently demonstrated that competent and gifted learners are known to independently apply their learning from one situation to other similar and novel situations (Sternberg & Davidson, 1989). In the present study, a clear lack of transfer was evident in the use of web diagrams. The students had been instructed in ways to use a webbing strategy to improve their written stories. The school materials that Ken brought to the assessment session included a completed web diagram for a story he had written on water pollution, and for which he had received a mark of 8 out of 10 from the teacher. After a brief discussion about the purpose and advantages of using web diagrams, the researcher asked Ken to draw a new web diagram based on his reading of the earthquake passage. He produced a very scant drawing with four sub-categories, and only two of these with any further detail. Subsequent questioning revealed that Ken had a minimal conceptual understanding of how to use web diagrams to facilitate his own learning, and that he was unable to transfer what he had learned by using a web diagram to augment his earlier writing task to the reading task on earthquakes.

Interestingly, if we refer back to the initial Stage One summary profile information, it was Ken who had attained the highest school achievement level of the three boys, indeed, he was performing significantly beyond his grade level in three out of four subjects. This inconsistency might be interpreted as supporting the idea that static assessment measures, alone, do not tell the whole story. Bransford and Schwartz (1999) have proposed an alternative notion of transfer, as preparation for future learning (PFL), and the distinction may have important implications for education. Typical views of transfer only deal with what children know and how children learn, whereas PFL is described as "knowing with," " a context" or "field" that guides noticing and interpretation (p. 92). Once again we can refer to the differences between Ken and Craig and their approach to the pre-reading activity prior to reading the earthquake passage. It seems apparent that Craig demonstrated a greater facility for PFL transfer in that instance than did Ken.

Using Feedback to Improve Learning

A final area that proved to be consistently observed in all three GLD students was a notable lack of interest or perhaps a failure to grasp the importance of using teacher and peer feedback to improve learning. Each of the students had brought previous assignments that had been marked by the teacher with them to the assessment sessions. When they were queried about why, for example, they scored a 2 out of 5 on a given part of the assignment, they were unable to give adequate reasons. In addition, in the majority of cases, they were unable to articulate what they would do differently to score a 5 out 5. Knowing how to assess one's own learning efforts and how to improve learning by using feedback from the teacher is considered to be a key link between assessment and learning (Gipps, 1999). Used as a way to help the student focus on the critical role they have in their own learning, teacher feedback can be highly instrumental in encouraging the student to take on greater learning responsibility.

SUMMARY AND IMPLICATIONS

The central argument of this chapter is that investigations of GLD learners have been too narrowly focused upon identification rather than in-depth assessment. Moreover, it has been shown that these students, who demonstrate such complicated learning abilities and limitations, are most likely to be under-identified and under-served in our schools. It was suggested that recent theories concerning children's learning and new alternative assessment approaches may serve the dual purpose of uncovering unique GLD individual learning needs, and contribute significantly to the instructional programming of regular teachers who are most likely to have these GLD students in their classrooms. This instrumental case study of three GLD adolescent boys consisted of a two-stage assessment process representing an attempt to bridge information sources from traditional static and contemporary dynamic procedures. The framework for data analysis was cognitive theory, specifically including information processing, Piagetian, and socio-cultural perspectives. Results confirmed the previously noted extreme variability of GLD students, and revealed numerous subtle cognitive, metacognitive, and contextual factors that appear to be highly relevant to learning success and transfer.

Although this study represents an initial exploration of the potential for cognitive theory-based, in-depth assessment procedures to inform GLD instructional practice, on the basis of the findings, a number of implications can be drawn. First, the obvious learning differences in these three students, despite their identical exceptional learner classification, suggests that for GLD students, intervention efforts should be determined on the basis of individual student needs as opposed to generic instructional programs. Second, cognitive theory and research can serve as a powerful framework to assess and analyze the subtle and complex learning strengths and challenges of GLD students, and has great potential to inform instructional practice. However, the application of such requires a considerable expertise more typically found in graduate students in developmental psychology, school psychology, or special education. Third, teachers are the key professionals who stand to benefit from the use of an in-depth assessment procedure as a natural process to determine appropriate instructional interventions for GLD students. However, they typically do not have the background expertise or experience to initiate these procedures on their own. Finally, GLD students, for the time being, can perhaps be best supported in schools through the collaborative teaming of support professionals such as resource teachers or school psychologists and regular classroom teachers.

REFERENCES

Andrews, J., & Lupart, J. L. (2000). *The inclusive classroom: Educating exceptional children.* (2nd edition). Scarborough, ON: Nelson.

Barton, J.M. and Starnes, W.T. (1989). Identifying distinguishing characteristics of gifted and talented/learning disabled students. *Roeper Review, 12*(1), 23–29.

Bassey, M. (1999). *Case study research in educational settings.* Buckingham:Open University Press.

Baum, S. (1994). Meeting the needs of gifted/learning disabled students. *The Journal of Secondary Gifted Education, 5*(3), 6–16

Baum, S.M., Cooper, C.R., & Neu, T.W. (2001). Dual differentiation: An approach for meeting the curricular needs of gifted students with learning disabilities. *Psychology in the Schools, 35*(5), 477–490.

Baum, S., Emerick, L.J., Herman, G. N., & Nixon, J. (1989). Identification, programs and enrichment strategies for gifted learning disables youth. *Roeper Review, 12*(1), 48–53.

Baum, S. & Owen, S. V. (1988). High ability/learning disabled students: How are they different? *Gifted Child Quarterly, 32*(3), 321–326.

Baum, S., & Kirschenbaum, R. (1984). Recognizing special talents in learning disabled students. *Teaching Exceptional Children,* 16, 92–98.

Baum, S., Owen, S.V., & Dixon, J. (1991). *To be gifted and learning disabled: From identification to practical intervention strategies.* Mansfield Center, CT: Creative Learning Press.

Bauman, P.L. (1988). *Expectations of educational programming and parent-school relations: A comparison of parents of gifted and talented learning disabled children and parents of other gifted and talented children,* Washington, DC: ERIC Clearinghouse ED 296 558

Boodoo, G. M., Bradley, C. L., Frontera, R. L., Pitts, J. R., & Wright, L. B. (1989). A survey of procedures used for identifying gifted learning disabled children. *Gifted Child Quarterly, 33*(3), 110–114.

Borkowski, J. G., & Day, J. D. (Eds.). (1987). *Cognition inspecial children: Comparative approaches to retardation, learning disabilities,, and giftedness.* Norwood, NJ: Ablex.

Borkowski, J. G., Schneider, W., & Pressley, M. (1989). The challenges of teaching good information processing to learning disabled students. *International Journal of Disability, Development, and Education, 36*(3), 169–185.

Bransford, J. D., & Schwartz, D. L. (1999). Rethinking transfer: A simple proposal with multiple implications. In A. Iran-Nejad & P. D. Pearson (Eds.), *Review of Educational Research, 24,* (pp. 61–100) Washington, DC: American Educational Research Association.

Bransford, J. D., Brown, A. L., & Cocking, R. R. (Eds.). (2000). *How people learn: Brain, mind, experience, and school.* Washington, DC: National Academy Press.

Bray, M. A., Kehle, T. J., Hintze, J. M. (1998). Profile analysis with the Wechsler Scales: Why does it persist? *School Psychology International, 19,* 209–220.

Brody, L. E. and Mills, C. J. (1997). Gifted children with learning disabilities: A review of the issues. *Journal of Learning Disabilities, 30*(3), 282–296.

Case, R. (1985). *Intellectual development: Birth to adulthood.* New York: Academic Press.

Chapman, J.W. (1988). Learning disable children's self-concepts. *Review of Educational Research, 58*(3), 347–371

Coleman, M.R. & Gallagher, J.J. (1995). State identification policies: Gifted students from special populations. *Roeper Review, 17*(4), 268–275.

Crawford, S. and Snart, F. (1994). Process-based remediation of decoding in gifted LD students: Three case studies. *Roeper Review, 16*(4), 247–252.

Cresswell, J. W. (1997). *Qualitative inquiry and research design: Choosing among five traditions.* Thousand Oaks, CA: Sage Publications

Fox, L. H., Brody, L., & Tobin, D. (Eds.) (1983). Learning-disabled/gifted children: Identification and programming. Austin, TX: PRO-ED.

Gipps, C. (1999). Socio-cultural aspects of assessment. . In A. Iran-Nejad & P. D. Pearson (Eds.), *Review of Educational Research, 24,* 355–392 Washington, DC: American Educational Research Association.

Hannah, C. L., Shore, B. M. (1995). Metacognition and high intellectual ability: Insight from the study of learning-disabled gifted students. *Gifted Child Quarterly, 39*(2), 95–109.

Hansford, S. J., Whitmore, J. R., Kraynak, A. R., & Wingenbach, N. G. (1987). *Intellectually gifted learning disabled students: A special Study.* Washington, DC: ERIC Clearinghouse ED 254 988

Howard, J. B. (1994). Addressing needs through strengths: Five instructional practices for use with gifted/learning disabled students. *The Journal of Secondary Gifted Education, 5*(3), 23–34.

Hoy, C., & Gregg, N. (1994). *Assessment: The special educator's role.* Pacific Grove, CA: Brooks/Cole.

Jeon, K. W. (1992). Gifted learning disabled and gifted underachievers: Similarities and differences. In A. H. Roldan (Ed.) *Gifted children and youth today, gifted adults of the 21st century: A Southeast Asian perspective,* (pp. 154–168). Manila, The Philippines: Reading Dynamics Centre.

Johnson, L., Karnes, M., & Carr, V. (1997). Providing services to children with gifts and disabilities: A critical need. In N. Colangelo & G. Davis (Eds.) *Handbook of gifted education* (2nd ed.). (pp. 516–527). Boston: Allyn & Bacon.

LaFrance, E.B. (1994). An insider's perspective: Teachers' observations of creative thinking in exceptional children. *Roeper Review, 16*(4), 256–257.

Lerner, J.W. (1981). *Learning disabilities: Theories, diagnosis and teaching strategies* (3rd ed.) Boston: Houghton Mifflin.

Lupart, J. L. (1990). An in-depth assessment model for gifted/learning disabled students. *Canadian Journal of Special Education, 6*(1), 1–14.

Lupart, J. L. (1991). A theory by any educational perspective, is still a theory. In A. McKeough & J. L. Lupart (Eds.). *Toward the practice of theory-based instruction* (pp.148–182). Hillsdale, NJ: Erlbaum.

Lupart, J. L. (1992). *The hidden gifted: Current state of knowledge and future research directions.* In F. J. Monks & W. A. M. Peters (Eds.) *Talent for the future: Social and personality development of gifted children: Proceedings of the Ninth World Conference on Gifted and Talented Children* (pp. 177–190). The Netherlands: Van Gorcum.

Lupart, J. L. (1995). Exceptional learners and teaching for transfer. In A. McKeough, J. Lupart, & A. Marini (Eds.). *Teaching for transfer: Fostering generalization in learning* (p. 215– 228). Mahwah, NJ: Erlbaum.

Lupart, J. L. (1998). Setting right the delusion of inclusion: Implications for Canadian schools. *Canadian Journal of Education, 23*(3), 251–264.

Lupart, J. L., McKeough, A., & Yewchuk, C. (Eds.). (1996) *Schools in transition: Rethinking regular and special education.* Scarborough, ON: Nelson.

Lupart, J. L., & Pyryt, M. (1996). Identifying the hidden gifted. *Journal for the Education of the Gifted, 20*(1), 7–16.

Lupart, J. L., & Webber, C. (1996). Schools in transition: Issues and prospects. In J. Lupart, A. McKeough, & C. Yewchuk (Eds.), *Scxhools in transition: Rethinking regular and special education* (pp. 3–39). Scarborough, ON: Nelson.

Maker, C. J. (1977). *Providing programs for the gifted handicapped.* Reston, VA: Council for Exceptional Children.

McCoach, D. B., Kehle, T. J., Bray, M. A., and Siegle, D. (2001). Best practices in the identification of gifted students with learning disabilities. *Psychology in the Schools, 35*(5), 403–411.

McGuire, K. L. and Yewchuk, C. R. (1996). Use of metacognitive reading strategies by gifted learning disabled students: An exploratory study. *Journal for the Education of the Gifted, 19*(3), 293–314.

McMillan, J. H. (2001). *Classroom assessment: Principles and practice for effective instruction* (2nd ed.). Boston: Allyn and Bacon.

Mercer, C.D. (1997). *Students with learning disabilities* (5th ed.) Columbus: Charles E. Merrill.

Miller, M. (1991). Self assessment as a specific strategy for teaching the gifted learning disabled. *Journal for the Education of the Gifted, 14*(2), 178–188.

Olenchak, F. R. (1995). Effects of enrichment on gifted/learning-disabled students. *Journal for the Education of the Gifted, 18*(4), 385–399.

Patton, M. Q. (1990). Qualitative evaluation and research methods. Newbury Park: Sage Publications.

Pressley, M., Harris, K. R., & Guthrie (Eds.). (1992). *Promoting academic competence and literacy: Cognitive research and instructional innovation.* San Diego: Academic Press.

Reis, S.M. (1997). Case studies of high-ability students with learning disabilities who have achieved. *Exceptional Children, 63*(4), 463–479.

Reis, S. M., Neu, T. W., & McGuire, J. M. (1997). Case studies of high-ability students with learning disabilities who have achieved. *Exceptional Children, 63*(4), 463–479.

Reis, S. M., McGuire, J. M., & Neu, T. W. (2000). Comprehension strategies used by high-ability students with learning disabilities who succeed in college. *Gifted Child Quarterly, 44*(2), 123–134.

Richert, E. S. (1997). Excellence with equity in identification and programming. In N. Colangelo & G. Davis (Eds.), *Handbook of gifted education* (2nd ed.) (pp. 75–88). Boston: Allyn & Bacon.

Salomon, G., & Perkins, D. N. (1998). *Individual and social aspects of learning.* In D. P. Pearson & A Iran-Nejad (Eds). *Review of Educational Research, 23,* (pp. 1–24). Washington, DC: American Educational Research Association.

Schiff, M. M, Kaufman, A. S., & Kaufman, N. L. (1981). Scatter analysis of WISC-R profiles for learning disabled children with superior intelligence. *Journal of Learning Disabilities, 14,* 400–404.

Senf, G. M. (1983). The nature an identification of learning disabilities and their relationship to the gifted child. In L.H. Fox, L. Brody, & D. Tobin (Eds.), *Learning disabled/gifted children: Identification and programming* (pp. 37–39). Austin, TX: Pro Ed.

Silverman, L. K. (1989). Invisible gifts, invisible handicaps. *Roeper Review, 12*(1), 37–42.

Skrtic, T. (1995). The organizational context of special education and school reform. In E. L. Meyen & T. M. Skrtic (Eds.), *Special education and student disability* (pp. 731–791). Denver, CO: Love.

Skrtic, T. (1996). School organization, inclusive education, and democracy. In J. Lupart, A. McKeough, & C. Yewchuk (Eds.) *Schools in transition: Rethinking regular and special education* (pp. 81–118). Scarborough, ON: Nelson.

Stake, R. E. (1995). *The art of case study research.* London: Sage Publications.

Starnes, W., Ginevan, J., Stokes, L., & Barton, J. (1988). *A study in the identification, differential diagnosis, and remediation of underachieving highly able students.* Washington, DC: ERIC Clearinghouse ED 298 730.

Sternberg, R. J. (1986). *Intelligence applied: Understanding and increasing your intellectual skills.* Orlando, FL: Harcourt Brace Jovanovich.

Sternberg, R. J. (2003). *Cognitive psychology* (3rd ed.). Belmont, CA: Thomson/Wadsworth.

Svec, H. J. (1985). *Learning disabled or selectively enriched? An application of student strengths to program planning.* Washington, DC: ERIC Clearinghouse ED 283 317.

Tallent-Runnels, M. K. and Sigler, E. A. (1995). The status of the selection of gifted students with learning disabilities for gifted programs. *Roeper Review, 17*(4), 246–248.

Tomlinson, C.A. (1995). Action research and practical inquiry: An overview and an invitation to teachers of gifted learners. *Journal for the Education of the Gifted, 18*(4), 467–484.

Treffinger, D. J. (1986). *Individualized program planning model. (PPM Teacher Referral Form).* New York: DOK Publishers Inc.

Trent, S. C., Artiles, A. J., & Englert, C. S. (1998). From deficit thinking to social constructivism: A review of theory, research, and practice in special education. . In D. P. Pearson & A Iran-Nejad (Eds). *Review of Educational Research, 23,* (pp. 277–307). Washington, DC: American Educational Research Association.

Vespi, L. and Yewchuk, C. (1992). A phenomenological study of the social/emotional characteristics of gifted learning disabled children. *Journal for the Education of the Gifted, 16*(1), 55–72.

Vygotsky, L. S. (1963). Learning and mental development at school age. In J. Simon & B. Simons (Eds.), *Educational psychology in the USSR* (pp.21–34). Stanford, CA: Stanford University Press.

Vygotsky, L. S. (1978). *Mind and society: The development of higher psychological processes* (M. Cole, V. John-Steiner, S. Scribner & E. Souberman, Eds.) Cambridge, MA: Harvard University Press.

Waldron, K.A., Saphire, D.G., & Rosenblum, S.A. (1978). Learning disabilities and giftedness: Identification based on self-concept, behavior, and academic patterns. *Journal of Learning Disabilities, 20,* 422–427.

Weber, P. & Battaglia, C. (1982). *The Identi-form System for gifted programs.* New York: D.O.K. Publishers Inc.

Whitmore, J. (1980). *Giftedness, conflict and underachievement.* Boston: Allyn and Bacon.

Whitmore, J. R. (1986). Conceptualizing the issue of underserved populations of gifted students. *Journal for the Education of the Gifted, 10*(3), 141–153.

Whitmore, J. R. (1989). Four leading advocates for gifted students with disabilities. *Roeper Review, 12*(1), 5–13.

William, F. (1980). *Exercise in divergent thinking: Exercise in divergent feeling:* New York: D.O.K.

Yates, C. M., Berninger, V. W. and Abbott, R. D. (1995). Specific writing disabilities in intellectually gifted children. *Journal for the Education of the Gifted, 18*(2), 131–155.

Yewchuk, C. (1986). Issues in the identification of gifted/learning disabled children. *British Columbia Journal of Special Education, 10,* 201–209.

Yewchuk, C., & Lupart, J. L. (2000). Inclusive education for gifted students with disabilities. In K. Heller, F. Monks, R. Sternberg, & R. Subotnik (Eds.) *International handbook of giftedness and talent.* (2nd ed.) (pp. 659–670). Amsterdam: Elsevier Science Ltd.

Yin, R. K. (1989). *Case study research: Design and methods.* London: Sage Publications.

Yin, R. K. (1994). Case study research: Design and methods. (2nd ed.). London: Sage Publications.

Chapter 4

LINKING ASSESSMENT AND DIAGNOSIS TO INTERVENTION FOR GIFTED STUDENTS WITH LEARNING DISABILITIES

Linda E. Brody
Carol J. Mills
Johns Hopkins University

INTRODUCTION

Jeremy stood up, walked, and talked at exceptionally young ages, and he showed a natural ability in math. His curiosity and oral communication made him stand out among age peers, and the adults in his life considered him gifted. Yet, after completing first grade and despite a strong preschool program, Jeremy was having difficulty learning to read. His self-esteem was suffering as he encountered trouble learning for the first time in his life.

Emily was about to enter eighth grade. As a seventh grader in the Johns Hopkins Talent Search, she scored 720 on the verbal section of the SAT-I. She learned to read early and is a voracious reader today. But some things are hard for her. She can't remember her multiplication facts, has poor motor and social skills, and rarely finishes anything in the time allocated. The discrepancy between Emily being so incredibly good at some things while struggling at others has baffled her parents and teachers alike as they have tried to meet her needs.

As a fourth grader, Marcus was exceptionally advanced in reading, math, and general knowledge. Yet he had difficulty focusing, was unorganized, and struggled with writing. His relationship with peers was deteriorating, and he was rapidly losing interest in school. Jeremy, Emily, and Marcus are all highly gifted in some ways, but undiagnosed learning disabilities were interfering with their achievement in school.

Unfortunately, many gifted students with learning disabilities remain undiagnosed and underserved because of a lack of understanding of the way these two exceptionalities interact and of how strengths and weaknesses can

73

mask each other. Some students may be identified as gifted but underachieve because their disabilities remain undiscovered. Others are diagnosed as having learning disabilities, but they languish unchallenged in remedial programs because their giftedness is not recognized. Still others are considered "average" but their cognitive profiles actually reflect talents and learning disabilities that are overlooked (Brody & Mills, 1997; Baum 1994; Baum, Owen, & Dixon, 1991). Although recent publications (e.g., Kaufmann, Kalbfleisch, & Castellanos, 2000; Neihart, 2000; Silverman, 2002) and the establishment of a few exemplary programs (e.g., see Kay, 2002; Weinfeld, Barnes-Robinson, Jeweler, & Shevitz, 2002) suggest increased interest in this population, better screening, diagnosis, and intervention strategies are needed to meet the needs of gifted students with learning disabilities.

CTY'S DIAGNOSTIC AND COUNSELING CENTER

Work at Johns Hopkins on this population dates back to the late 1970s, when researchers with backgrounds in gifted education and/or learning disabilities embarked on a collaborative effort to study students with these dual exceptionalities and to find ways to serve them. After reviewing the research literature, investigating resources, piloting programs, holding symposia, and analyzing the records of thousands of students with learning problems, the results were published in one of the first comprehensive texts to call attention to gifted students with learning disabilities (Fox, Brody, & Tobin, 1983; see also Daniels, 1983).

Interest in this population has continued at the Johns Hopkins Center for Talented Youth (CTY), which serves over 100,000 gifted students annually through talent searches, academic programs, and other services. While most of the students served by CTY are high achievers seeking academic challenge, some come to summer programs with a diagnosed learning disability, while others exhibit learning problems that suggest they may have an undiagnosed disability. When appropriate, accommodations are made for CTY students with learning disabilities (e.g., extra time, laptop computers). Meanwhile, researchers at CTY have been involved in a systematic study of this population and its needs (Brody & Mills, 1997; Mills & Brody, 1999).

After many years of working informally to assess and assist gifted students with learning difficulties, CTY established a Diagnostic and Counseling Center in 1997. While this center serves students with a variety of needs (including those seeking advice about acceleration), diagnosing learning disabilities in students who are gifted has become a particular focus of the center's mission. The staff's experience and expertise with gifted students has proven important in providing recommendations that focus on the students' high abilities, while also addressing their learning problems.

The following text will provide an overview of CTY's Diagnostic and Counseling Center's approach to assessing and diagnosing learning disabilities in students whose gifts often mask their problems, using Jeremy, Emily, and Marcus as case studies. This overview will demonstrate how recommendations for meeting the needs of students who have concomitant high abilities and learning difficulties must derive from comprehensive and targeted information gained from a professional psycho-educational evaluation.

Assessment and Diagnosis

Students who are both gifted and have a learning disability present a special challenge for parents and educators. Many times, because of the "masking effect" mentioned earlier, these students are not referred for evaluation, even when academic difficulties become apparent. It is often classroom teachers who must recommend further consideration and testing, but they may misinterpret behavior if they haven't been trained to recognize the special characteristics of gifted students with learning disabilities.

For Jeremy, who was considered by all to be gifted, but who was still struggling to learn to read at the end of first grade, the interpretation was "just give him time and it will eventually click for him." On the other hand, he was not recommended for screening for gifted services because of the emphasis on reading. For Emily, her high achievement was so evident that her teachers refused to acknowledge her struggles. She was recommended for gifted programs, but was refused services for students with learning disabilities. For Marcus, his struggles with attention and impulsive behavior so frustrated his teachers that they balked at advancing him academically, which only increased his behavioral problems.

When the need for an evaluation is recognized, it is important that a comprehensive assessment be done that includes measures designed to identify the full scope of any strengths and weaknesses. Too often, however, the assessment is conducted piecemeal by different professionals in the system (e.g., psychologist, learning specialist, occupational therapist) who fail to integrate the results. Ideally, a comprehensive psycho-educational evaluation should take place at one time and be coordinated by a lead diagnostician or a diagnostic team working closely together.

The defining characteristics that must be considered in identifying gifted students who have learning disabilities are: (a) the presence of an outstanding gift or talent, (b) evidence of a discrepancy between expected and actual achievement, and (c) an underlying processing deficit(s) that is at the heart of this discrepancy. To assess these diverse pieces of the diagnostic picture, a comprehensive battery of tests that measures ability, cognitive processing, achievement levels, and social–emotional functioning is needed.

Evidence of an Outstanding Talent or Ability

For students with learning disabilities, their strengths should be fully assessed, whether they are suspected of being gifted or not. In the process, it will be discovered that some of these students have exceptional abilities or academic talent. For students who are already seen as gifted but underachieving, it is essential to document the full extent and nature of their abilities or talents.

To assess a student's abilities, a measure of general ability, such as an IQ test, and/or measures of specific ability can be used. Practitioners need to recognize, however, that a learning disability can depress the test performance of students who are intellectually gifted. Consequently, cutoff scores on whatever measures are used for program eligibility may have to be adjusted to accommodate this effect (Karnes & Johnson, 1991; Silverman, 1989). On the other hand, students who manage to meet cutoff scores in spite of their disability should be recognized as having exceptional ability.

Within the field of gifted education, the use of intelligence tests to identify gifted students has been questioned on many fronts. One concern is that intelligence tests measure a limited range of abilities (Gardner, 2000; Sternberg, 2003). It has also been pointed out that they are not good measures for identifying students who are creatively gifted (Torrance, 1979), mathematically gifted (Stanley, 1979), or come from disadvantaged backgrounds (Ford, 2003). Using tests of specific aptitude instead of, or in addition to, an intelligence test sometimes can lead to more appropriate and justifiable instruction than when only an intelligence test is used (Durden & Tangerlini, 1993).

In practice, it is rare that IQ scores alone are used to identify gifted students. Instead, many school systems use multiple criteria in an attempt to be more inclusive. This practice, however, excludes most gifted students who have a learning disability. Because of their condition, it is almost impossible for these students to show evidence of high ability, have consistent records of exceptional achievement, *and* receive high ratings from their teachers for classroom performance.

The debate surrounding the use of intelligence tests reaches beyond the gifted field to include practitioners and researchers within the LD community (Siegel, 1989, 2003). The question of whether it is necessary or even useful to recognize a child's potential is still being debated. Of course, without recognition of a student's potential and gifts, there is no way those gifts can be addressed. For students who are both gifted and who have a learning disability, recognition of their high abilities can also be very important for building self-esteem and increasing motivation.

Opponents of intelligence testing argue that IQ scores are irrelevant and that all that is necessary for intervention purposes is to know the child's current skills. For example, it has been noted that two children with very different IQ scores, both exhibiting problems in learning to read, may not be fundamentally different in terms of their deficits (Siegel, 1989; Stanovich, 1986). Lyon (1989), however, noted that two children with very different IQ scores are "qualitatively and quantitatively different from each other on tasks assessing a range of 'intelligent' behaviors" (p. 505) that may be critical to how they learn and adapt. Furthermore, a child's level of intelligence can influence his or her emotional and behavioral responses to persistent failure, parent and teacher expectations, and, most importantly, remediation. For example, it has been found that children with a high verbal IQ who have a reading disability are able to depend less on phonetic coding and more on context and orthographic cues when reading continuous text (French, 1982; Olson, 1985).

For gifted students who have a learning disability, however, the critical issue is that some measure of high ability is necessary to document the presence of a discrepancy between expected and actual achievement. In addition, an individually administered intelligence test can provide extremely valuable information about a child's processing abilities that can be essential for diagnostic and intervention purposes.

Evidence of an Aptitude–Achievement Discrepancy

Although the concept of an aptitude–performance discrepancy is common in many operational definitions of learning disabilities, numerous objections to using a discrepancy to identify students with learning disabilities have been raised (Siegel, 1989; Stage, Abbott, Jenkins, & Berninger, 2003; Stanovich, 1993). Indeed, if proposed revisions to the Individuals with Disabilities Education Act are approved, the notion of establishing an aptitude–achievement discrepancy may be abandoned (U. S. Department of Education Office of Special Education and Rehabilitative Services, 2002).

For the gifted student who has a learning disability, the evidence of such a discrepancy is critical. Identifying students for intervention solely on the basis of very low achievement will not identify gifted students with a learning disability who function at or near grade level (Reynolds, Zetlin, & Wang, 1993; Siegel & Metsala, 1992). The relatively "normal" achievement of many of these students often masks a disability that only becomes apparent as the academic demands begin to exceed the child's ability to compensate. By then, precious years of needed remediation will have been lost, the child's self-esteem damaged, and behavior problems may have emerged.

Evidence of a Processing Deficit

Although the presence of an aptitude–achievement discrepancy may be a necessary prerequisite for identifying a gifted student with a learning disability, it is not sufficient for such a diagnosis because a discrepancy can result from many different causes (Krippner, 1968; Silverman, 1989; Whitmore, 1980). For example, a discrepancy could be due to poor instruction, emotional problems, or being chronically underchallenged. Evidence of a processing deficit can help to distinguish a learning disability from these other causes of underachievement.

Although the idea that a learning disability can and should be distinguished from other known causes of learning problems has been challenged in the LD literature (e.g., Kavale, 1980; Stanovich, 1993), a differential diagnosis is important for decisions regarding the need for, and type of, intervention. The analogy is a doctor treating a patient's symptoms without understanding and treating the underlying cause. A young child can develop a fever when cutting teeth, as well as when an ear infection is present, and only an accurate diagnosis and understanding of the underlying cause can lead to the appropriate treatment.

The Importance of Early Identification

Without early identification and intervention, gifted students with learning disabilities can fall so far behind their classmates that they can be permanently saddled with an academic gap that they can't overcome. Even more important, many remedial strategies are more effective with younger children so it is critical to find these students early. For example, multi-sensory instruction to help students compensate for processing problems, occupational therapy to address fine motor weaknesses, and speech and language therapy to address difficulties in oral communication tend to be more successful when begun as early as possible.

Appropriate intervention at a young age can also help prevent social and behavioral problems. A gifted child with a learning disability is at risk for developing a variety of behavioral and emotional problems including very low self-esteem, poor motivation, depression, anxiety, and discipline problems. Although any child with a learning disability can develop these problems, gifted children appear to be more prone because of their increased sensitivity, confusion caused by their ability to do many things easily while struggling with other tasks, and the assignment of negative labels (e.g., lazy; Levine, 2002). Jeremy, Emily, and Marcus all had some sort of emotional or behavioral problem as a result of not being properly identified.

Intervention

Ideally, all students should have an educational program that considers their individual strengths, weaknesses, and levels of achievement.

However, it is particularly important for gifted students who also have a learning disability to have such a program because their strengths and weaknesses are likely to vary so much. While these students would benefit from the establishment of special programs designed for this population (Weinfeld, Barnes-Robinson, Jeweler, & Shevitz, 2002), it is possible to provide appropriate services by modifying existing school resources.

In general, gifted students with learning disabilities need appropriate challenges in their areas of strength, remediation of their deficits, and grade-level instruction where achievement is above or below grade level. In addition, many students will need compensatory strategies or accommodations to ensure success in the most challenging settings possible. They will need social and emotional support because many of these students struggle with understanding why some things are so difficult for them while other things are easy. Finally, communication between parents and the school can also be critical (Bos, Nahmias, & Urban, 1999).

Challenge in Areas of Strength

All of the programmatic options available to serve gifted students should be considered and evaluated for gifted students who also have learning disabilities. To determine which services are appropriate for an individual student, consideration should be given to his or her specific abilities, achievement, social and emotional maturity, and any deficits that might impede success.

School-based programs for students designated as gifted and talented vary in scope, content, and delivery systems. They range from full-time programs to once-a-week pullout programs; they can serve to accelerate a student's progress or focus on enrichment. Depending on the nature of the program and the specific strengths and weaknesses of the student, the program may or may not be appropriate. It is important to note, however, that just being identified and included in a G/T program can have a positive effect on self-esteem and motivation for a gifted student who doubts his or her abilities because of a learning disability.

Recently, there has been an emphasis on differentiating instruction in the regular classroom for gifted students with or without learning disabilities (Tomlinson, 2001; Winebrenner & Espeland, 1996). While the practicality and efficacy of eliminating ability grouping in favor of diverse classes has been questioned (Brody & Mills, 1997), modifications can be made to the curriculum in mixed-ability classes to accommodate the needs of gifted students with learning disabilities. Depending on the student's needs, reading programs, spelling lists, and math assignments can all be modified to provide more challenge to a student with gifts in one or more of these areas. Gifted students with learning disabilities can also benefit from opportunities to conduct independent research (Moller, 1984).

Acceleration has been shown to be an effective method for facilitating students in need of advanced content (Rogers, 1992; Southern & Jones, 1991) and should be an option for gifted students with learning disabilities. Students who are globally gifted and advanced in content knowledge and skills may be candidates for advancing in grade placement, while many more students may benefit from being allowed to move ahead in an area of strength. Many factors should determine whether acceleration is appropriate for an individual student, but it is important not to let the presence of a disability alone eliminate acceleration as an option if it otherwise seems appropriate for a student. Difficulties in writing, for example, should not prejudice a teacher from allowing a mathematically talented student to accelerate in math. And a globally gifted student with ADHD can have the same behavior modification techniques applied in a more advanced grade as one that is age-appropriate but lacks challenge.

Many gifted students are served through enrichment programs, i.e., exposure to content not typically offered by the regular curriculum. Such enrichment opportunities have been shown to be effective in challenging and motivating gifted students who have learning disabilities (Baum, 1988). School-based enrichment programs (Renzulli & Reis, 1997), Saturday and summer programs (Olszewski-Kubilius, 2003), and extracurricular activities extend students' learning and expose them to peers with similar interests and abilities.

Grade-Level Instruction

While differentiation in the regular classroom that acknowledges individual strengths and weaknesses is important, it is worth noting that some grade-level work may also be appropriate for gifted students with learning disabilities. In areas where ability and achievement measures do not suggest that a student's performance is significantly above or below grade level, he or she can be part of the regular class. This strategy will allow the teacher to focus on differentiating instruction where it is really needed.

The assessment will be critical in determining which achievement areas are above, at, or below grade level for a particular student. Ability must also be considered, as it is possible that only lack of access to advanced work is keeping a gifted student from performing above grade level, in which case a more challenging program may be needed.

Remediation of Deficits

While it is important to emphasize the cognitive strengths possessed by a gifted student with learning disabilities, consideration must also be given to the student's weaknesses. In general, remediation should be emphasized more with a younger child when there is more likelihood of success. With older children, remediation is less likely to be effective, so the emphasis should be more on making accommodations for the learning disability to encourage success in the most challenging environments possible. Whatever options are chosen, extensive drill-and-practice is not the answer for most gifted students with learning disabilities, who may lose interest in learning if there is too much emphasis on repetition.

A learning disabilities specialist should work with students who exhibit poor achievement in basic skills such as reading, writing, or computation, using a variety of recognized and effective techniques. Such efforts should acknowledge the processing deficits that were identified in the assessment and build on the student's strengths. Other specialists may also be needed for individual students depending on the nature of the disability, e.g., occupational, physical, or speech and language therapists. Older students who have fallen behind in a content area may need to work with a tutor who can help them "catch up" on what they missed.

For some students, their disability is a more general processing deficit that affects multiple content areas, and multi-sensory instruction can be an important tool in helping them learn. Others who have poor organizational and study skills may benefit from a coach who can teach them strategies to be more successful. For students who have a memory deficit, strategies to promote memorization of facts can be helpful (Mastropieri, Sweda, & Scruggs, 2000).

Accommodations

An alternative to trying to "fix" the deficits is to provide accommodations to allow students to circumvent their disabilities. For gifted students with learning difficulties, accommodations will often allow them to be successful in settings that otherwise might pose an unrealistic challenge. In spite of this, many educators are suspicious of what they perceive as an "unfair advantage" if students with disabilities are provided with accommodations that aren't offered to other students. For gifted students with learning disabilities, however, such accommodation can be one of the most effective ways to address their needs (Brody & Mills, 1997; Fox, Tobin, & Schiffman, 1983).

The advent of technology has made learning and communicating easier for all of us, but it can be particularly valuable for students with disabilities (Tobin & Schiffman, 1983). A student with a fine motor weakness that impedes writing, for example, can often overcome his or her problem by using a computer for written assignments. If organizational problems or difficulties with spelling and grammar impede written communication, providing a student with the tools offered by a word processor will greatly enhance performance (Graham, Harris, & Larsen, 2001). It seems reasonable to offer access to a computer to any student whose achievement will be enhanced by using it, but for gifted students with written language disorders, computers can be the key to performing at a level commensurate with their intellectual abilities.

Similarly, gifted students with dyscalculia should be given access to a calculator so that they can move ahead in math according to their math reasoning abilities. Students with severe reading problems can be given books on tape so they don't miss content while struggling to read, and a tape recorder can be used to tape lectures for a student who has difficulty taking notes. The appropriate use of technology can allow many gifted students with learning disabilities to function as if the learning disabilities did not exist.

Students diagnosed with a processing disorder who need more time to process information should be given the additional time they need. If the goal of a test or assignment is to assess what students know, it doesn't make sense to let time limits prevent them from demonstrating that knowledge. For many gifted students with learning disabilities, this fairly simple accommodation can raise achievement levels dramatically. It may be particularly important to have extended time on standardized tests, since performing well on these tests can be the gateway to special programs for gifted students.

In addition to extended time, other modifications to assessment procedures are often necessary for students to show what they have learned. Some students may need alternative options (e.g., oral tests) to demonstrate their learning. Others may need to have the opportunity to answer in a test booklet rather than to use a separate answer sheet. The use of a laptop computer and/or a calculator may also be an appropriate testing accommodation depending on the student's disability.

Teachers can also adjust course requirements to help gifted students with learning disabilities succeed. For example, assigning students to work in small groups can allow the gifted student with a learning disability to participate in a way that uses his or her strengths. For students with processing difficulties that interfere with planning and organization, carving assignments into small chunks rather than giving one large long-term assignment can be helpful. And, if a student has difficulty producing a large quantity of work, an assignment might be reduced in scope while expectations for quality remain high. There are many possibilities for modifying assignments and testing procedures to help these students be more successful (e.g., see Winebrenner, 2002), but the intent is to circumvent the obstacle presented by the disability and allow students to show the full extent of their learning.

Social and Emotional Support

Gifted students with learning disabilities struggle with understanding why some things are so difficult for them, while other things are so easy. This struggle can diminish their self-esteem and impact on their relations with parents, siblings, teachers, and peers. In addition, difficulty with social relationships is itself a symptom of some specific learning disabilities (e.g., see Thompson, 1997).

Gifted students with learning disabilities often benefit from spending some time with a knowledgeable counselor who can work to enhance self-esteem, resolve family issues, and improve social relations (Brody & Mills, 1997; McEachern & Bornot, 2001; Mendaglio, 1993). Counselors are sometimes needed to work on problem behaviors that are the root cause of underachievement. In addition to individual counseling, group counseling with other students who face similar issues can be effective.

Peer relations can be particularly difficult for gifted students with learning disabilities if they feel like they don't belong with either the high achievers or with other learning disabled students. Students can be encouraged to find peers through common interests, such as sports, music, or other activities. Confidence gained in these situations is likely to carry over to other social environments and raise self-esteem generally for these students.

PUTTING THE PIECES TOGETHER: ASSESSMENT, DIAGNOSIS, AND INTERVENTION

Jeremy, Emily, and Marcus were referred for psycho-educational evaluations by their parents, who were concerned about their academic difficulties. The students' histories and presenting problems were all carefully reviewed to determine the specific measures that would be used for assessment. IQ and achievement tests were utilized in all cases, supplemented by additional measures of ability, cognitive processing, and social–emotional adjustment as needed. The results of the assessment batteries, along with the students' histories, informed the diagnoses. And the diagnoses, along with information gleaned from measuring their specific abilities and achievement levels, in turn determined the recommendations for intervention that were made.

Jeremy's Assessment and Diagnosis

Jeremy, who had been thought of as highly gifted for the first six years of his life and who had always learned everything so easily, was depressed and confused. By age 7, he had begun to develop stomachaches before school each day. Jeremy was very aware of how he had to struggle to learn to read compared to his classmates, and, as the year progressed, he watched those same classmates move farther and farther ahead of him in the development of their reading skills. His evaluation included the WISC-III, a full battery of achievement tests with a special emphasis on reading skills and language development, cognitive processing tests including tests of visual and auditory processing, and a variety of formal and informal social–emotional assessments.

Jeremy's Full Scale IQ score of 133 placed him within the gifted range. It was interesting to note that there was no practical difference between Jeremy's Verbal and Performance IQ scores (131 and 129, respectively), since it has been suggested that a split between Verbal IQ and Performance IQ is common among gifted children with a learning disability (Schiff, Kaufman, & Kaufman, 1981). Our research and others' (e.g., Barton & Starnes, 1989; Waldron & Saphire, 1990) have shown that gifted students with learning disabilities constitute an extremely diverse group and that no consistent pattern is typical of all. Since reading is not assessed with the WISC-III, it is not surprising that Jeremy had a very strong and balanced profile on the test.

The discrepancies within Jeremy's cognitive profile, however, were quite evident when he was given achievement and cognitive processing tests. On oral achievement tests, Jeremy scored exceptionally high (98th percentile), showing his strong thinking skills and good knowledge base. His reading and spelling scores, however, were below the 40th percentile, highly unexpected scores for a child with a Verbal IQ at the 98th percentile and a receptive language score at the 90th percentile. This degree of discrepancy is even more significant for a child Jeremy's age because of the low expectations for the development of reading skills in general for a child at the end of first grade. Without intervention, however, the discrepancy usually gets larger and larger. Another discrepancy was found between Jeremy's mathematics computation score (31st percentile) and his mathematics reasoning score (90th percentile). The most diagnostic pieces of Jeremy's assessment were his phonological processing, visual discrimination, and auditory discrimination scores, which were all below the 20th percentile. Jeremy was diagnosed with a *Reading Disorder or Dyslexia.*

Jeremy's Intervention and Individual Education Plan

Jeremy's strong general IQ qualified him for the gifted and talented student program in his school, and it was recommended that he be included. Such inclusion will help to enhance his self-esteem, allow him to interact with other bright students, and provide him with the intellectual stimulation he needs. In general, Jeremy's reading difficulties should not prevent him from being exposed to content at his comprehension level and participating in discussion groups with other bright students. His parents and teachers were encouraged to read books to him at his comprehension level, not his reading level, and it was suggested that they work with him to use context clues to recognize words, thus using his high intelligence to build sight vocabulary. Since science is a strong interest of Jeremy's, it was recommended that science be the basis of enrichment projects to keep him stimulated and interested in learning

In addition to enrichment and advancement opportunities, attention must be given to Jeremy's difficulties in reading before he falls farther behind his classmates. It was recommended that he work with a learning disabilities or reading specialist who is familiar with strategies to develop reading skills in students with a reading disorder. It was clear that Jeremy's phonological processing weaknesses must be addressed. In addition, Jeremy's deficits in both visual and auditory processing suggested that multi-sensory instruction would be beneficial, and such instruction was recommended.

Math reasoning is a particular strength, so it was suggested that Jeremy be placed with similarly advanced math students and given a challenging and fast-paced curriculum. Such placement will provide needed challenge and also help Jeremy see himself as a gifted child. In the assessment, his errors in math computation took place when he was presented with problems on paper (he knew his math facts when they were administered orally), so they were attributed to his difficulties with visual discrimination (e.g., he misread signs, reversed 6 and 9). Since Jeremy needs to show and check his work in math (as well as in any other subject where material is presented visually), extra time was recommended as an appropriate accommodation for him. Once Jeremy demonstrates his knowledge of math concepts and operations, he should be given a calculator to do computations, which will allow him to move forward to higher-level mathematics.

With regard to Jeremy's social and emotional needs, emphasizing his strengths and praising his successes will help enhance his self-esteem. It was suggested that he be encouraged to join activities that would provide access to other high-ability children. If self-esteem and/or peer relationships do not improve rather quickly, counseling should be provided. If his reading takes off, he may be fine emotionally, as that is the major source of frustration for him at this time.

Since Jeremy was so young when he was assessed, and reading is so critical, remediation for reading was stressed, while still challenging his intellect appropriately. With the following two cases of older children, however, there was less emphasis on remediation and more on accommodation to help them fit into challenging environments.

Emily's Assessment and Diagnosis

Emily's assessment was much more complicated than Jeremy's because of her age, the nature of her difficulties, and the fact that past assessments had misdiagnosed her problem. Although she had always achieved well in school despite anomalies in her academic development (e.g., unable to remember math facts), she was becoming highly anxious when asked to do math or writing assignments under timed conditions and her social problems were resulting in some social isolation. Emily's parents recognized that the large discrepancy between her SAT Verbal and Math scores in the Johns Hopkins seventh grade talent search was not a truly valid representation of her abilities; her math reasoning abilities were much stronger than she could demonstrate on the timed test. The looming prospect of SATs to be taken in eleventh grade for college admissions made the possibility of an undiagnosed learning disability of primary importance. They sought an independent evaluation to document the scope of Emily's abilities and to evaluate whether she had a learning disability.

Emily's evaluation included the WISC-III, a full battery of achievement tests with an emphasis on mathematics and written language (timed and untimed performance were assessed), several processing batteries (i.e., Detroit Test of Learning Aptitude and Woodcock-Johnson III–Tests of Cognitive Ability), parent and teacher rating scales for social–emotional and behavioral problems, an extensive background questionnaire asking about developmental history, and several parent interviews. Prior testing results, including SAT scores, were also evaluated and used to make Emily's diagnosis. The results of Emily's psycho-educational evaluation produced a great deal of data to integrate, making her diagnosis difficult.

Unlike Jeremy, Emily had a highly significant discrepancy between her Verbal and Performance IQ on the WISC-III (135 versus 108, respectively), making her Full Scale IQ score of 125 an unreliable estimate of her cognitive abilities and highly unrepresentative of what her cognitive profile revealed. While Jeremy's Full Scale IQ score of 133 would clearly qualify him for gifted programming, Emily's Full Scale IQ score would have missed most cut-offs for gifted identification. The discrepancy between her Verbal and Performance IQ scores, however, was not only diagnostic of a learning disability; it was also an important indicator of what type of learning disability she had.

Tests of cognitive processing revealed that Emily had difficulty on tests of visual processing (both visual discrimination and memory were below the 30th percentile), while her auditory processing scores were extremely strong (all were above the 95th percentile). Although Emily had strong scores on tests of general reasoning, including analysis and synthesis (85th percentile), she had difficulty with some abstract–conceptual tasks (below the 30th percentile).

On achievement tests, Emily scored at the 98th percentile on reading comprehension tests and had strong scores (above the 90th percentile) for the content and mechanical aspects of her written work. However, Emily needed a great deal of time to organize her thoughts on writing samples and to edit her work. On a timed (15 minute) writing sample, she was able to write only four sentences. Most telling was the difference between Emily's performances on a timed versus an untimed math test (28th percentile versus 98th percentile). Additionally, the difference between her math reasoning and math computation scores was highly significant. When doing math computations, Emily used a very unorthodox way of setting up her problems, transposed numbers, had difficulty seeing the sequence of steps necessary to solve the problems, and needed to repeatedly rework problems involving time and distance. But, given enough time, Emily was able to correct her mistakes and work through her unconventional process of solving problems so that she eventually came up with the correct answers.

For Emily, the results from her testing were highly diagnostic but not sufficient to come to the correct diagnosis. It was necessary to put these results together with her developmental and academic history, as well as her social development, and information about her behavior in non-academic settings (e.g., her poor gross motor development and pervasive difficulty working with time, distance, and space). Emily's diagnosis was *Nonverbal Learning Disability.*

Emily's Intervention and Individual Education Plan

Emily's advanced verbal reasoning abilities and achievement were clearly indicative of her need for greater academic challenges. While it was agreed that she could easily skip eighth grade with regard to content, there was concern that she needed time to develop social skills and deal with her deficits. So it was recommended that she remain officially in the eighth grade for the coming year. However, to provide more challenge, she would take English and Biology with the ninth graders at the high school, and the possibility of moving directly from eighth to tenth grade would be considered at the end of the year. It was also recommended that Emily take an individually paced mathematics course on the computer, allowing her to spend additional time on topics that are difficult for her while eliminating repetition when it isn't needed. She should also be allowed to use a calculator for math, accepting the fact that she is unlikely to ever memorize some basic math facts.

Access to a computer for writing assignments and extra time to complete them were also recommended for Emily. With these accommodations, Emily has the potential to be a very good writer. Extended time on tests, including standardized tests such as the SAT, was recommended. It was also suggested that she work with a coach or tutor to help with study skills and organization, and consider instruction and participation in a sport to help Emily with gross motor skills and balance.

Emily's social and emotional difficulties were of primary concern, so counseling was recommended to help her understand her individual cognitive profile (e.g., what she is good at and why some things are hard) and how she can bolster her self-esteem, which has suffered as her learning difficulties have increased. Specific social-skills training was suggested in order to teach her appropriate responses in social situations. Emily was advised to join extracurricular activities that might provide access to peers who share her interests. In particular, participation in a summer academic program for gifted students will provide her with a more challenging academic environment than she is likely to get in her school, as well as access to intellectual peers. Although Emily's nonverbal learning disability contributes to her social difficulties, some difficulties may also be due to lack of exposure to other intellectually advanced students. Finally, a mentor was recommended to serve as a role model for Emily and to help her develop long-term goals.

Marcus's Assessment and Diagnosis

Marcus's academic difficulties were related to his behavioral problems in the classroom. Because of these problems, his teachers refused to advance him academically (despite overwhelming evidence of his ability to work at a much higher level than his current placement) and so his behavioral problems got even worse. He began to throw temper tantrums at home about not wanting to attend school and he soon refused to do work in class that he felt was too easy for him. Although Marcus had not lost confidence in his abilities, he was becoming more and more frustrated at what he felt was unfair treatment from his teacher. Diagnosing the underlying problems behind Marcus' behavior was critical to recommending appropriate academic intervention.

In addition to the WISC-III, Marcus was given the *School and College Ability Test (SCAT)*, a test of specific verbal and quantitative reasoning ability. His evaluation also included a full achievement battery of tests to assess reading, mathematics and written language. The SCAT and all of the achievement tests that Marcus was given were above-level forms (i.e., forms developed for students who are older than him) to ensure that he did not "hit the ceiling" of these tests. The cognitive processing tests included the *Bender Gestalt* and the *Developmental Test of Visual–Motor Integration* (VMI). Other important diagnostic pieces of Marcus' assessment were the behavioral rating scales completed by his parents and teachers, a background questionnaire, a clinical interview with Marcus' parents, and classroom observations.

Marcus' Full Scale IQ score of 146 on the WISC-III revealed his remarkable abilities. His Verbal IQ score was 147 and his Performance IQ score was 137. In addition, Marcus' verbal and quantitative reasoning scores from the SCAT were both above the 97th percentile when compared to students *three grade levels above him.* There was some scatter, however, among Marcus' subtest scores on the WISC-III that was highly diagnostic. On several tests requiring sustained attention and focus, his subtest scores fell into the low average range—quite significant given that all of his other scores on the WISC-III were in the very superior range.

On achievement tests in reading and math, Marcus scored at an exceptionally high level (99th percentile when compared to *7th grade norms*). In stark contrast, on writing tests, Marcus had an average score (45th percentile) for writing mechanics, had exceptionally poor handwriting, and protested strongly when asked to produce a writing sample. However, his score on the VMI ruled out dysgraphia. Without evidence of poor performance in key areas in this assessment, one might have concluded that he was highly gifted and unchallenged, which he was. However, the assessment indicated that a diagnosis of *Attention Deficit Hyperactivity Disorder (ADHD)* with accompanying grapho-motor weaknesses was appropriate.

Marcus's Intervention and Individual Education Plan

Marcus's assessment showed that he was both exceptionally gifted intellectually and advanced in content areas. Although some of his behavioral problems stemmed from lack of challenging work, his attention deficits and poor impulse control were clear contributing factors.

To accommodate his intellectual needs, it was recommended that Marcus skip the fourth grade and enter the fifth. Even with this placement, however, he needed more advanced work. For math, it was suggested that he be placed with a small group of similarly advanced students or put in an individualized math program to allow him to work at his achievement level. In reading, placement with the most advanced fifth grade readers for group discussion was recommended, along with providing him with an individualized reading program at his reading level. Science is a strong interest for Marcus, so it was suggested that he work on a science research topic or science fair project whenever the class is working on a skill he has already mastered or as a reward for finishing his assigned work.

Marcus' weaknesses needed attention too, because they were interfering with achievement. It is important that his written language skills be developed and that his interest in writing be encouraged without his fine motor difficulties interfering, so it was recommended that Marcus be taught keyboarding and encouraged to use a computer for writing. An evaluation by an occupational therapist with regard to developing Marcus's fine motor skills was also suggested, though it is likely that therapy would have been more effective when he was younger.

Extra time for assignments and tests was endorsed as a way to help Marcus compensate for his handwriting problems. He must learn to check his work and needs the time to do so. A variety of supportive steps both at home and at school were also recommended to address Marcus's difficulties that result from ADHD including: making sure that expectations and assignments are clear, providing adequate communication between school and home, using study aids such as notebooks and assignment pads, being aware of Marcus' frustration with writing and giving him breaks as needed, seating him away from distractions, and providing reinforcement and rewards for success. It was also recommended that Marcus be evaluated by a physician for possible medication for ADHD.

Marcus' social and emotional issues were of particular concern since his peer relationships were deteriorating and his self-esteem appeared to be suffering. It was recommended that he spend time with a counselor who could help him understand himself better and work with him on modifying his behavior and developing social skills. Marcus was also encouraged to seek opportunities to meet and become friends with intellectual peers who share his interests, and Saturday classes at a local science museum were specifically suggested.

CONCLUSION

Children who are gifted and also have a learning disability have special characteristics and unique academic needs. These special characteristics make them difficult to identify and diagnose, while their unique academic needs necessitate an integrated approach on the part of numerous school personnel. Early intervention is important for any child with a learning disability and, yet, the gifted child with a learning disability is often overlooked for many years because he or she is not falling behind enough for anyone to acknowledge that a problem exists. Jeremy, Emily, and Marcus are illustrative of students whose gifts masked their disabilities and whose problems were exacerbated by social and emotional issues that arose from a misunderstanding of their cognitive abilities and needs.

Comprehensive psycho-educational assessments can identify extraordinary talents, delineate complex cognitive profiles, and reveal processing deficits that characterize gifted students with learning disabilities. Results from assessments can point to the programmatic interventions that are needed. As we seek a greater understanding of gifted students with learning disabilities and find more appropriate services to meet their needs, more of these now underserved students will have an opportunity to reach their full potential.

REFERENCES

Barton, J. M., & Starnes, W. T. (1989). Identifying distinguishing characteristics of gifted and talented/learning disabled students. Roeper Review, 12 (1), 23–29.

Baum, S. (1988). An enrichment program for the gifted learning disabled students. Gifted Child Quarterly, 32, 226-230.

Baum, S. (1994). Meeting the needs of gifted/learning disabled students. Journal of Gifted Secondary Education, 5 (3), 6–16.

Baum, S., Owen, S. V., & Dixon, J. (1991). To be gifted and learning disabled: From identification to practical intervention strategies. Mansfield Center, CT: Creative Learning Press.

Bos, C. S., Nahmias, M. L., & Urban, M. A. (1999). Targeting home–school collaboration for students with ADHD. Teaching Exceptional Children, 31 (5), 4–11.

Brody, L. E., & Mills. C. J. (1997). Gifted children with learning disabilities: A review of the issues. Journal of Learning Disabilities, 30 (3), 282–296.

Daniels, P. R. (1983). Teaching the gifted/learning disabled child. Rockville MD: Aspen.

Durden, W. G., & Tangherlini, A. E. (1993). Smart kids: How academic talents are developed and nurtured in America. Seattle: Hogrefe & Huber.

Ford, D. Y. (2003). Equity and excellence: Culturally diverse students in gifted education. In N. Colangelo & G. A. Davis (Eds.), Handbook of gifted education (3rd ed., pp. 506–520). Boston: Allyn & Bacon.

Fox, L. H., Brody, L., & Tobin, D., (1983). Learning-disabled/gifted children: Identification and Programming. Austin, TX: PRO-ED.

Fox, L. H., Tobin, D., & Schiffman, G. B. (1983). Adaptive methods and techniques for learning disabled/gifted children. In L.H. Fox, L. Brody, & D. Tobin (Eds.), Learning disabled/gifted children: Identification and programming (pp. 183–193). Austin, TX: PRO-ED.

French, J. N. (1982). The gifted learning disabled child: A challenge and some suggestions. Roeper Review, 4 (3), 19–21.

Gardner, H. (2000). Intelligence reframed: Multiple intelligences for the 21st century. New York: Basic Books.

Graham, S., Harris, K. R., & Larsen, L. (2001). Prevention and intervention of writing difficulties for students with learning disabilities. Learning Disabilities Research & Practice, 16 (2), 74–84.

Karnes, M. B., & Johnson, L. J. (1991). Gifted handicapped. In N. Colangelo & G. A. Davis (Eds.), Handbook of gifted education (2nd edition, pp. 428–437).

Kaufmann, F., Kalbfleisch, M. L., & Castellanos, F. X. (2000). Attention Deficit Disorders and gifted students: What do we really know? (RM00146). Storrs, CT: The National Research Center on the Gifted and Talented, University of Connecticut.

Kavale, K. A. (1980). Learning disability and cultural disadvantage: The case for a relationship. Learning Disability Quarterly, 3, 97–112.

Kay, K. (2002). Uniquely gifted: Identifying and meeting the needs of the twice exceptional student. Gilsum, NH: Avocus.

Krippner, S. (1968). Etiological factors in reading disability of the academically talented in comparison to pupils of average and slow-learning ability. Journal of Educational Research, 61 (6), 275–279.

Levine, M. (2002). The myth of laziness. New York: Simon and Schuster.

Lyon, G. R. (1989). IQ is irrelevant to the definition of learning disabilities: A position in search of logic and data. Journal of Learning Disabilities, 22, 504–506, 512.

Mastropieri, M. A., Sweda, J., & Scruggs, T. E. (2000). Teacher use of mnemonic strategy instruction. Learning Disabilities Research and Practice, 15 (2), 69–74.

McEachern, A. G., & Bornot, J. (2001). Gifted students with learning disabilities: Implications and strategies for school counselors. Professional School Counseling, 5 (1), 34–41.

Mendaglio, S. (1993). Counseling gifted learning disabled: Individual and group counseling techniques. In L. K. Silverman (Ed.), Counseling the gifted and talented (pp. 131–149). Denver: Love.

Mills, C. J., & Brody, L. E. (1999). Overlooked and unchallenged: Gifted students with learning disabilities. Knowledge Quest, 27 (5), 30–34.

Moller, B. W. (1984). Special techniques for the gifted LD student. Academic Therapy, 20, 167–171.

Neihart, M. (2000). Gifted children with Asperger's syndrome. Gifted Child Quarterly, 44 (4), 222–230.

Olson, R. K. (1985). Disabled reading processes and cognitive profiles. In D. B. Gray & J. F. Cavanaugh (Eds.), Biobehavioral measures of dyslexia (pp. 215–244). Parkton MD: York Press.

Olszewski–Kubilius, P. (2003). Special summer and Saturday programs for gifted students. In N. Colangelo & G. A. Davis (Eds.), Handbook of gifted education (3rd ed., pp. 219–228). Boston: Allyn & Bacon).

Renzulli, J. S. & Reis, S. M. (1997). The schoolwide enrichment model: A how to guide for educational excellence. Mansfield Center, CT: Creative Learning Press.

Reynolds, M. C., Zetlin, A. G., & Wang, M. C. (1993). 20/20 analysis: Taking a close look at the margins. Exceptional Children, 59, 294–300.

Rogers, K. B. (1992). A best-evidence synthesis of research on acceleration options for gifted students. In N. Colangelo, S. Assouline, & D. Ambroson (Eds.), Talent development (pp. 406–409). Unionville, NY: Trillium Press.

Schiff, M. M., Kaufman, A. S., & Kaufman, N. L. (1981). Scatter analysis of WISC–R profiles for learning disabled children with superior intelligence. Journal of Learning Disabilities, 14, 400–404.

Siegel, L. S. (1989). IQ is irrelevant to the definition of learning disabilities. Journal of Learning Disabilities, 22, 469–486.

Siegel, L. S. (2003). IQ-discrepancy definitions and the diagnosis of LD: Introduction to the special issue. Journal of Learning Disabilities, 36 (1), 2–3.

Siegel, L. S., & Metsala, J. (1992). An alternative to the food processor approach to subtypes of learning disabilities. In N. N. Singh & I. L. Beale (Eds.), Learning disabilities: Nature, theory, and treatment (pp. 44–60). New York: Springer-Verlag.

Silverman, L. K. (1989). Invisible gifts, invisible handicaps. Roeper Review, 12, 37–41.

Silverman, L. K. (2002). Upside down brilliance: The visual–spatial learner. Denver: DeLeon.

Southern, W. T. & Jones, E. D. (Eds.) (1991). The academic acceleration of gifted children. New York: Teachers College Press.

Stage, S. A., Abbott, R. D., Jenkins, J. R., & Berninger, V. W. (2003). Predicting response to early reading intervention from verbal IQ, reading-related language abilities, attention ratings, and verbal IQ–word reading discrepancy: Failure to validate discrepancy method. Journal of Learning Disabilities, 36 (1), 24–33.

Stanley, J. C. (1979). The study and facilitation of talent in mathematics. In A. H. Passow (Ed.), The gifted and talented: Their education and development (The 79th yearbook of the National Society for the Study of Education, pp. 169–185). Chicago: University of Chicago Press.

Stanovich, K. E. (1986). Cognitive processes and the reading problems of learning disabled children: Evaluating the assumption of specificity. In J. K. Torgesen & B. Y. L. Wong (Eds.), Psychological and educational perspectives on learning disabilities (pp. 87–131). Orlando, FL: Academic Press.

Stanovich, K. E. (1993). A model for studies of reading disability. Developmental Review, 13, 225–245.

Sternberg, R. J. (2003). Giftedness according to the theory of successful intelligence. In N. Colangelo & G. A. Davis (Eds.), Handbook of gifted education (3rd ed., pp. 113–123). Boston: Allyn & Bacon).

Thompson, S. (1997). The source for nonverbal learning disorders. East Moline, IL: Linquisystems.

Tobin, D., & Schiffman, G. B. (1983). Computer technology for learning disabled/gifted students. In L. H. Fox, L. Brody, & D. Tobin (Eds.), Learning disabled/gifted children: identification and programming (pp. 195–206). Austin, TX: PRO-ED.

Tomlinson, C. A. (2001). How to differentiate instruction in mixed-ability classrooms (2nd. ed.). Alexandria VA: Association for Supervision & Curriculum Development.

Torrance, E. P. (1979). Unique needs of the creative child and adult. In A. H. Passow (Ed.), The gifted and talented: Their education and development (The 79th yearbook of the National Society for the Study of Education, pp. 352–371). Chicago: University of Chicago Press.

U. S. Department of Education Office of Special Education and Rehabilitative Services (2002). A new era: Revitalizing special education for children and their families. Washington, DC: Education Publications Center.

Waldron, K. A., & Saphire, D. G. (1990). An analysis of WISC–R factors for gifted students with learning disabilities. Journal of Learning Disabilities, 23, 491–498.

Weinfeld, R., Barnes-Robinson, L., Jeweler, S., & Shevitz, B. (2002). Academic programs for gifted and talented/learning disabled students. Roeper Review, 24 (4), 226–233.

Winebrenner, S. (2002). Strategies for teaching twice exceptional children. Understanding Our Gifted, 14 (2), 3–6.

Winebrenner, S., & Espeland, P. (1996). Teaching kids with learning difficulties in the regular classroom: Strategies and techniques every teacher can use to challenge and motivate struggling students. Minneapolis: Free Spirit Publishing.

Whitmore, J. R. (1980). Giftedness, conflict, and underachievement. Boston: Allyn & Bacon.

Chapter 5

DYSLEXIA AND VISUAL SPATIAL TALENTS: ARE THEY CONNECTED?

Catya von Károlyi
University of Wisconsin–Eau Claire

Ellen Winner
Boston College and Harvard Project Zero

ABSTRACT

Although it has been claimed that with dyslexia comes visual–spatial gifts, the evidence relevant to this claim is mixed. Whereas individuals with visual–spatial gifts have a disproportionate incidence of reading deficits, including dyslexia, individuals with dyslexia do not consistently show superior visual–spatial abilities. Depending on the task and the study, individuals with reading disorders have been shown to perform at below average, average, and superior levels. The inconsistency in findings is likely due to the use of very different measures of visual–spatial ability. Recent studies from our lab suggest that when global (holistic) visual–spatial tasks are used, individuals with dyslexia excel. Future research is called for to test the hypothesis that dyslexia is associated with talent in global visual–spatial ability.

INTRODUCTION

It is often claimed that dyslexia is accompanied by visual–spatial gifts. In 1925, Dr. Samuel T. Orton, one of the first scholars to identify dyslexia, described a case in which visual–spatial giftedness and word reading problems co-occurred. The neurologist Norman Geschwind (1982) also noted the co-occurrence of dyslexia and talent in such visual–spatial areas as art, engineering, and architecture, and termed this association of a deficit with a talent as a "pathology of superiority" (pp. 22–23; see also Geschwind & Galaburda, 1987 pp. 65–66). The view that dyslexia is accompanied by visual–spatial gifts is echoed on Internet Web sites and in popular books and articles (e.g., Davis & Braun, 1997; Silverman, 2002; West, 1991). Individuals with dyslexia are commonly thought of as endowed with superior creativity, artistic ability, and mechanical skill.

What neurological model might lead us to predict an association between dyslexia and visual–spatial talents? Geschwind (1982) proposed the concept of *pathology of superiority* to describe such a co-occurrence. Geschwind and Galaburda (1987) went on to account for such a co-occurrence in terms of the *Testosterone Hypothesis*, suggesting that exposure to (or atypical sensitivity to) testosterone in utero could lead to left hemisphere language-related deficits and resultant compensatory growth in analogous regions of the right hemisphere. This was argued to lead to brains that were symmetrical (rather than the usual pattern of a larger left hemisphere). This set of events could then manifest itself as dyslexia accompanied by spatial talents (since the right hemisphere mediates many spatial abilities).

There is empirical evidence for Geschwind and Galaburda's (1987) prediction of greater symmetry in dyslexic brains: All seven of the dyslexic brains studied at autopsy by Galaburda and his colleagues showed symmetrical *plana temporale* (Galaburda, Sherman, Rosen, Aboitiz, & Geschwind, 1985; Humphreys, Kaufmann, & Galaburda, 1990). However, the original claim was that symmetrical brains would result from inhibited left-hemisphere growth along with enhanced right-hemisphere growth (Geschwind & Galaburda, 1987). Autopsied dyslexic brains show that the symmetry is not due to a smaller left hemisphere, but rather to a larger right hemisphere, likely due to incomplete neuronal pruning (Galaburda et al., 1985; Galaburda, Corsiglia, Rosen, & Sherman, 1987; see Beaton, 1997, for a critical review of the evidence). Humphreys, Kaufmann, and Galaburda (1990) speculate that the altered neuronal circuitry of symmetrical brains could result in altered cognitive capacities (whether superior or inferior is not specified).

The brains of individuals with dyslexia have also been found to have microscopic cortical abnormalities of two types: architectonic dysplasias (excessive folding, fused laminae and absent columnar organization) and neuronal ectopias (nests of neurons located in layer I, which is normally free of neurons) (Galaburda et al., 1985; Humphreys, Kaufmann, & Galaburda, 1990). These abnormalities were present on both sides of the brain. However, left hemisphere; in one of the three female dyslexic brains studied, abnormalities were more prominent on the right (Humphreys, Kaufmann, & Galaburda, 1990). (Two of the three female brains also had *glial scarring*, that is, zones without neurons.) Galaburda et al. (1985) argue that the lesions observed in these brains were acquired during the middle of gestation (during the time when neurons migrate to the cortex), and that such lesions lead to cerebral reorganization in the form of atypical growth and connectivity in the cortex.

Galaburda et al. (1985) speculate that the atypical findings in dyslexic brains could lead not only to dyslexia but also to the enhancement of other cognitive functions. They note that such a hypothesis is consistent with findings that cells compete for available synapses during development. Hence, lesions that inhibit language-related structures could lead to compensatory development of other structures. Because ectopias disrupt cortical development and lead to reorganization of neural pathways, the long-term developmental effects of ectopias could, in principle, result in enhancement of certain skills.

Studies of behavioral characteristics of mice with neuronal ectopias provide some support for the hypothesis that such lesions can lead to enhancement of certain functions, in this case, spatial ones. Mice with such ectopias have been shown to perform at a superior level on the Morris maze task, a spatial reference memory task in which one must remember a location that remains fixed across problems (Boehm et al., 1996; Waters, Sherman, Galaburda, & Denenberg, 1997). In contrast, ectopic mice performed worse than nonectopic mice on tasks that require working memory for information that changes from problem to problem. Given that ectopic mice show enhanced spatial reference memory, it is conceivable that human neuronal ectopias might also lead to enhanced spatial ability.

While it is possible that the kind of atypical brain development seen in dyslexia could result in enhancement of certain cognitive abilities, it seems equally likely that such atypical development could lead to deficits. In addition, the individual variability found in the brains of dyslexics studied at autopsy—in terms of the quantity and location of cortical abnormalities—suggests that there are likely to be considerable and unpredictable individual differences in the cognitive skills of dyslexics.

In what follows, we review evidence about the relationship between visual–spatial abilities and reading disorders. Most of the relevant studies focus on individuals identified as having dyslexia. However, some studies include individuals identified as having reading disabilities, reading disorders, or reading difficulties. We include these studies in our review when the participants were reported to have performed poorly on spelling or other measures of phonological processing, because this indicates that they probably had dyslexia. We also include a few studies that identified their participants as learning disabled if the participants were also described as having reading problems, and justify this decision because dyslexia is the most common learning disability (Springer & Deutsch, 1997). In what follows, we use the generic term *reading disorders* when referring to studies that did not specify that their participants had been diagnosed with dyslexia. Otherwise, our terminology reflects that used in each study.

The evidence relevant to our question takes two forms. First, one can observe whether individuals who are talented in visual–spatial areas exhibit dyslexia. Second, one can observe whether individuals with dyslexia exhibit visual–spatial strengths.

READING PROBLEMS IN INDIVIDUALS WITH VISUAL–SPATIAL TALENTS

Visual–Spatial Gifts and Reading Deficits Can Co-Occur

Reading difficulties have been noted in individuals known to have visual–spatial gifts. Aaron, Phillips, and Larsen (1988) reported that Thomas Edison, Leonardo da Vinci, and Hans Christian Andersen all showed both talent in visual–spatial areas and problems with spelling and syntax, problems that ran in their families. Writing samples gathered from the notes and letters of visual artists Auguste Rodin and Charles Marion Russell revealed spelling, syntax, and punctuation errors (Aaron & Guillemard, 1993). Similar findings can be found in case studies of inventors Michael Faraday, James Clerk Maxwell, and Nikola Tesla, artist and inventor Leonardo da Vinci, and others (West, 1991). None of these individuals had been clinically diagnosed with dyslexia, yet they showed evidence of some type of weakness in language, such as histories of difficulties in reading, spelling, and syntax, backwards writing, school problems, stuttering, and/or late language acquisition.

Retrospective case studies, however, are weak evidence for the claim that dyslexia is linked to visual–spatial talent. There are no recognized methods of diagnosing dyslexia using retrospective case studies and attempts to do so have been strongly criticized (Adelman, 1988). In addition, post-hoc analyses are particularly subject to hypothesis-confirmation bias. Finally, the fact that some individuals with spatial gifts have dyslexia tells us only that visual–spatial gifts and dyslexia *can* co-occur. Such findings tell us nothing about whether superior visual–spatial abilities and dyslexia are in fact related and therefore co-occur at a disproportionately high rate. For this kind of evidence, we must compare the incidence of reading problems in individuals with and without visual–spatial gifts, and we must compare levels of visual–spatial abilities in individuals with and without reading problems.

Consistent with the case studies described above, elevated prevalence of reading and language problems have been found in groups of individuals identified as having visual–spatial gifts when compared to control groups without reading problems. Such findings have been reported for artists, mathematicians, inventors, and children exhibiting spatial strengths.

Artists

Compared to students majoring in the humanities and social sciences and those majoring in math and science, art majors have been found more likely to report a past history of dyslexia, difficulty learning to read, difficulty reading quickly, and problems with reversing letters and numbers (Winner & Casey, 1993; Winner, Casey, DaSilva, & Hayes, 1991). When given a spelling test, these same art majors also made more spelling errors, including more nonphonetically-based spelling errors (common in dyslexia) than did the other two groups, even when controlling for differences in scholastic aptitude. An association between visual–spatial gifts and language difficulties was also reported by Hassler (1990), who found that artists performed at average on visual–spatial measures but fared poorly on a measure of verbal fluency.

Mathematicians

Mathematics has been argued to involve visual–spatial thinking (Krutetskii, 1976) and evidence suggests elevated prevalence of reading problems among mathematicians. Six of the 20 world-class mathematicians Bloom (1985) studied reported problems learning to read. None had learned to read before school, despite the fact that individuals with high IQs typically learn to read one or more years prior to entering school (Gross, 1993; Winner, 1996). And male college students majoring in math or science made significantly more nonphonetic spelling errors (the kinds of errors associated with dyslexia) than did students majoring in verbal areas (Martino & Winner, 1995)

Inventors

An elevated prevalence of language problems has also been noted among inventors, individuals who are likely to have high visual–spatial skills (Colangelo, Assouline, Kerr, Huesman, & Johnson, 1993). In spite of mathematics strengths, most of the of 34 inventors studied by Colangelo et al. reported weakness in writing and verbal areas and more than half described themselves as low achievers in school who had failed in at least one class.

Young Children with Superior Visual–Spatial Abilities

Very young children with high visual–spatial abilities have also been found to have language difficulties. Of 43 late-talking children studied by Sowell (1997), 72% were unusually good at puzzles. Most of the children had family members in spatial professions, and 60% had first- or second-degree relatives who were engineers.

Discussion

The disproportionate incidence of reading and language problems in individuals who choose careers that require visual–spatial skill may or may not predict that individuals with dyslexia should have higher than average visual–spatial skills. This finding may suggest that they have high visual–spatial skills, a hypothesis consistent with the concept of *pathology of superiority* (Geschwind & Galaburda, 1987). However, this finding may also be due to individuals with dyslexia entering visual–spatial professions not due of visual–spatial strengths, but to avoid professions requiring extensive reading. These individuals may have only average visual–spatial abilities, but may gravitate to visual–spatial professions because these abilities are stronger (relatively) than their language skills. This has been referred to as the *default hypothesis* (Winner, Casey, DaSilva, & Hayes, 1991).

Participation in a visual–spatial profession chosen by default could lead to heightened visual–spatial skills as a result of practice. Individuals with dyslexia might be more motivated to succeed in visual–spatial fields because of their relative lack of success in the verbal arena. Performance outcomes could also be affected by differences in the number of distractions outside of the field. Less time spent reading the newspaper could translate to more time in visual–spatial thinking. To test the default hypothesis, researchers should compare the visual–spatial profiles of individuals with and without dyslexia within a given spatial profession both at entry into the profession and after many years in the profession. If dyslexia drives people into spatial fields by default, those in spatial professions who have dyslexia should have lower spatial skills than those without dyslexia. If practice, motivation, or focus strengthens spatial skills, then individuals with dyslexia who go into spatial professions should ultimately attain higher visual–spatial skills than individuals with dyslexia who do not choose such professions. Alternatively, if individuals with dyslexia are more likely than individuals without dyslexia to excel at visual–spatial skills, then individuals with dyslexia in spatial professions should have visual–spatial gifts equal to individuals without dyslexia in these professions.

All we can assert on the basis of the above-reviewed evidence is that dyslexia can coexist with visual–spatial gifts. Because individuals with dyslexia may be drawn to visual–spatial fields because of reading deficits (i.e., by default) rather than because of visual–spatial ability, these studies cannot tell us whether individuals with dyslexia have superior visual–spatial abilities or whether they are simply avoiding verbal activities. These studies only inform us about relative, not absolute abilities. To determine whether individuals with dyslexia do indeed have superior visual–spatial abilities, we must turn to studies that compare spatial profiles of individuals with and without dyslexia.

VISUAL–SPATIAL ABILITY IN INDIVIDUALS WITH READING DISORDERS

Some researchers have argued that dyslexia, or at least some subtype of dyslexia is associated with weak rather than strong visual–spatial ability (i.e., Hooper & Willis, 1989; Ingram, 1964 cited in Naidoo, 1972; Morris, et al., 1998; Naidoo, 1972; also see Benton, 1984). Individuals with dyslexia who transposed or reversed letters, words or syllables, and read or wrote backwards have been considered deficient in visual–spatial skills (e.g. Naidoo, 1972). However, these tasks are not actually visual–spatial but are, rather, *visuoverbal* because they involve linguistic symbols (Benton, 1984). Like Benton, we do not consider these behaviors indicative of visual–spatial ability because they involve linguistic symbols.

Inferior performance on visual–spatial tasks by individuals with reading disorders has, however, been reported. The approach has been to administer visual–spatial tasks to individuals with and without dyslexia or other reading disorders. Unfortunately, taken together, these studies do not present a clear picture. On some visual–spatial tasks, those with reading disorders perform at below average levels; on many tasks, they perform at average levels; and they excel on only a few tasks. The picture is complicated because reading disorders have been inconsistently defined and because so many different kinds of visual–spatial abilities have been assessed through so many different types of measures. Some researchers assessed performance on major factors of spatial ability, such as those described by Carroll (1993) and Ekstrom, French, Harman, with Derman, (1976). Others have used measures that do not clearly map on to any of these identified spatial factors or that tap multiple factors, such as artistic ability and visual–spatial abstract reasoning. Below we organize the evidence into categories that represent three major factors of visual–spatial ability—spatial orientation, visualization, visual memory—and three more specific factors—flexibility of closure, speed of closure, and figural flexibility. To these categories we add artistic ability and visual–spatial abstract reasoning.

Spatial Orientation

Spatial Orientation is defined as "the ability to perceive spatial patterns or to maintain orientation with respect to objects in space" (Ekstrom et al., 1976, p. 149). It has also been defined as the ability to imagine how an image will appear from another perspective (Carroll, 1993).

The Boats Test assesses spatial orientation (Guilford & Zimmerman, 1953). On this test, one must imagine how a landscape would look from an altered orientation, a skill that we reasoned would be associated with navigational skill. In this (very difficult) task, participants are presented with a landscape scene viewed from the front of a speedboat. Below this scene is a second scene reflecting a change in the boat's position. The task is to determine how the position of the boat has changed, given the changed view. Position of the boat is demonstrated by selecting one of five diagrams representing the change in the boat's position. When we administered this task in its standard timed version, high school students with dyslexia performed equivalently to the control group (Winner et al., 2001). To test the hypothesis that allowing unlimited time might enhance dyslexic performance, the task was also administered with no time limits. Contrary to hypothesis, however, individuals with dyslexia performed worse in the untimed condition than did the control group.

The Judgment of Line Orientation task requires participants to compare the orientations of lines and match those oriented at the same angle. Morris et al. (1988) administered this task to 232 7.5 to 9.5 year olds (71% male). Using cluster analysis, Morris et al. identified one group of participants consisting of 31 students with phonological deficits and reading disorders—20 students with reading disabilities and 11 students whose reading disorders did not meet the criteria for being classified as a disability. On the Judgment of Line Orientation Test, this group performed at an average level for the sample. Similarly, on a pattern-matching task, in which participants must match patterns made up of two to seven small dots on index cards (i.e., [* * * * *] compared with [*   * * *   *]), children identified as having learning disabilities performed equivalently to controls (Rudel & Denckla, 1976).

We also administered a spatial reference memory task that we hypothesized was likely also to assess spatial orientation (Winner et al., 2001). This task was based on the Morris Maze task, a task on which mice with neuronal ectopias (mentioned earlier) outperform those without (Waters, Sherman, Galaburda, & Denenberg, 1997). Given that ectopic mice show enhanced spatial reference memory, and given that the same kinds of ectopias have been found in dyslexic brains, we reasoned that this might be a task on which individuals with dyslexia would excel. Our task assessed the ability to recall relations between locations of familiar landmarks. Students were asked to imagine themselves facing in a particular direction and standing at a particular place in one of their school buildings (e.g., with their back to the door to the third floor elevator). They were then asked to imagine pointing towards another location in their school (e.g., from where you are now standing, point to the door of the gym). Participants indicated the direction in which they would point by marking an X on a circle. Contrary to hypothesis, high school students with dyslexia performed significantly worse than individuals without dyslexia on this task (Winner et al., 2001). Individuals with dyslexia missed the target by a mean of 24.251 degrees; individuals without dyslexia missed the target by only 11.192 degrees. Thus the responses of individuals with dyslexia were twice as far off target as those without dyslexia.

Mental Rotation

Mental rotation tasks typically involve comparing a target figure to an array and determining which figure in the array is identical to the target. The difficulty comes from the orientation of the correct figure in the array. One must mentally rotate the figure to determine whether it is a match to the target. Some mental rotation tasks are made up of drawings of two-dimensional objects and others of drawings of three-dimensional objects.

On the Card Rotation Test (Ekstrom et al., 1976) one must compare a target line drawing to eight other drawings and determine in each case whether each of the eight is the same or different from the target. The ones that are different are the same shapes but they are flipped over (i.e., mirror images). The ones that are the same are simply at a different angle of rotation and can be recognized to match if one mentally rotates the image in two-dimensional space. We carried out a study comparing high school students with and without dyslexia on a wide range of spatial tasks. This study was conducted to test the hypothesis that individuals with dyslexia have above average visual–spatial ability (a finding that would explain the disproportionate incidence of individuals with reading problems in fields requiring visual–spatial skill). On the Card Rotation task, students with dyslexia performed significantly worse than those with no reading problems. This finding was not due to the speeded nature of the task because even when presented in an untimed form, dyslexic high school students were found to perform significantly worse (Winner, et al. 2001).

The Flags Test of Spatial Thinking (Thurstone & Jeffrey, 1956) is another test of mental rotation abilities. In this task, one must make rapid same/different judgments of drawings of a target flag and six competing flags. The six competing flags differ from the target in spatial orientation or position. Sinatra (1988) found that right-handed male university students with dyslexia performed in the normative-average range on Flags. (The normative group for this measure was made up of 278 male industrial workers.)

A more difficult mental rotation test, the Vandenberg Test of Mental Rotation (Vandenberg & Kuse, 1978), yielded similar findings in our study (Winner et al., 2001). On this test, participants view a target figure, which is a line drawing of a three-dimensional complex figure, along with four choices.

Two of the choices are drawings of the same figure rotated in three-dimensional space. The other two choices are drawings of different but very similar figures (sometimes mirror images). The task is to indicate which two of the four choices are identical to the target. As with the Card Rotation test, high school students with dyslexia in our study performed significantly worse than a non-reading impaired control group even when the test was presented in untimed form (Winner, et al. 2001).

Similar findings were reported by Johnson and Ellis Weismer (1983) who found that children with language disorders had longer latencies on a mental rotation task compared to a control group, though their accuracy rates were no different from the control group. In this task, children were presented with drawings of linear arrays of geometric forms (two at a time), and were asked to make same/different judgments. One of the forms was rotated about its center 45°, 90°, or 135°. The fact that the children with reading disorders took longer to solve the problems correctly might suggest that deficiencies on mental rotation tasks are simply due to the requirement of working quickly. However, the findings reported above, showing that individuals with dyslexia perform worse even under untimed conditions, allow us to rule out this hypothesis.

On the basis of the above-reviewed research, there is no evidence for enhanced spatial orientation ability in individuals with dyslexia, and there is evidence that individuals with dyslexia are impaired in this ability.

Visualization

Visualization is defined as "the ability to manipulate or transform the image of spatial patterns into other arrangements" (Ekstrom et al., 1976, p. 173). It has also been defined as the ability to apprehend, encode, and mentally manipulate spatial forms (Carroll, 1993). This factor is considered similar to Spatial Orientation. However visualization requires that parts of a figure be manipulated mentally, while orientation requires that the entire figure be manipulated mentally.

The Form Board Task (Ekstrom et al., 1976) was administered by Winner et al. (2001) to assess this capacity in high school students with and without dyslexia, again to test the hypothesis of superior spatial ability linked to dyslexia. In this task, a geometric design is presented, along with five shapes underneath the design. The participant must indicate which of the five pieces, when put together, would form the top design. Students with dyslexia performed equivalently to the control group on a timed version of this task. On an untimed version, hypothesized to improve the performance of individuals with dyslexia, the dyslexia group performed worse (but not significantly so) than controls.

We also designed a task that we hypothesized was likely to assess visualization. On this task, called the "Archimedes Screw Task," participants examine a series of four line drawings representing a screw-based device invented by Archimedes to raise water from a lower to a higher level. Two of the drawings are correct in their depiction of both the direction in which the screw must turn to raise the water and the resultant flow of the water. Two of the drawings are incorrect, depicting impossible screw-turn and water-flow combinations. Participants were asked to decide which way the screw would have to turn in order to bring water up. To solve this task one must form a mental image of the screw, and one must then try out turning the screw in each of two directions, all the time visualizing which direction water inside the tube would move (up or down) given the turning of the screw. While this itself is not an ordinary task that people confront in the real world, the skills required seem to be the kinds of skills that an inventor would use in imagining how a new device would actually work. On this task, we found no difference between the performance of students with and without dyslexia. Those with dyslexia performed as well as, but no better than, those without dyslexia.

Hermelin and O'Connor (1986) tested the ability of individuals with dyslexia to solve verbally presented problems whose solution appears to us to call for spatial visualization. For example, one problem used required participants to visualize a cube and imagine cutting it up into smaller cubes: "A painted wooden cube with an edge of 9 cm is cut up into little cubes each of a 3 cm edge. There will be 27 of these little cubes. How many of them will have only two painted sides?" (Correct answer is 12.) Clearly, to solve this task (whose correct answer is 12), one must form an image of the cube and imagine cutting it up, and then imagine how many of the smaller cubes would have only two painted sides. On this task, individuals with dyslexia performed significantly worse than controls.

On the basis of the above-reviewed research, there is evidence that individuals with dyslexia are either normal or impaired in visualization. Most importantly for our purposes, we have found no convincing evidence for enhanced visualization ability in individuals with dyslexia.

Visual Memory

Visual memory is defined as "the ability to remember the configuration, location, and orientation of figural material" (Ekstrom et al.., 1976, p. 109). A preponderance of evidence suggests that deficits in working memory accompany dyslexia, and visual memory is not immune (Swanson, Mink & Bocian, 1999). We found no research suggesting that dyslexia is associated with deficits in visual–spatial working memory in the absence of other deficits in working memory. Therefore, this chapter does not review the literature on visual memory. Some of the studies we reviewed on visual–spatial abilities in dyslexia, however, included tasks that tap visual memory. The following studies, therefore, must be considered as merely a sampling of the research on visual memory in dyslexia.

The Rey Osterrieth Complex Figure is a test of perceptual organization and visual memory (Osterrieth, 1944; Rey, 1941). Participants are shown a line drawing of a complex figure and are asked to copy the figure using a pencil and paper (Copy Condition). The target figure is then removed and participants are asked to reproduce the figure from memory (Immediate Recall Condition). Twenty minutes later, participants are asked to reproduce the figure from memory again (Delayed Recall Condition). No advance warning is given that the figure will have to be drawn from memory for either memory condition. Winner et al. (2001) found that college students with dyslexia performed as well as those without dyslexia on the copy task, but performed significantly worse than those without dyslexia on the immediate recall task. In a second study, Winner et al. added the delayed recall component and administered the task to high school students with and without dyslexia. Again, those with dyslexia performed worse than the controls.

A task assessing visual memory was also included in Koenig, Kosslyn, and Wolff's (1991) study of right-handed male 16– to 18–year-olds with and without dyslexia. Participants memorized simple line patterns made up of "X"s in a 4 x 5 grid and subsequently judged whether an "X" presented on an otherwise empty grid would have been part of the memorized pattern. No difference in error rates or response times were found between groups for memory for novel patterns. These findings (showing average rather than impaired performance in individuals with dyslexia) might be seen to conflict with the inferior performance of individuals with dyslexia on the Rey Osterrieth task described above. Both involve memory for designs. However, the Rey is a far more complex task: The image is more complex, and the task requires reproduction.

The Target Test is a visual memory task that involves "the ability to reproduce graphically a pattern previously pointed out by the examiner" (Rourke & Finlayson, 1978, p. 126). On the Target Test, students with reading disorders in Rourke and Finlayson's study scored significantly higher than average readers who had arithmetic weakness. However, no norms were reported for this test and there was no comparison made to an average control group.

A test of visual memory for nonsense designs was included in a study by Libeman, Mann, Shankweiler and Werfelman (1982). In this study poor readers (not clinically diagnosed as disabled) were compared to good readers. There was no significant difference between the performance of poor and good readers on this task.

We did find one study reporting superior performance on a visual memory task by disabled readers. Swanson (1984) presented both unnamed nonsense pictures and nonsense pictures with either relevant or irrelevant names to matched groups of skilled and disabled readers who were asked to reproduce the shapes and, where appropriate, recall the associated names. Disabled readers were significantly better than skilled readers at reproducing unnamed complex shapes. Training participants to use a semantic strategy (naming the unnamed figures to improve recall) improved recall by skilled readers more than by disabled readers. Compared to the disabled readers, skilled readers were better able to recall and name the complex shapes in both the relevant and irrelevant naming conditions, but not in the unnamed condition. Note that when verbal memory was not invoked, disabled readers had better visual memory for complex shapes than did skilled readers.

Swanson's (1984) findings suggest that individuals with reading disorders may have absolute strengths in visual memory for novel complex shapes that do not lend themselves to recall using semantic strategies. However, other studies failed to find absolute strength in visual memory in individuals with dyslexia. What is needed is research that disentangles visual memory from working memory in general. Two factors that should be explored in any investigation of visual memory in dyslexia are the roles of stimulus complexity and novelty.

In sum, we found no convincing evidence for enhanced abilities in three major visual–spatial factors on measures tapping spatial orientation, visualization ability, or visual memory.

Flexibility of Closure

Flexibility of closure is defined as "the ability to hold a given visual percept or configuration in mind so as to disembed it from other well defined perceptual material" (Ekstrom et al., 1976, p. 19). In tests of this factor, participants must search a distracting design in order to find a target design. We administered the Hidden Figures Test (Ekstrom et al., 1976), a test of flexibility of closure, to college students with and without dyslexia (Study 1) and to high school students with and without dyslexia (Study 2) (Winner et al., 2001). (In Study 2 we simplified the measure, reducing the number of possible target shapes to three.) The test involves searching a visual array in order to find one of five given target shapes. To succeed, one must be able to hold a target shape in mind in order to disembed it from a more complex array. The task is difficult because one does not know which of the five shapes is the embedded one, so that each option must be tried until one is found embedded in the complex array. In both studies, students with dyslexia performed equivalently to controls on this measure. We can conclude that there is thus no evidence for enhanced flexibility of closure in individuals with dyslexia. But nor are such individuals impaired on this ability, in contrast to their impairment in spatial orientation.

Speed of Closure

Speed of closure is defined as "the ability to unite an apparently disparate perceptual field into a single concept" (Ekstrom et al., 1976, p. 25). This factor differs from flexibility of closure because here one sees no obvious image to begin with and one does not know what to search for. Carroll (1974) defines closure speed as requiring "a search of a long-term memory visual-representation memory store for a match for a partially degraded stimulus cue" (cited in Ekstrom et al., 1976, p. 25). We administered the Gestalt Completion Test (Ekstrom et al., 1976) (a test of closure speed) to high school students with and without dyslexia (Winner et al., 2001). This test assesses the ability to access spatial representations in long-term memory given only partial cues. Participants see an incomplete drawing of a familiar object and are asked to identify the object as quickly as possible (by saying its name). We found that, contrary again to our hypothesis of enhanced ability, individuals with dyslexia performed equivalently to controls both in accuracy and in response time. Thus, we conclude that as yet there is no evidence for enhanced speed of closure associated with dyslexia.

Figural Flexibility

Figural flexibility is defined as "the ability to change set in order to generate new and different solutions to figural problems" (Ekstrom et al., 1976). This ability is thought to be closely related to flexibility of closure (Caroll, 1974). The Storage Task (Ekstrom et al., 1976) was administered by Winner et al. (2001) to assess this capacity in high school students with and without dyslexia. In this task, participants are given a drawing of a three-dimensional cubic space and are asked to show (by drawing) as many different ways as possible in which to arrange rectangular objects in this space. On a timed version of this test, individuals with dyslexia performed nearly significantly worse than controls. On an untimed version, there was no difference between groups. Thus, we conclude that there is no evidence for enhanced figural flexibility associated with dyslexia.

Consistent with the evidence on task performance on major visual–spatial factors, we found no evidence of enhanced visual–spatial abilities on tasks tapping flexibility of closure, speed of closure, or figural flexibility. Not all studies of visual–spatial abilities in individuals with and without dyslexia have used tasks that can be neatly fit into any of the categories described above. We therefore describe these separately.

Artistic Ability

Given the disproportionate incidence of individuals with dyslexia in art school (Winner & Casey, 1993; Winner, Casey, DaSilva, & Hayes, 1991), we expected to find superior artistic ability in those with dyslexia (Winner et al. 2001). We therefore assessed drawing ability in high school students with and without dyslexia. Participants were given a sheet of paper and a sharp pencil and were asked to draw their own hand as accurately as possible. Drawings were classified as showing some talent, as average, or as primitive by two independent judges blind to whether the drawing was by a participant who had dyslexia or by one who did not have dyslexia. Of the six drawings classified by both judges as talented, two were by dyslexics and four were by control participants. Thus, 13% of the dyslexic group and 18% of the control group showed some artistic talent. Of the 15 drawings classified by both judges as primitive, eight were by dyslexics and seven were by control participants. Thus, 53% of the dyslexic drawings, and 32% of the control drawings were classified as primitive. Chi-square tests revealed no differences between groups in terms of level of drawing ability. Thus, despite their over-representation in art schools, our sample of individuals with dyslexia showed no more drawing ability than did those without dyslexia on this task.

Visual–Spatial Abilities Measured on Tests of Intelligence

Some visual–spatial abilities are tapped in most intelligence tests: recognizing, reproducing, or inferring patterns; completing incomplete pictures; mathematical, mechanical, and engineering abilities. Many of the claims about visual–spatial abilities in dyslexia, both positive and negative, are based on performance on such components of intelligence tests.

The Matrices subtest of the Kaufman Brief Intelligence Test (K-BIT) (Kaufman & Kaufman, 1990) entails completing a matrix of patterns. Each matrix is made up of a series of figures that follow on another in a logical pattern. The task is to choose from an array of figures the one that continues the logical pattern established in the matrix. Winner et al. (2001) found that high school students with dyslexia performed significantly worse than those without dyslexia on this task.

Numerous other studies have examined performance by individuals with dyslexia on the Wechsler Intelligence spatial subtests. It is to these we now turn.

Wechsler Intelligence Scales and Subtests

A number of studies have investigated whether individuals with reading problems show either relative or absolute strength on certain spatial subtests of the Wechsler Intelligence Scale for Children. Bannatyne (1971) grouped WISC subtests to create Spatial, Conceptual, and Sequential categories. The Spatial category was composed of Picture Completion, Object Assembly, and Block Design (all timed tests that contribute to the Performance Scale IQ score). Picture Completion assesses the ability to determine what piece is missing from pictures of common objects. Object Assembly assesses the ability to assemble puzzles depicting common objects such as a tree or a dog. Block Design assesses the ability to duplicate drawings of increasingly complex block arrangements with bi-colored cubes. The Conceptual category was made up of three subtests that contribute to the Verbal Scale: Comprehension, Similarities, and Vocabulary. The Sequential category was made up of Coding, Picture Arrangement, and Digit Span. The first two of these subtests contribute to the Performance Scale whereas Digit Span is an optional subtest of the Verbal Scale.

Bannatyne (1971) hypothesized that individuals with dyslexia have a visual–spatial orientation characterized by a preference for three-dimensionality, and are thus likely to choose occupations calling for three-dimensional thinking. He found that individuals with dyslexia scored highest on the Spatial and lowest on the Sequential subtests; their scores on the Conceptual subtests fell between these two. Bannatyne demonstrated that individuals with dyslexia are relatively stronger in spatial than verbal ability (which is hardly surprising given their verbal problems) but tells us nothing about whether individuals with dyslexia actually have superior visual–spatial ability.

Numerous other studies have reported similar findings (relative strength on the Spatial Category subtests by individuals with dyslexia) and have also found that individuals with dyslexia perform at an above average level on these subtests (thus showing absolute strengths) (Naidoo, 1972; Rugel, 1974). Rugel (1974) reported in a review of 25 studies that in 11 of these studies, disabled readers scored significantly higher than control groups on the Spatial subtests. However, a note of caution is in order. In some cases, the mean scaled WISC subtest scores of the disabled readers were not significantly higher than WISC norms. In some of these studies, the participants were learning disabled—not specifically reading disabled. In other studies, the sample included individuals with retarded IQ levels. These circumstances could depress scores in comparison to the norms. Because not all of the WISC subtest results are reported in scaled scores (i.e., rank order, group deviation scores) it is not possible to obtain an exact count of the studies that do find visual–spatial abilities above the norm for disabled readers. In addition, there was at least one case in which disabled readers scored no higher than the control group of average readers on Block Design and Picture Arrangement, yet did score higher than the WISC norms on these subtests. Thus, the visual–spatial strengths Rugel found associated with disabled compared to average readers may not in fact actually demonstrate that visual–spatial strengths are associated with reading disabilities.

In response to the 1974 revision of the WISC (WISC-R), Bannatyne recategorized his Spatial, Conceptual, and Sequential categories. The same relative strength on the spatial subtests was replicated by Smith, Coleman, Dokecki, and Davis (1977) in 43% of 208 students with learning disabilities not limited to reading disabilities.

On the WISC-R, four studies report results that fail to support the finding of absolute strength in individuals with dyslexia on the spatial subtests. Studies by LaFrance (1997), Rourke and Finlayson (1978), Sinatra (1988) and Siegel and Ryan (1989) found only average performance by reading-disabled individuals on the Spatial subtests; and Morris et al. (1988) found that students with reading problems performed worse than a non-disabled control group on Block Design. (Unfortunately it is impossible to determine from the way this study reported its data whether the poorer performance by the reading-disabled students was due to their having below average abilities, or to the control group having above average ability.)

Taken together, these subtest-based approaches allow us only to conclude with certainty that individuals with dyslexia perform better on the Spatial than on the Verbal subtests of the Wechsler Intelligence Scales. There is simply no clear and consistent evidence that individuals with dyslexia perform at an above average level on these spatial subtests compared to normal readers.

Cognitive Laterality Battery

The *Cognitive Laterality Battery* (CLB) was devised to determine whether individuals with dyslexia excel on tasks calling on putatively right-hemisphere abilities—Block Design, a task requiring identification of common objects from incomplete drawings, and a mental rotation task (Gordon, 1983). CLB tasks intended to measure left-hemisphere functions included the WISC Digit Span subtest and measures based on *sequenced* sounds, recall of *serial* presentations of circles, and the fluency of word production. Harness, Epstein, and Gordon (1984) found that 97% of a reading-disabled group of children scored above average on the CLB right-hemisphere tasks and below average on the CLB left-hemisphere tasks. Gordon (1983) described this pattern of performance as indicative of a right shift, or a shift towards a "right hemisphere profile" (p. 34). Harness, Epstein, and Gordon (1984) represented these results on a normal curve (where the control group's mean score, by definition, would be zero), and showed that the reading-disabled groups' mean score was centered at +1.12 standard deviations. Although one could achieve a right shift solely by performing poorly on the CLB left-hemisphere tasks, or solely by performing well on the CLB right-hemisphere tasks, the reading-disabled group's right shift was the result of *both* below average performance on CLB left-hemisphere tasks and above average performance on CLB right-hemisphere tasks. Harness, Epstein, and Gordon, interpret their results as showing that reading-disabled individuals tend to use a right-hemisphere processing approach.

A note of caution is in order, however. The reading-disabled group was disproportionately male (4:1). Since the control group was made up of three school classes, it is likely that the sex ratio was fairly even, or at least more heterogeneous than the reading-disabled sample. Given the male advantage on certain spatial tasks (Linn & Petersen, 1985; Springer & Deutsch, 1997), the superior performance of the reading-disabled group could simply be due to the confound with sex. Thus, like the results from studies using the spatial category subtests of the WISC, the results from Harness, Epstein, and Gordon (1984) do not allow the conclusion that individuals with dyslexia have absolute spatial strengths.

Global Visual–Spatial Abilities

We have saved for last the one piece of evidence that we believe suggests there might indeed be some truth to the claim that individuals with dyslexia have enhanced visual–spatial capacity. In our lab, we have been able to demonstrate superior performance by individuals with dyslexia on a task we employed to assess a global visual–spatial ability (von Károlyi, 2001). On a computer screen, we showed high school students with and without dyslexia line drawings of figures and asked them to indicate which represented possible objects (that could exist in three-dimensional space) and which represented impossible ones (that could not exist in three-dimensional space, such as those in an Escher drawing). (See Figure 1.) Scanning an impossible figure part by part, but failing to integrate the parts, yields the illusion that the figure is possible (Mottron & Belleville, 1993). Only by scanning globally, which we refer to as *holistic inspection,* does one recognize that the parts conflict and that the figure is therefore impossible (Schacter, 1992).

The findings of this study were surprising: individuals with dyslexia proved significantly faster than controls at identifying impossible figures, and their greater speed did not lead to a sacrifice in accuracy. These results were recently replicated on a new sample of high school students (von Károlyi, Winner, Gray, & Sherman, in press), and suggest that the deficit of dyslexia is accompanied by a very specific kind of visual-spatial talent—rapid and accurate holistic inspection.

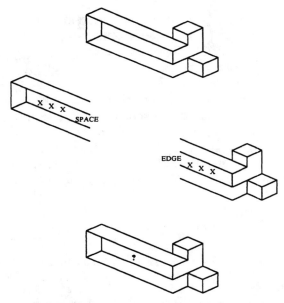

Figure 1. Impossible figures rely on ambiguity. (*Reprinted with permission from the* Journal of Learning Disabilities; *figure source: Schacter, Cooper, and Delaney, 1990*)

Many components make up visual–spatial skill and levels of ability within individuals can vary widely across areas. For example, one can have a wonderful sense of design and a poor sense of color, or excellent attention to detail combined with a poor sense of proportion. Global visual–spatial abilities may be distinct from other kinds of visual–spatial abilities.

Given that individuals with dyslexia typically read slowly and often exhibit slow naming speeds (Wolf & Bowers, 2000), the finding that individuals with dyslexia are faster than controls on any task is surprising. The compelling implication of this finding is that dyslexia should not be characterized only by deficit, but also by talent. Global visual–spatial processing may underlie important real-world activities such as mechanical skill, carpentry, invention, visual artistry, surgery, and interpreting x-rays or Magnetic Resonance Images (MRI). We suggest that none of the other tasks administered to individuals with dyslexia and reviewed above have called for the same kind of holistic perception, or global spatial processing, as did this task.

Linking dyslexia to talent casts this condition in far more optimistic light than linking it to a deficit only. Further research in our lab is now being conducted to investigate whether individuals with dyslexia are faster on other global visual–spatial processing tasks besides identification of impossible figures. Many of the lab-based approaches to assessing visual–spatial abilities fail to translate, for example, to on-the-job performance. For ecological validity, researchers should compare the performance of individuals with and without dyslexia on other "real world" tasks. Brain imaging and visual half-field studies could add much to our understanding of visual–spatial processes in dyslexia. The discovery of talent associated with dyslexia, if upheld, may eventually lead to more effective educational strategies and help guide individuals with dyslexia to professions in which they can excel. But if indeed we eventually can conclude with certainty that visual–spatial talent is associated with dyslexia, this review should have made clear that such talent will not be any across-the-board kind of visual–spatial ability, but rather will be one or more highly specific visual–spatial talents. The challenge for researchers now is to determine whether holistic inspection is one kind of visual–spatial talent that differentiates individuals with dyslexia.

NOTES

1. Research for this paper was supported by a grant from the International Dyslexia Association awarded to Ellen Winner (Principal Investigator) and Catya von Károlyi (Co-Principal Investigator), a Boston College Research Expense Grant awarded to Ellen Winner, and funding provided by Gordon Sherman to replicate the study of global visual–spatial abilities. We thank Gordon Sherman for his support, Maryanne Wolf for her advice in the design or our studies, Daphna Malinsky for her part in conducting some of our studies, and Theresa Deeney and Alan Kaufman for informative dialogues about the WISCs.

REFERENCES

Aaron, P. G., & Guillemarde, J.-C. (1993). Artists as individuals with dyslexia. In Dale M. Willows, Richard S. Kruk, & E. Corcos (Eds.), *Visual processes in reading and reading disabilities* (pp. 393–415). Hillsdale, NJ: Lawrence Erlbaum Associates.

Aaron, P. G., Phillips, S., & Larsen, S. (1988). Specific reading disabilities in historical men of eminence. *Journal of Learning Disabilities, 21*(9), 523–538

Adelman, H. (1988). Reaction to Aaron, Phillips, and Larsen. *Journal of Learning Disabilities, 21*(9), 538, 545.

Bannatyne, A. (1971). *Language, reading and learning disabilities: Psychology, neuropsychology, diagnosis and remediation.* Springfield, IL: Charles C. Thomas.

Beaton, A. A. (1997). The relation of planum temporale asymmetry and morphology of the corpus callosum to handedness, gender, and dyslexia: A review of the evidence. *Brain and Language, 60*, 225–322.

Benton, A. L. (1984). Dyslexia and spatial thinking. *Annals of Dyslexia, 34*, 69–85.

Bloom, B. S. (1985). *Developing talent in young people.* New York: Ballantine.

Boehm, G., Sherman, G., Hoplight, B., Hyde, L., Waters, N., Bradway, D., Galaburda, A., & Denenberg, V. (1996). Learning and memory in the autoimmune BXSB mouse: Effects of neocortical ectopias and environmental enrichment. *Brain Research, 726,* 11–22.

Carroll, F.B. (1993). *Human cognitive abilities.* Cambridge, UK: Cambridge University Press.

Chase, C. (1996). A visual deficit model of developmental dyslexia. In C. Chase, G. Rosen, & G. Sherman (Eds.), *Developmental dyslexia: Neural, cognitive, and genetic mechanisms* . Baltimore, MD: York Press.

Colangelo, N., Assouline, S. G., Kerr, B., Huesman, R., & Johnson, D. (1993). Mechanical inventiveness: A three phase study. In G. Bock & K. Ackrill (Eds.), *The origins and development of high ability* (pp. 160–174). New York: Wiley.

Davis, R. D., & Braun, E. M., (1997). *The gift of dyslexia: Why some of the smartest people can't read and how they can learn.* New York: Perigee Books, Berkley Publishing Group.

Denenberg, V. H., Sherman, G. F., Schrott, L. M., Rosen, G. D., & Galaburda, A M. (1991) Spatial learning, discrimination learning, paw preference and neocortical ectopias in two autoimmune strains of mice. *Brain Research, 562,* 98–104.

Ekstrom, R., French, J., Harman, H., with Dermen, D. (1976). *Kit of factor-referenced cognitive tests.* Princeton, NJ: Educational Testing Service.

Galaburda, A. M., Corsiglia, J., Rosen, G. D., & Sherman, G. F. (1987). Planum temporale asymmetry, reappraisal since Geschwind and Levitsky. *Neuropsychologia, 25,* 853–868.

Galaburda, A., Sherman, G., Rosen, G., Aboitiz, F., & Geschwind, N. (1985). Developmental dyslexia: Four consecutive cases with cortical anomalies. Annals of Neurology, 18, 222–233.

Geschwind, N. (1984). The biology of cerebral dominance: Implications for cognition. *Cognition, 17,* 193–208.

Geschwind, N. (1982). Why Orton was right. Annals of Dyslexia, 32, 13–30.

Geschwind, N., & Galaburda, A. M. (1987). *Cerebral lateralization.* Cambridge, MA: MIT Press.

Gordon, H. W. (1983). The learning disabled are cognitively right. *Topics in Learning & Learning Disabilities* (April), 29–39.

Gross, M. U. M. (1993). *Exceptionally gifted children.* New York: Routledge.

Guilford, J.P., & Zimmerman, W.S. (1953). *Guilford-Zimmerman Aptitude Survey.* Orange, CA: Sheriden Psychological Services.

Hassler, M., (1990). Functional cerebral asymmetric and cognitive abilities in musicians, painters, and controls. *Brain and Cognition, 13,* 1–17.

Harness, B. Z., Epstein, R., & Gordon, H. W. (1984). Cognitive profile of children referred to a clinic for reading disabilities. *Journal of Learning Disabilities, 17*(6), 346–352.

Hermelin, B., & O'Connor, N. (1986). Spatial representations in mathematically and in artistically gifted children. *British Journal of Educational Psychology, 56,* 150–157.

Hooper, S. R., & Willis, W. G. (1989). *Learning disability subtyping: Neuropsychological foundations, conceptual models, and issues in clinical differentiation.* New York: Springer-Verlag.

Humphreys, P., Kaufmann, W., & Galaburda, A. (1990). Developmental dyslexia in women: Neuropathological findings in three patients. Annals of Neurology, 28(6), 727–738.

Johnston, J. R., & Elis Weismer, S. (1983). Mental rotation abilities in language-disordered children. *Journal of Speech and Hearing Research, 26,* 397–403.

Kaufman, A.S. (1979) WISC-R research: Implications for interpretation. *School Psychology Review,8*(1), 5–27.

Kaufman, A., & Kaufman, N. (1990). *Kaufman Brief Intelligence Test.* Circle Pines, MN: American Guidance Service.

Koenig, O., Kosslyn, S. M., & Wolff, P. (1991). Mental imagery and dyslexia: A deficit in processing multipart visual objects? *Brain and Language, 41,* 381–394.

Kosslyn, S. M., Maljkovic, V., Hamilton, S. E., & Thompson, W. L. (1995). Two types of image generation: Evidence for left and right hemisphere processes. *Neuropsychologia, 33*(11), 1485–1510.

Krutetskii, V. A. (1976). *The psychology of mathematical abilities in school children.* New York: Free Press.

LaFrance, E. B. (1997). The gifted/dyslexic child: Characterizing and addressing strengths and weaknesses. *Annals of Dyslexia, 47,* 163–182.

Libeman, I.Y., Mann, V.A., Shankweiler, D. & Werfelman, M. (1982).Children's memory for recurring linguistic and nonlinguistic material in relation to reading ability. *Cortex, 18,* 367–375.

Linn, M. C., & Petersen, A. C. (1985). Emergence and characterization of sex differences in spatial ability: A meta-analysis. *Child Development, 56,* 1479–1498.

Martino, G., & Winner, E. (1995). Talents and disorders: The relationship between sex, handedness, and college major. *Brain and Cognition, 29,* 66–84.

Morris, R. D., Stuebing, K. K., Fletcher, J. M., Shaywitz, S. E., Lyon, G. R., Shankweiler, D. P., Katz, L., Francis, D. J., & Shaywitz, B. A. (1998). Subtypes of reading disability: Coherent variability around a phonological core. *Journal of Educational Psychology, 90,* 1–27.

Mottron, L., & Belleville, S. (1993). A study of perceptual analysis in a high-level autistic subject with exceptional graphic abilities. *Brain and Cognition, 23,* 279–309.

Naidoo, S. (1972). *Specific dyslexia.* New York: Wiley & Sons.

Orton, S. T. (1925). "Word blindness" in school children. *Archives of Neurology and Psychiatry, 14,* 581–613.

Osterrieth, P.A. (1944). Le test de copie d'une figure complexe. *Archives de Psychologie. 30,* 206–356.

Rey, A. (1941). L'examen psychologique dans le cas d'encephalopathie traumatique. *Archives de Psychologie, 28,* 286–340.

Rourke, B. P. & Finlayson, M. A. J. (1978). Neuropsychological significance of variations in patterns of academic performance: Verbal and visual spatial abilities. *Journal of Abnormal Child Psychology, 6*(1), 121–133.

Rudel, R. G., & Denckla, M. B. (1976). Relationship of IQ and reading score to visual, spatial, and temporal matching tasks. *Journal of Learning Disabilities, 9*(3), 42–51.

Rugel, R. (1974). WISC subtest scores of disabled readers. *Journal of Learning Disabilities, 7*(1), 46–65.

Schacter, D. L. (1992). Understanding implicit memory: A cognitive neuroscience approach. *American Psychologist, 47*(4), 559–569.

Schacter, D. L., Cooper, L. A., & Delaney, S. M. (1990). Implicit memory for unfamiliar objects depends on access to structural descriptions. *Journal of Experimental Psychology: General, 119,* 3–19.

Siegel, L. S., & Ryan, E. B. (1989). Subtypes of developmental dyslexia: The influence of definitional variables. *Reading and Writing: An Interdisciplinary Journal, 2,* 257–287.

Silverman, L.K. (2002) Upside-down brilliance: The visual spatial learner. Denver, CO: DeLeon.

Sinatra, R. (1988). Styles of thinking and literacy proficiency for males disabled in print acquisition. *Reading Psychology: An International Quarterly, 9,* 33–50.

Smith, M. D., Coleman, J., Dokecki, P. R., & Davis, E. E. (1977). WISC-R scores of learning disabled children. *Journal of Learning Disabilities, 10*(7), 437–443.

Sowell, T., (1997). *Late-talking children.* New York: Basic Books.

Springer, S. P., & Deutsch, G. (1989). *Left brain, right brain.* (3rd ed.). San Francisco: W. H. Freeman.

Springer, S. P., & Deutsch, G. (1997). *Left brain, right brain: Perspectives from cognitive neuroscience.* (5th ed.). San Francisco: W. H. Freeman.

Swanson, H. L. (1984). Semantic and visual memory codes in learning disabled readers. *Journal of Experimental Child Psychology, 37,* 124–140.

Swanson, H. L., Mink, J., & Bocian, K.M., (1999). Cognitive processing deficits in poor readers with symptoms of reading disabilities and ADHD: More alike than different? *Journal of Educational Psychology, 91*(2), 321–333.

Thurstone, L. L. & Jeffrey, T. (1956), *Flags Test of Spatial Thinking.* Education Industry Service.

Vandenberg, S., & Kuse, A. (1978). Mental rotation: A group test of three dimensional spatial visualization. *Perceptual Motor Skills, 47,* 599–604.

von Károlyi, C. (2001). Visual spatial strength in dyslexia: Rapid discrimination of impossible figures. *Journal of Learning Disabilities. 34*(4), 380–391.

von Károlyi, C., Winner, E. Gray, W. & Sherman, G. (in press). Dyslexia linked to talent: Global visual spatial ability. *Brain and Language.*

Waters, N., Sherman, G.F., Galaburda, A.M., & Denenberg, V.H. (1997). Effects of cortical ectopias on spatial delayed matching-to-sample performance in BXSB mice. *Behavioral Brain Research, 84*, 23–29.

Wechsler, D. (1949). *Wechsler Intelligence Scale for Children (Manual)*. New York: The Psychological Corporation.

Wechsler, D. (1974). *Wechsler Intelligence Scale for Children--Revised*. New York: The Psychological Corporation.

Wechsler, D. (1991). *Wechsler Intelligence Scale for Children: Third edition manual*. San Antonio, TX: The Psychological Corporation.

West, T. G. (1991). *In the mind's eye: Visual thinkers, gifted people with learning difficulties, computer images, and the ironies of creativity*. Buffalo, NY: Prometheus.

Winner, E. (1996). *Gifted children: Myths and realities*. New York: Basic Books.

Winner, E. & Casey, M.B. (1993) Cognitive profiles of artists. In G. Cupchik & J. Lazlo (Eds.), *Emerging visions: Contemporary approaches to the aesthetic process* (pp. 154–170). New York: Cambridge University Press.

Winner, E., Casey, M., DaSilva, D., & Hayes, R. (1991). Spatial abilities and reading deficits in visual art students. *Empirical Studies of the Arts, 9*(1), 51–63.

Winner, E., & von Károlyi, C. (1998) Artistry and aphasia. In M. T. Sarno (Ed.), *Acquired aphasia*. (3rd. Edition). New York: Academic Press.

Winner, E., von Károlyi, C., Malinsky, D., French, L., Seliger, C., Ross, E., & Weber, C. (2001). Dyslexia and visual-spatial talents: Compensation vs. deficit model. *Brain and Language, 76*, 81–110.

Wolf, M. & Bowers, P. (2000). The question of naming-speed deficits in developmental reading disability: An introduction to the Double-Deficit Hypothesis. *Journal of Learning Disabilities, 33*, 322–324.

Chapter 6

TO READ BUT NOT TO READ: IDENTIFYING AND UNDERSTANDING THE NATURE OF POOR READING COMPREHENSION IN CHILDREN

Kate Nation
Oxford University

INTRODUCTION

Very broadly, it is possible to think of two sets of skills a child needs to master in order to become a skilled reader of an alphabetic language. First and foremost, they need to learn to <u>decode</u>. Learning that letters map to speech sounds in a systematic way provides children with a rudimentary reading system that allows them to read words, even novel words they have never seen before. With practice and exposure to print, children's decoding skills soon become fast, flexible, and efficient. However, the ultimate goal of reading is to understand what has been written, and although good decoding skills are an essential component of skilled reading, they are no guarantee that successful comprehension will follow. Thus, the other set of skills children need if they are to read successfully are concerned with <u>comprehension</u>. As encapsulated in Gough and Tumner's (1986) simple model, skilled reading requires adequate decoding and comprehension: Neither skill alone is sufficient. Generally, there is a strong association between decoding and comprehension: Children who are good at decoding tend to be good at comprehending and similarly, children with weak decoding skills tend to have difficulty comprehending. For some children however, their proficiency at reading words and texts stands in stark contrast to the difficulty they have with understanding what they have read. Of course, there are many children who have difficulty with reading comprehension <u>and</u> decoding (sometimes referred to as garden-variety poor readers), but it is children who have poor comprehension <u>despite</u> normal decoding who are the focus of this chapter.

IDENTIFYING CHILDREN WITH POOR READING COMPREHENSION

Researchers interested in investigating children with specific reading comprehension difficulties tend to recruit children into experiments following fairly intensive screening. Typically, a large number of children are given a battery of tests. We then select out children who perform poorly on some tests (tapping reading comprehension) but do well on other tests (tapping decoding and the ability to read words). These "multivariate outliers" are then classed as poor comprehenders (e.g. Stothard & Hulme, 1992; Oakhill, 1994). Before giving a little more detail, it is worth noting why we use this time-consuming approach. Is it not easier to ask teachers to refer children who have poor reading comprehension to us, or for us to go to special classrooms for children with poor reading comprehension? The answer to this question is a very simple no. In our experience, most poor comprehenders are not recognized as having a reading difficulty; for those few children who are causing teachers some concern, problems with behavior, peer relations or other areas of learning such as mathematics are occasionally noted, but problems with reading or language are not. One exception concerns children with autism and related disorders. There is a relatively small proportion of autistic children who show good reading accuracy but poor reading comprehension and for these children, difficulties with reading comprehension do tend to be noticed. But for most poor comprehenders, reading impairments tend to go unnoticed, at least during the primary years (ages 7–11).

Our approach to selecting poor comprehenders builds on one developed by Oakhill and colleagues (Oakhill, 1982; Yuill & Oakhill, 1991 for review). The Neale Analysis of Reading Ability (NARA-II; Neale, 1997) provides a measure of reading comprehension that is relatively independent from reading accuracy. A sample passage is shown in Table 1. Children read aloud the passage and any mistakes they make are corrected by the tester. It is possible to convert the number of words they read correctly to a reading accuracy standard score. Children are then asked questions about the passage. Some of these can be answered by direct reference to information in the passage whereas others require children to make inferences based on real-world knowledge. The number of questions answered correctly is then used to derive an age-referenced reading comprehension standard score. Children whose reading comprehension scores fall substantially below their (normal range) score on tests tapping decoding skills can be classified as having specific reading comprehension difficulties. Using this basic methodology, approximately 10% of children are identified as poor comprehenders when unselected samples of 7- to 11-year-olds are screened (Nation & Snowling, 1997; Stothard & Hulme, 1992; Oakhill, 1994).

This is a time-consuming and labor-intensive method for recruiting participants to take part in experiments (with approximately 250 children needing to be screened to produce an experimental group of approximately 20 children). But methodologically, the advantage of this approach is clear: We can be certain that children recruited in this way have at least average reading accuracy skills. Thus, for these children, limitations in decoding or basic word recognition processes cannot be responsible for their poor comprehension (cf. Perfetti, 1985). The very existence of poor comprehenders makes clear that skills beyond those required for word recognition are needed, if adequate comprehension is to follow.

Table 1. Sample passage and questions from the Neale Analysis of Reading Ability-Revised (NARA-II; Neale, 1997). *Children read aloud the passage (accompanied by a picture) and are then asked questions (which are asked and answered orally).*

Kim stopped on her way to school. In the middle of the traffic lay two children. Their bicycles had crashed into each other. Kim ran quickly to help. She saw that no one was hurt. The children pointed to a television camera. "We are taking part in a road safety lesion," they said.	1. Where was Kim going? 2. Why did Kim stop? 3. What had happened to the bikes? 4. How do you think Kim felt? 5. What did Kim do? 6. Were the children hurt? 7. What were the children really doing? 8. How did Kim find out what was happening?

Good progress has been made toward understanding strengths and weaknesses of children classified as poor comprehenders. Oakhill, Cain, and colleagues have identified a variety of text-level processes that poor comprehenders find difficult. For example, they are poor at making inferences and at integrating information in text. They are also poor at monitoring their own comprehension, and tend not to be sensitive to story structure (for example, see Cain & Oakhill, 1996, 1999; Cain, Oakhill, Bryant, & Barnes, 2002; Yuill & Oakhill, 1991). Given that children are selected as poor comprehenders on the basis of having poor reading comprehension, it is perhaps not surprising that they show such text-level weaknesses when experimental measures are used. Nevertheless, this work is making important progress in delineating which aspects of the reading comprehension process poor comprehenders find difficult.

A different approach has been taken by Nation, Snowling, and colleagues. We have focused on poor comprehenders' oral language skills. Although their phonological skills, that is, their sensitivity to the structure of spoken language, are normal, we have identified relative weaknesses in "broader" aspects of language. Most generally, poor comprehenders have depressed verbal IQ, relative to both a control group and their own nonverbal abilities (Nation et al., 2002). They tend to have less well-developed vocabulary knowledge and weaknesses in semantic processing. For example, they are slower and less accurate at deciding whether two words are synonymous, they produce fewer exemplars in semantic fluency tasks and they may organize semantic information differently, as evidenced by differential effects in semantic priming tasks (Nation & Snowling, 1998, 1999). There is also some evidence pointing to relative weaknesses with syntactic awareness and syntactic comprehension (Nation & Snowling, 2000; Stothard & Hulme, 1992), and with aspects of verbal memory (Nation, Adams, Bowyer-Crane & Snowling, 1999).

From the studies reviewed above, it is not clear whether poor comprehenders have impaired language skills, or whether language is just relatively low, relative to control children matched for age, nonverbal ability, and reading accuracy. To address this issue, we assessed 23 poor comprehenders (aged between 8 and 9 years) using tests tapping four general domains of language, namely phonology, semantics, morphosyntax and language use (Nation, Clarke, Marshall & Durand, under review). Consistent with previous work, the poor comprehenders had normal phonological skills. However, in addition to scoring significantly below the controls on all other aspects of language, 20 of 23 poor comprehenders showed language skills at least 1.25 standard deviations below population norms on at least one measure, and 11 of 23 showed deficits in excess of –1.25 standard deviations on at least two language measures. These data illustrate that most poor comprehenders have some element of spoken language weakness, and that for some children, language impairments are severe.

So how might poor comprehenders' spoken language skills relate to their reading development? We have suggested that while their normal phonological skills provide a firm foundation for the development of reading accuracy, weaknesses in those aspects of spoken language concerned with meaning may constrain how well children can understand what they have read. An important direction for future research is to chart how these weaknesses in spoken language relate to reading comprehension difficulties.

INDIVIDUAL DIFFERENCES IN POOR COMPREHENSION

A major drawback to the approach we use for screening and selecting poor comprehenders is that comprehension as measured by the NARA test of reading comprehension taps a variety of skills, including the activation of word meanings and relevant background knowledge, generation of inferences, and monitoring of both ongoing comprehension and the internal consistency of text (Hannon & Daneman, 2001; Palinscar & Brown, 1984). It follows from this that children may fail to understand what they have read for a variety of different reasons. Thus, any population of poor comprehenders selected via the screening method outlined above is likely to be heterogeneous. Likewise, children with a variety of developmental difficulties may show reading comprehension deficits. Although we find that poor comprehenders as a group are characterized by language weaknesses, it is certainly not the case that all poor comprehenders have significant language impairments. Similarly, although reading comprehension tends to be low in groups of children with spoken language impairments, not all children with poor spoken language skills have poor reading comprehension (Bishop & Admas, 1990; Catts, Fey, Tomblin & Zhang., 2002). To illustrate the heterogeneity of poor comprehenders, four children will be described who all show substantial gaps between their at least average-for-age decoding and their impaired reading comprehension. All of them would be "flagged" as poor comprehenders according to their pattern of reading performance. Yet, in other areas of development, the children are quite different and arguably, the reasons why they find reading comprehension difficult may also be different.

Poor Comprehenders with Relatively Weak Language Skills

David is fairly typical of the poor comprehenders we recruit into our experimental studies (e.g. Nation & Snowling, 1998, 1999, 2000). At age 9, his ability to read aloud single words presented one-at-a-time out of context was average: He obtained a standard score of 100 on the British Ability Scales (BAS-II; Elliot, Smith & McCulloch, 1996) reading test. However, his reading comprehension was poor: He achieved a standard score of only 70 on the NARA-II.[1] His comprehension difficulties were still apparent two years later: On this occasion his word reading score was 103 and his comprehension score was 80. Like many of the poor comprehenders described by Nation et al. (2002), David's word recognition was in line with his overall IQ but his reading comprehension was significantly lower than expected. He also demonstrated a cognitive profile that is fairly typical for poor comprehenders (Nation et al., 2002): his visuo-spatial ability and nonverbal ability were average (100 and 101) but his verbal ability was below average (80). He also showed weakness on a range of tests tapping vocabulary knowledge and aspects of spoken language comprehension. For children like David, it is tempting to suggest that weaknesses in verbal ability constrain reading comprehension. Put simply, if a child has problems understanding spoken language, then difficulty understanding written language is not surprising.

Poor Comprehenders with Weak Cognitive Ability

Edward presented with a similar reading profile to David. At age 8.5, his single-word reading score was 103 but his reading comprehension score was

84. Like David, his poor comprehension persisted and he achieved almost identical standard scores two years later. He also had poor verbal ability, achieving a standard score of 71 on the BAS-II verbal ability scale. Unlike David however, Edward had general cognitive weaknesses that extended to the nonverbal (62) and visuo-spatial domains (80). In Edward's case, the gap between decoding and comprehension was not caused by surprisingly low reading comprehension: His poor reading comprehension was perfectly in line with IQ expectations. However, his reading accuracy was significantly <u>higher</u> than one would expect, given his IQ. Given that Edward has extremely well-developed word recognition skills, relative to both his comprehension and general cognitive ability, his reading is characteristic of what one sees in children labeled as hyperlexic, a term used to describe exceptional word recognition skills in children who have otherwise limited cognitive abilities and behavioral abnormalities (for review, Nation, 1999).

Poor Comprehenders with Nonverbal Learning Difficulties

Although sharing a similar reading profile to both David and Edward, the source of Beth's difficulties appear to be very different. At age nearly 10, Beth showed the classic poor comprehender dissociation, achieving standard scores of 78 on a test of reading comprehension and 106 on a test of word recognition. Her vocabulary knowledge and other linguistic skills, including phonological skills, were average, and her verbal IQ was 97. However, her nonverbal abilities were less strong. On the British Abilities Scale, she achieved a standard score of 86 on the nonverbal measures, and 77 on the visuo-spatial measures. Thus, her cognitive profile is consistent with that typically seen in children described as having a nonverbal learning difficulty (NLD; Rourke, 1989). Although there have been no detailed studies of reading in children with NLD, the dissociation between normal word-level reading skills and impaired reading comprehension has been highlighted in clinical neuropsychological diagnostic schedules (e.g. Pelletier, Ahmad & Rourke, 2001; Rourke, 1989). Furthermore, researchers interested in hyperlexia have described a sub-group of hyperlexic children who have nonverbal learning difficulties (Richman & Wood, 2002).

It is interesting to note that we originally saw Beth when she was 7 years old. At that time, she appeared to have normal reading skills with standard scores of 105 and 103 on tests of word reading and comprehension respectively. Indeed, she was a member of our control group of normal readers until further testing revealed that she did not meet our criterion of normal-range nonverbal ability. Why did her reading comprehension decline over time? One possibility is that her apparent decline is an artifact of test measurement error. This possibility seems unlikely: Not only do the tests have good psychometric properties, but her pattern of reading behavior was consistent across a number of different tests administered at each time point. We suspect that declines in reading comprehension over time may be part of the developmental course of NLD. To have "normal" reading comprehension at age 7 is not necessarily the same as having "normal" reading comprehension at age 10. In the early years, "normal" reading comprehension may be achieved by capitalizing on adequate linguistic knowledge (for example, vocabulary, sensitivity to grammatical word order). Children with NLD are not considered to have impairments with these aspects of language processing (e.g. Pelletier et al., 2001). Arguably, however, as children get older, they are expected to be adept at the more complex aspects of comprehension such as inference making based on real-world knowledge and experience. Given the difficulties that children with NLD have with aspects of discourse, conversation, and social perception (Worling, Humphries & Tannock, 1999), difficulty with "higher level" aspects of reading comprehension are not surprising. Similar pragmatic impairments have been reported in other groups of children who also have poor reading comprehension, such as high-functioning children with autism (Dennis, Lazenby & Lockyer, 2001) and children with early-onset hydrocephalus (Dennis & Barnes, 1993).

These ideas are speculative but could be tested empirically by assessing the reading comprehension skills of children with NLD longitudinally. In line with Beth's reading profile, we predict drop-offs in reading comprehension, relative to normally developing children, as the demands placed on reading comprehension increase as children get older. Additionally, it would be interesting to see whether NLD children's comprehension varies according to particular text properties. For example, they may have a reasonable understanding of those aspects of the text that are fairly literal. On this view, comprehension only breaks down when understanding relies on the ability to make inferences.

Although David, Edward, and Beth all have similar profiles of reading behavior, and in particular, all have substantial reading comprehension deficits despite having normal reading accuracy, the origins of their comprehension impairments may well be different. One feature that does unite these children is that none of them were recognized by their teachers as having a reading difficulty. David was thought to be a little fidgety, and Edward was considered to be unimaginative. Some concerns had been raised about Beth's clumsiness, and her slightly insensitive social behavior. But, in no case were these concerns serious enough to warrant referral to external specialist services, and in no case were difficulties with reading and language suspected. This was not the case for the next child, whose difficulties were well recognized.

Poor Comprehenders with Autism Spectrum Disorder

We saw Duncan when he was almost 15 years old. His developmental difficulties were well documented and he had been diagnosed with atypical autism during early childhood. His verbal and nonverbal skills were considered average, and his reading accuracy skills were well developed: He achieved standard scores of 115 on the two tests of reading accuracy we administered. However, his reading comprehension was very poor. On the NARA test described above, his reading comprehension standard score was 70, barely at the level expected for a 6–year-old child. Unlike the children described above, our findings were entirely consistent with teacher and parent reports: Duncan's good reading accuracy had not been assumed to be an index of good reading comprehension.

There is a strong association between autism and hyperlexia. Many children who have a hyperlexic reading profile are autistic, or show features of autism (Grigorenko, Klin, Pauls, Senft, Hooper & Volkmar, 2002). It is not clear why this may be the case. Nation (1999) speculated that a number of factors may be important: a particular pattern of cognitive and linguistic strengths and weaknesses, a tendency to be interested in local features rather than global coherence, and a preoccupation with text and reading. As these features tend to cluster together in people with autism, patterns of hyperlexic reading are therefore more common in this group. An interesting question is whether these features also tend to characterize non-autistic children who have poor reading comprehension but good reading accuracy.

Although there is a large body of literature on hyperlexia, it is limited mainly to descriptions of the condition rather than attempts to understand the nature of reading behavior in those children considered to be hyperlexic. This is an important direction for future work. Similarly, it is important to keep in mind that although hyperlexia is more common in autistic children than non-autistic children, most children with autism do not show hyperlexic reading. Very little is known about the characteristics of reading in non-hyperlexic autistic children.

CONCLUSIONS AND FUTURE DIRECTIONS

Identifying children who read well but fail to understand what they have read raises many theoretical questions, and of course, practical concerns. First and foremost, poor comprehenders exist. Our screening methods suggest that approximately 10% of the population of 7- to 11-year-old children have specific reading comprehension weaknesses. These children demonstrate very clearly that the possession of fluent and accurate reading accuracy is no guarantee that successful comprehension will follow. In our experience, many of these children are not identified as having a reading comprehension difficulty. Why might this be? Arguably, the most obvious index of a child's reading ability is how accurate they are at reading words and texts. Children with these obvious difficulties are likely to be very noticeable in the classroom. In contrast, poor comprehenders read accurately and fluently. Their difficulties are seldom recognized in the classroom and it is only when tested that their underlying difficulties with reading comprehension are revealed.[2]   Thus, one practical application of our work is to suggest that classroom assessments of children's reading make every effort to assess comprehension of extended text, not just word recognition or sentence comprehension (Nation & Snowling, 1997).

A related point concerns the developmental course of poor reading comprehension. With the exception of some of the studies investigating extreme cases of hyperlexia in clinically referred children, most studies of poor comprehenders have been concerned with children aged 7–11. An interesting and important question concerns what happens to these children as they get older. We speculate that their difficulties are not transient. Both David and Edward showed consistent patterns of poor reading comprehension over time. Preliminary data from our longitudinal sample suggest that David and Edward are not atypical: 78% of poor comprehenders originally tested at age 8–9 still had significant comprehension impairments when tested later at age 13–14; a further 13% continued to have milder weaknesses with reading comprehension. These numbers are concerning given that as children get older, so much of the curriculum comes to depend heavily on reading comprehension. Although it is an empirical question, it seems likely that poor comprehenders will face educational difficulties across the whole curriculum as they get older.

It is clear that reading comprehension is a complex process and a corollary of this complexity is that children may fail to comprehend for a number of different reasons. The four children considered in this chapter all showed reading comprehension skills that lagged well behind their ability to decode and recognize print. However, it is clear that the four children are very different, and potentially, the reasons why they fail to comprehend may be different. Many poor comprehenders have spoken language limitations and for some, the level of language impairment is fairly severe. For other children however, difficulties may be a consequence of more general factors such as poor attention, while for others, poor reading comprehension may be related the presence of a nonverbal learning difficulty. For some children, reading profiles need to be considered alongside their more pervasive developmental difficulties. Another possibility is that some poor comprehenders may potentially suffer from lack of environmental input. An important job of future research is to begin to tease apart these different routes to poor comprehension. Such research will help to identify early risk factors associated with poor reading comprehension and in turn, should point the way to methods of effective intervention for children with poor reading comprehension.

NOTES

1. The British Ability Scales is very similar to its American equivalent, the Differential Ability Scales. All standard scores reported in this chapter have a mean of 100 and a standard deviation of 15.
2. For a similar discussion concerning the status of poor comprehenders' spoken language skills, see Nation et al. (under review).

REFERENCES

Bishop, D.V.M., & Adams, C. (1990). A prospective study of the relationship between specific language impairment, phonological disorders and reading retardation. *Journal of Child Psychology and Psychiatry, 31*, 1027–1050.

Cain, K., & Oakhill, J. (1996). The nature of the relation between comprehension skill and the ability to tell a story. *British Journal of Developmental Psychology, 14*, 187–201.

Cain, K., & Oakhill, J.V. (1999). Inference making and its relation to comprehension failure. *Reading and Writing, 11*, 489–503.

Cain K., Oakhill J.V., Barnes M.A., Bryant P.E. (2001). Comprehension skill, inference-making ability, and their relation to knowledge. *Memory & Cognition, 29*, 850–859.

Catts, H.W., Fey, M.E., Tomblin, J.B., & Zhang, X. (2002). A longitudinal investigation of reading outcomes in children with language impairments. *Journal of Speech, Language and Hearing Research, 45*, 1142–1157.

Dennis, M. & Barnes, M.A. (1993). Oral discourse after early-onset hydrocephalus: linguistic ambiguity, figurative language, speech acts, and script-based inferences. *Journal of Pediatric Psychology, 18*, 639–652.

Dennis, M., Lazenby, A.L., & Lockyer, L. (2001). Inferential language in high-function children with autism. *Journal of Autism and Developmental Disorders, 31*, 47–54.

Elliot, C. D., Smith, P., & McCulloch, K. (1996). *British Ability Scales*. Second Edition. Windsor, UK: NFER-Nelson.

Gough, P. B., & Tunmer, W. E. (1986). Decoding, reading, and reading disability. *Remedial and Special Education, 7*, 6–10.

Grigorenko, E.L., Klin, A., Pauls, D.L., Senft, R., Hooper, C. & Volkmar, F. (2002). A descriptive study of hyperlexia in a clinically referred sample of children with developmental delays. *Journal of Autism and Developmental Disorders, 32*, 3–12.

Hanon, B., & Daneman, M. (2001). A new tool for measuring and understanding individual differences in the component processes of reading comprehension. *Journal of Educational Psychology, 93*, 103–128.

Nation, K. (1999). Reading skills in hyperlexia: a developmental perspective. *Psychological Bulletin, 125*, 338–355.

Nation, K., Adams, J. W., Bowyer-Crane, C. A., & Snowling, M. J. (1999). Working memory deficits in poor comprehenders reflect underlying language impairments. *Journal of Experimental Child Psychology, 73*, 139–158.

Nation, K., Clarke, P., Marshall, C., & Durand, M. (under review). Hidden language impairments in children: parallels between poor reading comprehension and specific language impairment?

Nation, K., Clarke, P., & Snowling, M. J. (2002). General cognitive ability in children with poor reading comprehension. *British Journal of Educational Psychology, 72*, 549–560.

Nation, K., & Snowling, M. J. (1997). Assessing reading difficulties: the validity and utility of current measures of reading skill. *British Journal of Educational Psychology, 67*, 359–370.

Nation, K. & Snowling, M. J. (1998). Semantic processing skills and the development of word recognition: evidence from children with reading comprehension difficulties. *Journal of Memory and Language, 39*, 85–101.

Nation, K. & Snowling, M. J. (1999). Developmental differences in sensitivity to semantic relations among good and poor comprehenders: evidence from semantic priming. *Cognition, 70*, B1–13.

Nation, K. & Snowling, M. J. (2000). Factors influencing syntactic awareness in normal readers and poor comprehenders. *Applied Psycholinguistics, 21*, 229–241.

Neale, M. D. (1997). Neale Analysis of Reading Ability-Revised (NARA-II). Windsor, UK: NFER.

Oakhill, J.V. (1982). Constructive processes in skilled and less-skilled comprehenders' memory for sentences. *British Journal of Psychology, 73*, 13–20.

Oakhill, J.V. (1994). Individual differences in children's text comprehension. In M.A. Gernsbacher (Ed.), *Handbook of Psycholinguistics*. San Diego, CA: Academic Press.

Palincsar, A.S. and Brown, A. L. (1984) Reciprocal teaching of comprehension-fostering and comprehension-monitoring activities. *Cognition and Instruction, 1*, 117–175.

Pelletier, P. M., Ahmad, S. A., & Rourke, B. P. (2001). Classification rules for basic phonological processing disabilities and nonverbal learning difficulties: formulation and external validity. *Child Neuropsychology, 7*, 84–98.

Perfetti, C.A. (1985). *Reading ability*. New York: Oxford University Press.

Richman, L.C., & Wood, K. M. (2002). Learning disability subtypes: classification of high functioning hyperlexia. *Brain and Language, 82*, 10–21.

Rourke, B.P. (1989). Nonverbal learning difficulties: the syndrome and the model. New York: Guildford Press.

Stothard, S.E., & Hulme, C. (1992). Reading comprehension difficulties in children: the role of language comprehension and working memory skills. *Reading and Writing, 4*, 245–256.

Worling, D. E., Humphries, T., Tannock, R. (2001). Spatial and emotional aspects of language inferencing in nonverbal learning difficulties. *Brain and Language, 70*, 220–239.

Yuill, N., & Oakhill, J. V. (1991). *Children's problems in text comprehension*. Cambridge, UK: Cambridge University Press.

Chapter 7

GIFTED ADULTS WITH LEARNING DISABILITIES IN POSTSECONDARY SETTINGS

Mary K. Tallent-Runnels
Carol A. Layton
Texas Tech University

INTRODUCTION

There is much research reported on children with learning disabilities and less reported on children who are gifted and have learning disabilities (Brody & Mills, 1997). However, there are even fewer published studies about adults with learning disabilities in postsecondary programs (Kovach & Wilgosh, 1999) and even less about gifted adults with learning disabilities. This chapter highlights these gifted adults with learning disabilities and describes and analyzes their postsecondary experiences particularly as they relate to their learning and study strategies. These strategies were chosen as a focus because they are necessary for success in college, and because we believe an examination of how these twice-exceptional people survived or did not survive in college will serve to inform others how to succeed beyond their high school careers. This understanding can help improve effectiveness in all learners (Vaidya, 1993).

This population was also chosen because students in postsecondary situations face more obstacles than they did from Kindergarten through 12th grades (Stodden, Whelley, Chang, & Harding, 2001). For example, there is less teacher/student contact, more academic competition, different student support networks, and a greater expectation that students will be more autonomous learners.

We will briefly describe related research about general characteristics of learning and study strategies of gifted people with learning disabilities and relevant research about characteristics of postsecondary gifted learners with learning disabilities. Gifted people with learning disabilities, as defined here, will be those who demonstrate exceptional ability or talent in one or more areas but who also display a discrepancy between expected and actual achievement resulting from a processing deficit (Dole, 2001).

Next, we will describe interviews with three gifted adults with learning disabilities. One of these is an assistant professor, another is a presidential appointee who recently received his bachelor's degree, and the third is a junior in college. Following the interviews and their analysis, we will offer advice on how to better prepare and serve these young adults.

SELECTED CHARACTERISTICS OF GIFTED LEARNERS WITH LEARNING DISABILLTIES

Since most of the research on gifted learners with learning disabilities has been on children in K–12 schools, we will share that first. One characteristic of note about this population of gifted learners with learning disabilities is that they constitute a heterogeneous group and may be very different from each other (Brody & Mills, 1997). However, in general they have extensive vocabularies (McEachern & Bornot, 2001); have higher-order thinking skills of a high quality (Vaidya, 1993), superior reasoning and problem solving skills (Cohen & Vaughn, 1994), and good abstract thinking and communication skills (Cohen, & Vaughn, 1994). They are also adept at using verbal skills to conceptualize (Cohen & Vaughn, 1994), and they dislike drill and repetition (Robinson, 1999).

Some of the research about postsecondary gifted learners with learning disabilities reveals characteristics similar to those of the K–12 students we described. However, one study noted that postsecondary gifted learners with learning disabilities reported higher motivation and time management skills on Weinstein's Learning and Study Strategies Inventory (Kovach & Wilgosh, 1999) than other non-gifted postsecondary learners with learning disabilities. These results confirmed those of another study of ninth graders comparing gifted learners with typical students. In that study, motivation was the primary characteristic that separated these two groups (Tallent-Runnels, Olivárez, Jr., Candler-Lotven, Walsh, Gray, & Irons, 1994), with the gifted learners reporting higher motivation than the typical learners.

Like younger students in this population, postsecondary gifted learners with learning disabilities also had extensive vocabularies, large backgrounds of general knowledge, and were creative and divergent thinkers (Ferri, Gregg, & Heggoy, 1997). In general, they were also abstract thinkers (Silverman, 1989).

Both of these groups, younger and older learners, may have problems with reading, written expression, spelling, rote memorization, and organizational skills (Cohen & Vaughn, 1994; Silverman, 1989). They may fail to complete assignments and become frustrated with classroom demands (Robinson, 1999). Therefore, they can also be disruptive in class (Ferri,

Gregg, & Heggoy, 1997), and their experiences with failure and frustration can lead to poor self-efficacy (Dole, 2001).

One of the disturbing findings about gifted learners with learning disabilities is that they are not usually identified as both gifted and having a learning disability. If one label is placed on them, usually they do not receive services for the other (Tallent-Runnels & Sigler, 1995). In addition, in a study of 95 college students demonstrating learning disabilities with and without giftedness, the learning disabilities of those who were gifted were not always identified early (Ferri, Gregg, & Heggoy, 1997). Half of the men who were gifted were identified as having learning disabilities in elementary school, but only 30% of the gifted women were identified as having a learning disability that early. Also, 34% of those who were gifted were not identified with learning disabilities until they were in college.

With so few studies about postsecondary gifted learners with learning disabilities, we needed more to convey what they are really like by the time they had lived with this dual exceptionality for so many years and survived long enough to get to college and beyond. There were other questions we needed to answer. How did they grow and change? Did their disability go away when they became older? What were the keys to their survival up to, during, and after college? What are those who succeed like, and what can we learn from them?

We thought the best way to answer those questions was to take a look at some of their lives. We wanted to offer a glimpse into their struggle through the maze of education. To do this we thought that interviews were a clear choice for further investigation and a vehicle for learning from the untold story of several individuals who are gifted as well as learning disabled.

Through the scant amount of research conducted with persons who are learning disabled and gifted, several themes did emerge. Some of these themes included: motivation, higher-order thinking skills and abstract thinking, late identification of learning disabilities, verbal skills, time management, and rote memorization. Much of this review focused on the selection of study methods and the way that individuals who are gifted and learning disabled mediate their cognitive abilities/patterns to adapt to learning settings and specific challenges in pursuit of academic success.

INTERVIEWS

These postsecondary students and graduates were asked to talk about their study skills selections, emergence as gifted learners, and the adaptation of coping mechanisms that their learning disabilities required. These interviewees possessed unique gifts and unparalleled learning disabilities. All had a personal story to relate, encapsulating their own journey as learners.

These stories allowed us a glimpse into the intricacies of learning with a gifted intellect and a significant learning disability.

Claudia

Claudia, our former student, began her story with a description of herself. Thoughtfully, she answered by stating that she is a professor, a mother, a wife, an ex-military member, and a person with learning disabilities. Claudia went on to explain that, for her, none of these facets took precedence over another, and all were equally responsible for the person she is today. Claudia's vita was strong, indicating good use of her giftedness and perhaps the unusual gift of being able to circumvent her disabilities. She had won student awards for her undergraduate work, master's work and doctoral student work. Five years out of her program, she is in her second year as an assistant professor of educational psychology with six articles published in scholarly journals, two funded grants, and four national presentations. Her career was postponed until her husband separated from his full-time military career.

School Experience

School was never a pleasant experience for Claudia, although one might not see that as the case, since she spent so much time as a student. From her earliest memories, she was self-conscious about her ability to perform academically. She always felt unable to reach her "intellectual potential" in the classroom. Claudia knew she was "smart," but on the classic assessments of academic performance she consistently fell short. In her undergraduate program she received a 2.8 GPA. She phrased her frustration with this GPA and called it "a far cry from what I felt I learned during my four years."

Claudia remembered several teachers as exemplary because they acknowledged her strengths and provided her with opportunities to demonstrate her ability through alternatives other than traditional paper-and-pencil tests. She felt these experiences were rewarding and meaningful. Claudia noted that one thing that stands out in her mind was the fact that even the other students picked up on her life long paradox. She clearly remembered one classmate in ninth grade asking her, "Why are you so smart in class and so stupid on the tests?" Claudia felt that this comment described her academic experiences rather well.

It was not until her graduate school career that she began to feel academically competent. Claudia thinks it was a combination of participating in a program comprised of graduate "educators" and the fact that reliance on classic tests was greatly reduced. However, she resigned herself to the fact that she needed to do "other things" in order to pass her classes. These "other things" consisted of behavior that she engaged in such as extra note taking, and different and more extreme study habits.

Discovering Her Giftedness

Thinking back, Claudia always believed that she was able to "out think" others. However, she was unable to demonstrate this ability. Her parents said that when she was three she built a working gum machine out of tinker toys and Lego blocks. Her parents seemed to sense her gifted abilities. They were bewildered at the paradox of her gifted behavior and her difficulty with schoolwork. Claudia was placed in a gifted program in elementary school, which operated much like an independent study class. Claudia felt that the school personnel did not know exactly how to approach her gifts and learning difficulties.

Describing Her Giftedness

Claudia chose to describe her giftedness in terms of Howard Gardner's Theory of Multiple Intelligences. She reported her gifted areas as Interpersonal and Intra-personal intelligence. She possessed good knowledge about her giftedness and understood others well. This knowledge allowed Claudia not only to pursue a successful career but also gave her the ability to "read" her students, understand them, and actively help them learn.

Discovering Her Learning Disability

From the time she was very young, Claudia knew that she had a learning disability. Feelings of inadequacy pervaded every memory of her schooling. She cannot recall not feeling "disabled." She was not officially diagnosed with learning disabilities until she was in the 10th grade, after she obtained low scores on the SAT. School personnel suggested that she was not "college-bound material." The school suggested to Claudia's parents that she take up a trade, because she would never make it through college.

Describing Her Learning Disability

Claudia described her learning disability well. More specifically, she reported having multiple "symptoms" that all revolve around mathematics, writing, and reading. She once was referred to as dyslexic. That is, she said that she exhibited all the classic letter inversions and reversals, substitutions, jumps and breaks in text. In addition, she had many processing problems that interfered with her ability to sequence, hold numbers and letters "in her head," view information containing perceptual cues accurately, and process written text. Interestingly, she knew that her ability to remember facts and terms was directly related to her choice of input devices. Claudia further exhibited her self-awareness of metacognitive skills. She knew if she read information, chances were that she would not remember it. If she heard information, and it was meaningful, she would remember it. Claudia was also aware of her ability to recall and organize meaningful information and effectively retrieve it later. However, the information must have been meaningful for her to use it effectively. Names or numbers, due to their inherent lack of meaning, were extremely difficult for Claudia to recall.

Having a learning disability affected everything Claudia did. She could not write a note to a colleague without misspelling words. She could not read a newspaper and glean the information she needed to understand the story...at least not the first time through. She had trouble understanding all directions and even required assistance following simple recipes to prevent substitutions and misunderstandings. Claudia never read orally in front of anyone if she could help it.

As a professor, Claudia used her computer to produce her lectures, either in narrative or with PowerPoint to avoid having to write on the board. She read every paper, every class project, with a dictionary in hand so that she was able to ensure her corrections were spelled correctly. She read everything aloud (her papers and student papers) so that she could hear the words. The list of these personal compensatory strategies was extensive.

Claudia followed a group of researchers evaluating the causes of learning disabilities. These researchers think that blue backgrounds or "filters" are effective with the addition of altered lighting. Claudia used these modifications. She altered her computer background from white to blue and reduced the "brightness" on the computer and in her office. These strategies seemed to help with her processing and she believes they reduced the jumps and breaks of the text while reading and writing.

Study Strategies

Claudia said she was not "taught" study strategies in school. She reported that during the time she was in elementary and secondary school no one seemed to think about teaching learning and study strategies to her or at least help her with them. By the time she was in graduate school and learning about strategies, she had already discovered what worked for her. Claudia knew that she was not a visual learner. Clearly she had used her giftedness to explore how her brain best processed information.

Her time management and planning or goal-setting skills were excellent. One example of these skills came during the semester she gave birth to her second son by caesarean section. Because she knew when the C-section would happen, she planned and worked ahead in her classes. She had her son the week before spring break, took a week off after the break, and then began working again. She completed all assignments and made all A's that semester. Also, in order to turn assignments in on time and still have time to edit them, she would occasionally request permission to turn in drafts of them for initial review by her instructors.

Most of Claudia's compensatory skills were discovered by trial and error. Her knowledge of her own disability and gifts offered her the ability to find ways to learn effectively. Keys to learning and the ability to study were dependent on meaningful learning and deep processing. Claudia demonstrated her awareness of her metacognitive processes by describing her ability to use her cognitive strengths/gifts to learn effectively. Meaningful learning was not just a catch phrase for Claudia. It was a reality and a necessity. If she could not find meaning in something and personalize it, she had great difficulty learning it. She systematically and meticulously combed through each piece of information to be learned, personalizing the content with prior knowledge. As an assistant professor, Claudia used a peg word method to remember her students' names. As she compensated for her learning disability daily, she creatively developed methods to accomplish and learn needed information on a constant basis.

Writing was a tedious task for Claudia. Sequencing, spelling, and grammar were her weaknesses. Her ability to organize her thoughts and the quality of her ideas were a clear strength. She had an editor correct her spelling, examine the grammar, and check for correct syntax. Writing, though time-consuming, seemed to be one way for Claudia to express her giftedness. The obstacles presented by her learning disability were circumvented through editing, allowing Claudia to express ideas and process information at a complex level.

Claudia described other compensatory strategies. She used monocular visual cues when she drove or rode a bike. That is, she did not have a natural sense of where she was within the lines when she drove. So she would do things like making sure the center stripe of the road was even with the line on the hood of her car. She noted the positioning of the door handles of the cars next to her so that she could gauge how close she was to them. She had difficulty with directionality. She often used and made maps to get places and then another map to return home.

Relying on her husband to read the paper and mail, Claudia used auditory stimuli to comprehend and understand. She chose a watch with an analog face to prevent reversing the numbers. A spell check and grammar check were a part of every written document that Claudia produced. Even though this method was not foolproof, it still caught a multitude of errors.

When given a choice of words in the spell checker, she could not always tell the difference in the word choices...that is; she could not see the difference in the spellings. Sometimes when given three words that looked the same, she picked the wrong word. Once she wrote a paper for a class while working on her doctorate and every place she had the word "public" she replaced it with the word "pubic." She never caught the error, and no one was available at that time to help her edit. The professor caught the error and put smiley faces by each mistake—all 14 of them! It was an embarrassing situation then, yet later, it seemed a bit humorous.

Claudia would rewrite everything...in her own words. In graduate school she often had two notebooks for each class, one for the class notes and one for her note translations. She stressed her reliance on meaningful information. She never applied rote or rehearsed methods of memorization. Retaining visual material was difficult, if not impossible. She had to be able to recall a personal example or go through the process to remember it. She talked aloud in order to retain the information. Claudia said her disability was almost like not being able to hear yourself think; self-talk greatly reduced the problem.

Claudia studied weeks in advance for every test. She learned well with a partner. She typically picked a study partner who was doing poorly in class so that she could teach them the information. It improved her ability to learn. If she was with someone who knew the information better then she, Claudia never seemed to learn as much. Claudia thought that working with others who had trouble mastering material better enabled her to increase her self-confidence.

Evaluations as Guides to Study

Claudia received several professional assessments through the years. Unfortunately, these assessments did little to help her understand how to study effectively given her cognitive abilities and disabilities. Acquiring a method to study for tests was simply trial and error. In hindsight, she feels she should have discerned what to study by the way the material was presented, but this strategy did not occur to her. Additionally, her instructors were not always skilled at test construction, and often the content to be tested was not indicated clearly.

When asked about the best form of assessment, Claudia felt best about evaluations that were multifaceted. She liked assessments that allowed her to demonstrate what she knew without time constraints or confusing questions. For example, she cannot say that she did poorly on multiple-choice tests. Her performance depended on the construction of the test. If the test consisted of long questions, items taken verbatim from the text, questions that contained confusing language, or questions that had good answers and then better answers, she would not do well. If the questions dealt with meaningful learning, understanding concepts, and application, she would perform better.

Writing assignments as evaluation tools, such as papers and presentations, allowed Claudia to utilize her strengths and compensate for her weaknesses (using proofreaders and editors). Although writing was still very difficult, she was able to "work around" her difficulties. Time to organize and rewrite allowed Claudia time, a precious commodity, to filter through her disabilities.

Factors for Success

Claudia did not enjoy attending school, testing, or evaluations of her ability. She loved learning. To her, they were not equivalent. In terms of success, she separated learning from school. However, as a younger student, it was difficult for Claudia to detach "grades" from "learning." She was not able to do separate the two until she was much older. A class where she learned but received an "A" made her feel successful. A class where she received a lower grade, even if she learned a lot, made her feel inadequate. Claudia later learned that her success had more to do with how much she learned in the setting as opposed to the grade she received.

Advice for Other Who Are Gifted and Learning Disabled

Claudia has always been sensitive to the needs of others. One of her sons also has learning disabilities. She viewed his disability as one that was far more pervasive than hers but she could envision his difficulties and possible success.

Claudia helped her son with his assignments from school by creating a beneficial learning climate at home. She concentrated on meaningful learning, helping to make connections with learning for her son. She also aided him in learning how to make these connections for himself. Together, they did a lot of multiple-modality learning. A homework assignment that would normally take a few minutes for others, often took an extensive amount of time. Claudia learned that processing must occur at a higher-order level for her son to master concepts. Higher-order thinking, or processing at a deep level, could key learning success.

Claudia offered other bits of expertise she had learned. She emphasized that other aspects of successful learning must be adequately supported and reinforced. Instead of attempting to learn by trial and error, adults should explain weaknesses and strengths to children and demonstrate ways to combine their gifts and abilities to become successful learners. In order to meet the challenge of a learning disability, children must have a thorough understanding of their disability and their giftedness. Understanding both can illuminate many avenues to learning as well as methods to using higher-order thinking skills that are productive for learners and possibly more critical for those with learning disabilities.

For Claudia's students at the university, she presented her classes as though all students were learning disabled. She used multiple modalities of learning for every lecture. She presented her lecture notes on PowerPoint. Then she took those notes and placed them on a web page, so students could download them and come to class with a written copy already in hand. The notes highlighted the most important parts of the text, so they could use these notes not only to follow along during class, but also as a study guide. Claudia read the notes directly off the board for those who needed to hear the words in order to process the information. Additionally, she continuously attempted to give meaning to all information and encouraged students to make the information "their own" by assigning their own examples and meanings. Claudia worked individually with any students who needed clarification, not necessarily teaching the information, but teaching them how their brain processes information and how to make a connection with the class material. She encouraged paraphrasing of concepts and discouraged rote memorization.

Her individual style of teaching was a culmination of all the methods used by Claudia's previous professors that directly benefited her ability to learn and grow as a student and her discovery of how she processes information. Her students who did not have learning difficulties simply did not notice the accommodations. Those who really needed the assistance continually pointed out how her class methods allowed them to meet their full potential.

Michael

Michael was a recent college graduate from an honors program at a major university. Upon graduation he secured an excellent position that he found challenging and rewarding as a presidential appointee in our nation's capital. His curriculum vita was impressive. He graduated magna cum laude from a major university. He was a Presidential Scholar and a graduate of the Honors College. He had rich experiences and significant responsibilities working in various government offices. His story presented an interesting perspective on his gifts and on his learning disability.

School Experience

Michael began his school experience in a private preschool and continued there through kindergarten. He attended a magnet school for gifted and talented learners during his lower elementary grades. Throughout upper elementary, junior high school and high school he attended neighborhood schools. Michael's family moved during these years; however, he made only one transition between elementary and junior high and then relocated again when he was a junior in high school. Teachers noted his dual perplexities: problems with learning and his strong intellectual ability.

Discovering His Giftedness

Michael's mother had a master's degree in early childhood development, and she noticed anecdotal signs of high intelligence very early in his life. Michael reported that his mother said that he could speak in short sentences at age one. Early in life Michael's vocabulary was extensive and his use of language was at a sophisticated level. The rate of his development was well advanced in comparison to developmental charts and same age peers.

Describing His Giftedness

Michael had an excellent memory and a strong ability to place new ideas and concepts into context with respect to his existing knowledge. He expanded rapidly on those new ideas by adding his own independent thoughts. He used his extensive vocabulary and his ability to communicate as an avenue to add to his growing body of knowledge. Michael was a great problem solver. His ability to analyze and evaluate information and situations was clearly outstanding. Based on the information that he provided, it was evident that he examined his giftedness and knew how to use his own ability. Michael reported that he takes new information; applies it to what he knows; then uses it in addition to his original thoughts to arrive at good solutions valued by others.

Michael's abilities, combined with desire and motivation, have allowed him to excel in school and in the work environment. Michael stated that he synthesizes and interprets large amounts of information very quickly. His excellent visual skills allowed him to develop a superior sight-word vocabulary that compensated for his lack of auditory discrimination. His impressive current career appointment required a high level of expertise. His work was highly detailed, and there was little room for error. The information had to be completely accurate, because people at the highest levels of our government relied upon it.

Discovering His Learning Disability

Michael's mother became aware of his disability at age four. While Michael was well advanced in many areas, he had difficulty following sequential directions and discriminating auditory information. He had difficulty with phonics and reading skills. His mother took him to a major university to be evaluated. Not only did they document his gifted intelligence level, but they also discovered his learning disability, which encompassed auditory discrimination, a component of reading. When Michael was in first grade, his teacher began to notice similar problems with auditory skills; these were manifested in his results on standardized group testing.

Describing His Learning Disability

Michael described his learning disability as difficulty with auditory discrimination, following sequential directions, coupled with Attention Deficit Hyperactivity Disorder (ADHD). Michael's attention was focused on and diverted to many sounds in his classroom. His inability to discriminate made phonics difficult, and his attention often focused on others and on surrounding sounds. Through the years, he relied on his strong visual modality, sight words for reading, and visual cues for following sequential information. He also relied on visual data, such as facial expressions and body language, when listening; these visual prompts helped him to attend well to what was being said. When he was a young student, Michael took medication to control ADHD and his impulsive behavior. He stated that his medication allowed him to think before acting.

Study Strategies

When Michael was in college, he did not study a great deal by going over notes and reading the text. Instead, he attended class regularly and participated heavily in classroom discussion. This strategy allowed him to place the information in context, so that he could recall it effectively when necessary. He also took advantage of accommodations that allowed him to receive classroom notes from his professors or fellow students. He focused his attention on learning in the classroom, using the visual information to couple with listening rather than the cumbersome task of taking notes. If the information delivered in the classroom was not adequate to ensure success, then he would augment that information by reading portions of the assigned text and speaking with the professors on unclear points. For Michael, individual studying was not a time to learn new information; it was a time to review information he had already learned.

Michael preferred to compose papers at the computer so he could control the flow of his ideas. His approach was to come up with a broad idea for the paper in his mind and decide how he would organize his thoughts to convey specific concepts in writing. Then he would begin putting those ideas into text. As he typed, he often rewrote sentences several times, and he always returned to previous sentences and paragraphs to change word choices or to rearrange sentences to ensure clarity. When he finished, he read the entire paper to make sure it flowed in a logical order and conveyed his thoughts effectively. He paid particular attention to this flow, making sure that his ideas were sequenced well.

Unlike Claudia, learning an effective way to study was based on techniques introduced by an early evaluation. Michael used past knowledge and self-discovery to study effectively. He combined his desire to make good grades with his enjoyment of spending time with friends. He tried not to waste time studying alone, because he learned best in a collaborative and cooperative situation. Michael liked the activity of being in an interactive classroom where discussion was the primary mode of learning.

Michael always excelled when teachers or co-workers recognized his desire to succeed. Other times teachers were quick to dismiss his comments and concentrate on his lack of control in sharing his thoughts. Before college, when he had ideas or questions, he would blurt them out without raising his hand and being recognized by the teacher. As a student, Michael always learned better when he actively participated in classroom discussions, especially on complex or difficult issues. In college, he felt there was a common attitude that it was "uncool" to speak out in class. His peers would make fun of him for talking so much in class, but he always felt that it was natural to interact with teachers. He developed social skills that helped him control his desire to interrupt or blurt out answers. Many students tried to absorb lectures without asking questions when they did not understand the material. Then they performed poorly on exams because they did not have the whole picture. Michael also did well with teachers who helped put ideas in a context he could understand.

Michael did not like assignments that required memorization. He found these assignments pointless and unhelpful. Like Claudia, memorization did not help him learn anything unless it was attached to his thoughts and personal knowledge. When preparing for a test, Michael would review lecture notes based on the material covered by the test. Also like Claudia, his most effective study method was to find a classmate who needed assistance with the material covered in the classroom and to review the notes with that person. Because he usually had a grasp of the concepts, he would explain the ideas involved in the lesson to his peer. By doing that, he would recall and solidify facts in his own memory. If he did not study with a peer, he would simply look over his notes and make sure he understood each concept from the notes.

Evaluations as Guides to Study

When Michael was in upper elementary school he received an evaluation of his giftedness and learning disability. The evaluator made several recommendations to his family and to Michael as to how to improve his academic success. The evaluator worked with Michael, his teachers, and his parents to come up with concrete suggestions. She explained to Michael how his disability affected his cognitive abilities, as well as how to use his giftedness and strengths to help him overcome any disadvantage that his disability presented. Michael reported that he and his parents used this information to help him achieve in school. From his evaluation Michael had a clear understanding of his disability and was given the knowledge to modify his study habits to enable him to grasp concepts and command of the curriculum at school.

Factors for Success

Michael was very successful at the university level. His motivation and support from his parents were integral factors in this success. Armed with the understanding of Michael's strengths and weaknesses, his parents worked with him to develop effective study strategies. Michael accepted his disabilities and understood his giftedness. He never pretended to learn like everyone else. He took his unique cognitive profile and developed ways to study that were uniquely his. He accepted the accommodations offered him through the Individuals with Disabilities Act (IDEA) as well as the Americans with Disabilities Act (ADA). Although these accommodations did not offer him an advantage, they did offer him a way to show his expertise. He stated that if he tried to pretend he learned like everyone else, he was much less productive. If he accepted his own profile of learning, he was much more successful in course work and the amount of mastery achieved in each class.

Advice for Others

Michael conveyed the importance for other twice-exceptional individuals to seek out information about their own giftedness and disabilities. When talking to evaluators, he said that others should make sure that they understood their findings and could use information as a useful tool for themselves. He considered knowledge of learning preference to be a powerful tool. Michael was clear about not being embarrassed about unique and creative study methods. He encouraged others to explain their specific needs to teachers. He felt most teachers would appreciate self-knowledge and want to help students in their endeavor.

Natalie

Natalie was a 20-year-old college junior majoring in international business at a major state university. Although she needed only three semesters to graduate with her degree, she considered changing her major. Since Natalie was currently attending a postsecondary institution, she presented a different perspective from the previous stories of college graduates.

School Experience

Early recollections of school for Natalie included constant reminders from teachers to increase her organization skills. From her earliest recollections of school, her teachers admonished her about not turning in her homework on time. She had difficulty finding assignments and keeping up with school materials. This disorganization became a pattern that continued through junior high and high school. Her grades were poor, C's and D's. She did not like school and continued not to turn in her homework through her secondary school setting. She admits that if she had completed her work she would not have had as many problems making adequate grades. Natalie stated that school was not a fun place to be; it was tedious. She did not care for the activities or the school curriculum.

Upon applying to a private university, Natalie stunned her parents and high school guidance counselor by scoring a 1410 on her SAT. Her scores were so high that she was admitted to the academically challenging setting of a university and given a scholarship. At the time, the school admission counselor said that although her entrance essay was not adequate, they felt that she had great potential. During the year at the small private university, she struggled with bad grades and would have failed, but her university professors allowed her to turn in papers late. Subsequently, Natalie transferred to a major state university with a center for students with learning disabilities.

Discovering Her Giftedness

Natalie was tested in early elementary school and received an intelligence test score of 167. Their seemingly intelligent child who continually received low scores on her report card baffled her parents. Natalie also attended a gifted program while in elementary school. Later she was evaluated again and received a 147 on a different intelligence test. Her entrance exam for college again placed her in a gifted category. Her intellectual ability was exceptional yet she had trouble with simple organizational skills.

Describing Her Giftedness

Natalie described her giftedness as being able to memorize easily. She loved to study words and use them effectively. She was able to remember many little details. She felt that her giftedness and good cognitive ability allowed her to "slide" through school. She viewed her gifted ability as a negative. She perceived her cognitive strengths as a vehicle that has allowed her to slip through school without developing good organizational skills.

Discovering Her Learning Disability

Natalie had been tested several times throughout her childhood; teachers and parents felt she was not living up to the previous intelligence test scores. She had and continues to have a significant difference between verbal and performance scores. She had many organizational problems. Although she was able to memorize easily, most often the memorization related only to words. In school she was able to memorize facts easily. She often could remember many small facts, yet she missed the main idea. Her disability was compounded by her inattentiveness. She had also been diagnosed as having ADHD. Her poor organizational skills, lack of attentiveness, and inability to see main points all contributed to her difficulty with writing.

Describing Her Learning Disability

Like Claudia, although Natalie had trouble throughout her early school career, she was not diagnosed with a learning disability until she was in high school, in the ninth grade. She described characteristics of her disability in the following words: easily distracted, inability to concentrate, difficulty with social relationships, poor organization skills, and an inability to grasp the main concept. Her writing ability lacked organization. Note taking was a difficult task. She described writing as a "pain," and papers drove her nuts. Her outlines were thorough and time consuming so she usually did not make a rough draft.

Study Strategies

Natalie said that she had not discovered her most effective way to study. The method she used to study depended on what she studied. In languages, she used vocabulary cards and constructed sentences with different verbs. In math, she worked problems with ease, because she tended to remember the process as she solved problems. Natalie took extensive notes and highlighted her texts. Her study habits changed at will. She attempted to study with different methods and had not hit upon one with any consistency. Natalie noted that concentrating with isolated noise was extremely difficult, unless that noise was constant. For example, turning a page in a book could ruin her concentration, but studying in the student center with music and lots of talking seemed not to be bothersome.

Like Michael, Natalie liked classrooms where there was a great deal of verbal interaction. She believed she learned best in that type of environment. Debating, which she referred to as arguing, was a tool that she found really helped her capture the major issues in a class. She loved arguing with her professors. She worked hard to formulate different perspectives so that she could interact with others. To prepare for an exam, Natalie read through the text a couple of times. She thought that she took superfluous notes; however, the exercise of note taking helped her more than studying. Natalie was not fond of school and still struggled to enjoy her time at the university.

Evaluations as Guides to Study

Unfortunately, Natalie felt that her evaluations were not helpful in deciding how to compensate for her learning disability. She was unaware of how to use her giftedness to increase her study effectiveness. Her lack of organizational skills and ability to capture main ideas interfered with this process. She lacked clear, precise explanations about the effect of her learning disability and the impact it had on her giftedness.

Factors for Success

Natalie felt that individual tutoring had offered her the best help she had received at the university level. She liked the fact that a tutor could drive her method of study. Her ability to learn was directly affected by the tutor's ability to match her learning style. Her tutors tried to keep her schedule, checked daily on her progress on assignments and reviewed with her material she should have mastered. Through the tutoring center she attended, she had assigned study hours and obtained good advice on course selection. Her tutors served as coaches, keeping her on track during the semester.

Advice for Others

When asked for some sage advice for other gifted and learning disabled individuals who are pursuing higher education, Natalie was quite frank. She simply stated, "Find someone who will kick your butt to get your stuff in on time." Apparently, Natalie continued to be frustrated by her lack of organizational skills and inability to turn assignments in on time. Her problems with organization extended to writing assignments, an essential skill in postsecondary education. She was obviously concerned over meeting deadlines and improving her organizational skills.

ANALYSIS OF THE THREE STORIES

Based on the central themes that emerged from the review of literature, the stories were analyzed to see if the importance of motivation, necessity of early identification, well-developed organizational skills, dislike of rote memorization, and the use of higher-order thinking skills and verbal skills surfaced in the lived experience of three gifted individuals with learning disabilities. We added metacognition to this list because it emerged so clearly from the interviews. Each story was examined and compared to the other two lived experiences.

Metacognitive Knowledge

When examining all three stories, it was evident that Michael and Claudia made significant use of their knowledge of how their brains process information and the relationship between their giftedness and their learning disabilities. Michael had an evaluator explain his gifted and learning disabled characteristics and subsequent learning style and strengths. His evaluator extended that knowledge to his teachers at school and to his parents. Michael used this cadre of tools, specific information about his strengths and weaknesses, to develop ways to study and excel in school.

Claudia discovered her personal information in a more circuitous manner, trial and error. While evaluators did little to demystify her learning disability or giftedness, she pursued her quest to learn about her disability and her ability to "out think" others. Claudia investigated her own abilities to formulate solutions to her own learning puzzles. Both Claudia and Michael used their metacognitive knowledge to become successful learners. Both individuals graduated from university and achieved many of their short-term goals and were progressing toward the completion of some long-term goals.

Conversely, Natalie indicated that she did not understand her own abilities, strengths, and weaknesses. She knew that she had a memory for details, yet she failed to use this information productively to make the most of her giftedness and minimize the effect of her disability. Natalie indicated that she had not gained useful information from evaluations.

The three stories demonstrate the importance of teaching students about their disabilities and ways to circumvent, enhance, and utilize cognitive processes. A qualified professional evaluator with the ability to give meaningful feedback was extremely important to Michael and could have made a significant difference for Claudia and Natalie. After much expended energy and time, Claudia gained this knowledge through her own quest for mediating her abilities and honing her expertise in learning. As was evidenced in the interview, Natalie had not yet discovered how to use her gifted abilities and how to work with her weaknesses.

The Importance of Motivation

Within each of the three stories, motivation played a valuable role. Motivation propelled Claudia through her doctorate and continued to push her forward toward her lifelong goals. Successful endeavors were fraught with hard work, yet Claudia persisted in adapting to her learning situations and achieving small steps that led to her current success. Interestingly, Claudia differentiated learning from the concept of school. She was motivated to learn yet disliked school.

Like Claudia, Michael did not enjoy school, yet he was motivated to graduate with honors and upon graduation, obtained a highly competitive position with a great deal of authority. His interview indicated that he was still learning on the job and continued to pour over material thoroughly, because others depended on his ability to solve problems, and synthesize and evaluate information. Motivation was a major factor in his achievement and continues to be an integral part of his success.

Natalie's interview allowed us to see her determination to get a degree. She was unclear about her major. The very fact that she changed universities, enrolled in a program that would help her, and took advantage of tutoring, indicated strong motivation. Natalie, too, did not enjoy school. All three interviewees stressed this salient point: School was painful.

The interviewees indicated that liking school did not alter their motivation to eventually succeed there. Claudia and Michael used school as a vehicle to achieve graduation and later success. It was as if school was the most difficult hurdle, and specific job-related tasks promised to be more enjoyable and intriguing because of personal choices and interests. While Natalie was still seeking a degree and had no clear goals for the future, she was focused on getting out of school with a degree.

The Necessity of Early Identification

Identification of gifted abilities and learning disabilities were mentioned within the interviews. Claudia was identified as gifted much earlier than she was identified as having a learning disability. The same pattern was evident in Natalie's story. Michael was identified as gifted early on and his learning problems were pinpointed in first grade. The struggle to discern methods of approaching learning was much easier for Michael. Claudia relied on herself to discover her learning style and best modalities to learn. Natalie continued to rely on the help offered through her study center and tutors.

Claudia and Natalie both indicated frustration. Michael did not express the same amount of frustration that the Claudia and Natalie did. Claudia overcame her frustration with excellent learning and study strategies. She showed us that she met learning challenges with adequate time and self-taught skills. Natalie continued to be perturbed with school, yet she had discovered the necessity of using a tutor to mediate her problems. As opposed to acquiring learning skills as Claudia did, Natalie relied on others to ease her frustration. Michael, armed with early identification and evaluation help in explaining his abilities, seemed to avoid this level of troublesome annoyance.

Well-Developed Organizational Skills

The importance of organizational skills was evident in Michael and Claudia's stories. They each listed compensatory strategies used to master their school and course requirements. Claudia kept separate notebooks, one for note taking and the other for translating her notes into meaningful information. She had a system for learning that required her to place as much material as possible into an auditory format. She also retaught the material to others who experienced difficulty with class concepts. These strategies demonstrated a well-organized system to alleviate weaknesses in her cognitive processing.

Michael also had a well-ordered system for his own learning. He talked his way through new concepts. Michael listened intently in class, discussed the information, and reviewed new concepts after class. He adapted to his learning environment by extracting the information in a format that was conducive to learning. Like Claudia, he also liked to explain the material to others who might not know it well.

Natalie's story does not demonstrate organizational skills. She relied on tutors to organize her assignments and study sessions. Natalie did learn enough about her metacognitive processes to mediate her strengths and weaknesses in an organized fashion. She related that missing assignment deadlines cost her dearly in terms of higher grades. She found difficulty in adhering to a schedule, and time had little meaning for her.

The three stories differ significantly. The successful experiences of Claudia and Michael demonstrated well-developed organization skills adapted to their personal learning profiles. Natalie's lack of success indicated that she needed to develop organizational skills that were compatible with her gifts and disabilities. Again, the evaluation completed with Natalie should have given her the basic structure that she needed to develop a workable system to organize her assignments and choose appropriate study methods.

Dislike of Rote Memorization and Possession of Extensive Vocabularies

Both Claudia and Michael expressed a dislike of rote memorization. Claudia had to relate all learning to something meaningful to remember it. She said she personalized it with prior knowledge. She would also rewrite everything from classes in her own words. Michael also placed new ideas in context with respect to existing knowledge. He used his participation in class discussions as a vehicle to help him understand and remember the content. His extensive vocabulary and verbal skills helped him accomplish this task. Natalie had not learned her best way to remember without a tutor and did not discuss this aspect of her learning.

Use of Higher-Order Thinking Skills

The ability to learn and master concepts at a high level was illustrated in Claudia's story. Claudia continually reminded us about her mastery of learning to such an extent that she could use the information well. She analyzed, synthesized, and evaluated information to make concepts meaningful. She also mastered concepts to such a degree as to be able to teach them to others. She would take information and apply it in a personalized way. Her use of higher-order thinking skills to retain information in a usable format was evident. Michael also used higher-order thinking when he worked with others and talked his way through concepts. By thoroughly discussing and thinking through issues, Michael used higher-order skills such as analysis, synthesis, and evaluation to create meaningful learning opportunities.

Natalie did not indicate that she was employing higher-order thinking to mediate her learning. Reliance on tutors to help organize her learning for her was not helpful in terms of higher-order thinking skills. Natalie continued to struggle to grasp main ideas, and the use of higher-order thinking skills was not substantiated.

INSIGHTS FROM THE STORIES

We related the lived experience of three twice-exceptional individuals, learning disabled and gifted. We can glean numerous lessons from their stories. What we learned about them and from them will help others in their struggle to be educated. Based on the themes and the interviews, the following suggestions can be derived from the analysis of the stories.

1. Students should have adequate self-knowledge regarding their own cognitive abilities and learning preferences. Learning disabled and gifted students should be given extensive explanations regarding any of their assessments with an emphasis on how to functionally use the information. Any concerns over how best to learn should be addressed. It is possible that Claudia's struggles might have been lessened had she understood her disabilities earlier and how they related to her strengths.

2. Development of metacognitive abilities places power to learn within the grasp of each learner. Clearly, Claudia and Michael had exceptional metacognitive strengths. These same strengths might help Natalie manage her own learning better instead of relying on others to do that for her. Others have pointed out the need for gifted learners with learning disabilities to develop metacognitive skills also (Montague, 1991).

3. Teachers and parents need to be involved in providing extra support for students who are twice exceptional and understand their abilities and disabilities. Claudia and Michael found a real sense of support from their parents, and Claudia continues to receive that same support from her husband. Emotional encouragement and assurance are essential for these learners (McEachern & Bornot, 2001).

4. School should be a place where students are comfortable with learning. Accommodating someone's specific learning style would help his or her learning immensely. Providing information in differing modalities and giving evaluation alternatives must be considered.

5. Good explanations of cognitive strengths and weaknesses should provide encouragement regarding how to constructively use gifted processes. Discovery of potential successful endeavors should help develop motivation. This discovery was the key to the perseverance of these learners. Students should have opportunities to develop areas of strength and use them to compensate for weaker processing areas.

6. Early identification of learning problems and giftedness should enable students and their parents to seek ways to avoid failure. Often, special education evaluations do not show students with learning disabilities areas of strength or giftedness. As with Michael and Claudia, these

were critical components to developing their gifted abilities. Would Claudia and Natalie have had less difficulty if their learning disabilities had been identified as early as Michael's? Compensatory strategies should be taught early to these students (Dole, 2001; Stormont, Stebbins, & Holliday, 2001).

7. Both Claudia and Michael had very well-developed organizational skills. Due to their learning disabilities, these organizational skills were integral to their success. Natalie still suffered due to a lack of organizational skills. Teaching organizational and study skills to students is imperative (Hoover, 1989). Had these three students had this advantage, they might have struggled less in school.

8. As is evidenced by the stories, teaching simplistic or watered-down instruction is not what gifted individuals with learning disabilities need. Using higher-order thinking skills enabled Claudia and Michael to take their knowledge and apply it at sophisticated levels. This ability helped them achieve success; they were able to use new concepts and apply the knowledge at a personalized, creative level. Learning in an evaluative and analytical structure utilized their gifted abilities.

CONCLUSIONS

The learning and study strategies of gifted adult learners with learning disabilities are crucial to their success in school. Teaching learning strategies to all students helps improve their success in school, but students with learning problems, in particular, must be armed with a repertoire of strategies from which to choose. They should also learn when to best use them.

Clearly more research must be conducted about gifted postsecondary students with learning disabilities. They are distinct from the other learners with learning disabilities who are served on college campuses. We have no way of knowing how many of them have failed to complete school because they tired of the very hard work needed to succeed. These learners have to work more hours and more cleverly than typical students and than other gifted students who do not have learning disabilities. They are truly twice exceptional.

REFERENCES

Brody, L. E., & Mills, C. J. (1997). Gifted children with learning disabilities. *Journal of Learning Disabilities, 30*, 282–296.

Cohen, S. S. & Vaughn, S. (1994). Gifted students with learning disabilities: What does the research say? *Learning Disabilities, 5*, 87–94.

Dole, S. (2001). Reconciling contradictions: Identity formation in individuals with giftedness and learning disabilities. *Journal for the Education of the Gifted, 25,* 103–137.

Ferri, B. A., Gregg, N., & Heggoy, S. J. (1997). Profiles of college students demonstrating learning disabilities with and without giftedness. *Journal of Learning Disabilities, 30,* 552–559.

Hoover, J. J. (1989). Study skills and the education of students with learning disabilities. *Journal of Learning Disabilities, 22,* 455–461.

Kovach, K., & Wilgosh, L. R. (1999). Learning and study strategies, and performance anxiety in postsecondary students with learning disabilities: A preliminary study. *Developmental Disabilities Bulletin, 27,* 47–57.

McEachern, A. G., & Bornot, J. (2001). Gifted students with learning disabilities: Implications and strategies for school counselors. *Professional School Counseling, 5,* 34–41.

Robinson, S. M. (1999). Meeting the needs of students who are gifted and have learning disabilities. *Intervention in School & Clinic, 34,* 195–204.

Shormont, M., Stebbins, M. S., & Holliday, G. (2001). Characteristics and educational support needs of underrepresented gifted adolescents. *Psychology in the Schools, 38,* 413–423.

Silverman, L. K. (1989). Invisible gifts, invisible handicaps. *Roeper Review, 12,* 37–42.

Stodden, R. A., Whelley, T., Chang, C., & Harding, T. (2001). Current status of educational support provision to students with disabilities in postsecondary education. *Journal of Vocational Rehabilitation, 16,* 189–198.

Tallent-Runnels, M. K., Olivárez, Jr., A., Candler-Lotven, A. C., Walsh, S., Gray, A., & Irons, T. (1994). A comparison of learning and study strategies of gifted and average ability junior high students. *Journal for the Education of the Gifted, 17,* 143–160.

Tallent-Runnels, M. K., & Sigler, E. A. (1995). The status of the selection of gifted students with learning disabilities for gifted programs. *Roeper Review, 17,* 246–248.

Vaidya, S. R. (Summer, 1993). Gifted children with learning disabilities: Theoretical implications and instructional challenge. *Education, 113,* 568–573.

Chapter 8

COMPENSATION STRATEGIES USED BY HIGH-ABILITY STUDENTS WITH LEARNING DISABILITIES

Sally M. Reis
University of Connecticut

Lilia M. Ruban
University of Houston

INTRODUCTION

Recent research has provided fascinating examples of the problems faced by high-ability students with learning disabilities (LD), as well as the compensation strategies they used to address and overcome the challenges associated with specific learning disabilities (Reis, McGuire, & Neu, 2000; Ruban, McCoach, McGuire, & Reis, in press). For example, Reis et al. (2000) found that these students often received content remediation that they did not need, rather than instruction in compensatory strategies, in their elementary and secondary school learning disabilities programs. Many academically talented young people with learning disabilities never qualify for programs for gifted and talented learners and fail to succeed in school, but those who do often learn strategies that help them to succeed, despite their learning problems.

In this chapter, current research about compensation strategies is discussed, as are the strategies used by successful high-ability college students who have learning disabilities. When these students succeed in challenging academic environments, it is because they have learned to compensate for their deficits as well as to develop their gifts and talents. The use of these compensation strategies is essential for academic success, especially in the areas of study and performance strategies, self-regulation and time management strategies, opportunities for counseling, self-advocacy, and the development of an individual plan using metacognition and executive functions. Of particular note is the emerging understanding of the role of self-regulation in the successful academic performance of students with LD. The importance of academic self-regulation to achievement in this population cannot be understated, as self-regulated learning (SRL) is "a pivotal construct in contemporary accounts of effective academic learning" (Pintrich, 1995, p. 173). A synthesis of research in different fields such as giftedness, learning disabilities, and academic self-regulation provides insights into the nature and idiosyncrasies of academic self-regulation among high-ability students with LD (Ruban, 2000; Ruban et al., in press).

Only two studies have identified compensation strategies used by successful students with LD in a college environment and whether college students with LD (including high-ability students with LD) use similar or different learning and study strategies to succeed in a challenging learning environment, as compared to their non-disabled peers (Reis et al., 2000; Ruban, 2000). Few studies have investigated the question of how different populations of college students acquire SRL strategies and study skills, and how and in what contexts they choose to use them in their academic work (Pintrich & De Groot, 1990; Wolters, 1998). This chapter will provide a summary of the limited research conducted on SRL strategies and compensation strategies used by high-ability students with LD who succeed in challenging academic settings.

COMPENSATION STRATEGIES USED BY SUCCESSFUL HIGH-ABILITY STUDENTS WITH LEARNING DISABILITIES

Hannah and Shore (1995) suggested that the study of gifted students with LD provides deep insights into the nature of giftedness and the combination as well as interaction of exceptionalities. According to these researchers, the increasing interest in the study of these twice-exceptional students is particularly noteworthy, especially because giftedness and learning disabilities until recently have been studied separately from a cognitive perspective. In reviewing the relatively limited research in this area, Hannah and Shore (1995) concluded that research has been conducted primarily in the following three areas: case studies (Baum, 1984; Rosner & Seymour, 1983; Suter & Wolf, 1987); comparisons of test performance of gifted/LD students to that of populations of gifted and LD students (Barton & Starnes, 1989; Suter & Wolf, 1987); and educational programming options (Baum, 1984, 1988; Baum, Owen, & Dixon, 1991; Suter & Wolf, 1987). Baum and Owen (1988) found that some high-ability students with LD had unique characteristics related both to persistence and individual interests; they also demonstrated lower academic self-efficacy (Bandura, 1986) than their peers who had not been identified as gifted and learning disabled. Baum and Owen also found that 36% of the students in their study who had been identified as having a learning disability simultaneously demonstrated behaviors associated with giftedness. Hannah and Shore's (1995) study showed that, in terms of metacognitive knowledge and strategy use, gifted students with LD performed in a manner that was more similar to their gifted peers than their peers who had learning disabilities, providing support for the hypothesis that a strong relation exists between metacognition and giftedness.

Newer theories of intelligence (Gardner, 1983, 1993, 1999; Sternberg, 1981, 1995, 1997) and expanded conceptions of giftedness (Renzulli, 1978; 1986) suggest that the talents and abilities of some students are not accurately measured by the instrumentation currently used. Learning disabilities in high-ability students with LD are difficult to identify (Baum, 1984; Baum & Owen, 1988; Baum & Olenchak, 2002; Reis, Neu, & McGuire, 1995), as students often perform extremely well in some areas and poorly in others. Some will never be identified as gifted because their high abilities mask their disabilities or their learning disabilities mask their talents, resulting in average or below average school performance (Baum, et al., 1991; Tannenbaum & Baldwin, 1983). Students with LD identified as gifted using traditional methods may demonstrate different profiles: Some display problems in school from a young age, while others encounter frustration only when the material and content become increasingly more challenging (Baum et al., 1991; Daniels, 1983; Whitmore & Maker, 1985). Some students with severe reading problems, for example, develop excellent auditory memories that enable them to memorize books and passages, and this ability helps them to mask their inability to read until late in elementary school (Reis et al., 1995). Accumulated research evidence supports the contention that gifted students with LD represent a very heterogeneous group of students, which makes it difficult to make canned generalizations about this unique population (Baldwin, 1999; Hannah & Shore, 1995; Olenchak, 1994; Reis et al., 2000).

Researchers report that some high-ability students with LD can be quite productive in nonacademic settings (Baum, 1984; Fox, Brody, & Tobin, 1983; Reis et al., 1995; Schiff, Kaufman, & Kaufman, 1981; Whitmore, 1980). Baum (1984) investigated the use of an enrichment program based on the Enrichment Triad Model (Renzulli, 1977) that was successfully implemented for gifted students with LD, and then suggested four educational implications that could guide the development of special programs for this population. First, these students need focused attention on their gifts and talents, rather than the usual singular focus on their disabilities. Second, talented students with LD thrive in a supportive environment in which their individual abilities are valued and appreciated. Third, students need to obtain a unique set of strategies to compensate for their learning problems in addition to the content instruction they so often receive. Finally, gifted students with LD must understand their unique pattern of academic and learning strengths as well as weaknesses in order to learn to compensate for these discrepancies. More recent studies provide evidence that disruptive behaviors of high-ability students with LD improve or even disappear when these students participate in talent development programs designed to identify and nurture their special gifts and talents (Baum & Olenchak, 2002; Baum, Owen, & Oreck, 1996; Baum, Renzulli, & Hebert, 1994; Olenchak, 1994, 1995).

A conflict exists between the types of remedial strategies used in special education and the academic needs of high-ability students with LD: These students do not respond favorably to the remedial approach of special education, such as the repetition of basic skills to ensure mastery (Baum, 1984; Baum & Owen, 1988; Daniels, 1986; Jacobson, 1984; Reis et al., 1995; Whitmore, 1980). Current research has found that successful adults with learning disabilities emphasize their potential to achieve rather than focusing on the deficits caused by their disability (Reis et al., 1995; Gerber & Reiff, 1991). Factors such as persistence, self-confidence, the will to conquer adversity, and strong character have been cited as contributing to the success of individuals with disabilities (Gerber & Reiff, 1991; Maker, 1978; Reis et al., 1995). Gerber and Reiff (1991) studied highly successful adults with learning disabilities from 24 states and Canada and identified several themes associated with career success, of which the most prevalent was the desire and effort to gain control of one's life. They found a correlation between higher degree of control and an increased likelihood of success in life. Other themes that emerged from Gerber and Reif's extensive interviews with adults included the desire to succeed; goal-orientation; reframing or reinterpreting the disability in a positive sense; persistence; goodness of fit between strengths, weaknesses, and career choice; learned creativity or divergent thinking; and a social ecology of support systems, including family and friends. Learning how to premeditate or conquer their learning disability was not a major factor in the lives of these successful adults; rather they learned to compensate for their disability and move forward.

SPECIFIC COMPENSATION STRATEGIES

Little has been written about compensation strategies for gifted students with LD in elementary and secondary schools. Crux (1991) referred to compensation strategies as a broad class of learning strategies that "describe study, cognitive, spatial, memory, or learning strategies" (p. 7), and explained that students with LD use compensation strategies because they provide effective methods for processing information when thinking, remembering, storing, and making sense of old and new information. She found variations in the characteristics of compensatory methods and strategies, which was understandable, as the purpose of these strategies is "to provide ways of compensating for a learning problem" (Crux, 1991, p. 5). Baum et al. (1991) suggested that successful high-ability students with LD who are able to work in their interest areas use compensation strategies as a way to address their disabilities. Since the remediation approach used in so many K–12 intervention programs have been shown to be ineffective for high-ability students with LD, an effective model for considering compensation strategy service delivery systems can be found in the education of university students with LD (Shaw, Brinckerhoff, Kistler, & McGuire, 1991). The postsecondary framework requires that students gain the autonomy seldom learned in elementary or secondary special education programs. At the postsecondary level, more colleges and universities provide services for an increasing number of students with LD who are pursuing higher education (Mangrum & Strichart, 1997). In some university settings, students participate in a program to learn to understand their specific learning needs and gain assistance in using compensatory strategies to circumvent academic disabilities and become independent and successful learners in academically challenging college or university settings (Brinckerhoff et al., 2002; McGuire et al., 1991; Vogel & Adelman, 1993).

COMPENSATION STRATEGIES TAUGHT IN SUCCESSFUL UNIVERSITY PROGRAMS: STUDY STRATEGIES AND SKILLS

In one study documenting the specific activities of university students with LD, McGuire et al. (1991) found that the areas most commonly addressed in a successful university program for students with LD included study strategies, course-related performance strategies (e.g., reading comprehension and written expression), counseling, and self-advocacy training. Study strategies and specific skills to compensate for a learning disability emerged as the primary need of university students with LD, including specific types of note-taking strategies, time management, test-taking preparation, and library skills. Note-taking strategies are seldom taught in the regular university curriculum, yet were found to be critical for the organization of information delivered in classes.

Time management was the most frequently occurring objective among study strategies in successful university programs for students with LD (McGuire et al., 1991). The use of one-month organizers and semester overview calendars was consistently modeled and further enhanced in weekly, and sometimes daily meetings that included discussions about how to maximize the use of time. Successful time management depends on students' abilities to self-monitor their activities and make appropriate decisions, and self-monitoring of time management must also include understanding the need for extra time to complete academic tasks in the area of the specific disability.

Instruction in test-taking skills is rarely provided in students' educational experiences (Bragstad & Stumpf, 1987), but successful university students with LD must plan for test preparation. Learning specialists in university centers often model strategies for analyzing multiple-choice questions, suggest methods to reduce test-taking anxiety, and help students to learn to use an error-analysis approach to review tests and pinpoint reasons for incorrect answers. Strategies related to classroom performance, such as written expression, reading comprehension, and mathematical processes, are also taught by learning specialists in university LD programs (McGuire et. al, 1991). Written-expression instruction helps students in the development of skills such as the organization of written assignments, proofreading, and sentence structure and mechanics.

Counseling and Self-Advocacy

Counseling for university students with LD can include academic, personal, and career concerns, and has been found to absorb one third of learning specialists' instructional time (McGuire et al., 1991; McGuire & Madaus, 1999). Academic counseling may help some students to consider balancing their academic course load in light of their learning strengths and weaknesses. If, for example, pace and depth in reading is a problem, students may be advised to adjust their selection of courses to avoid a class schedule in which overwhelming amounts of reading are required in every class. Students are also advised of the other, more clinical counseling services available to them at the university, if personal counseling is required.

High-ability students with LD often need guidance in understanding their profile of strengths and weaknesses in order to utilize appropriate strategies and advocate for academic accommodations (Tannenbaum & Baldwin, 1983). Self-advocacy requires an understanding of these strengths and weaknesses and the students' skills in presenting their abilities as well as weaknesses in their communication with faculty. This self-awareness enables students to request accommodations such as extra time on tests, alternative testing environments, or extensions for assignments. Self-monitoring is essential, as students use metacognition to both monitor and adjust for their individual areas of strengths and weaknesses (Brinckerhoff et al., 2002).

Academic Self-Regulation

According to Bandura (1997), a major advance in the study of lifelong cognitive development relates to the mechanisms of self-regulated learning in academic settings. *Academic self-regulation* is the process in which students activate and sustain cognitions, behaviors, and affects that are systematically oriented toward the attainment of goals (Schunk & Zimmerman, 1998; Zimmerman, 1989; 1998a, 1998b; Zimmerman & Schunk, 1989). Self-regulated learners are characterized as active learners who efficiently and effectively manage the metacognitive, motivational, and behavioral aspects of their learning (Zimmerman, 1989). Zimmerman identified the hallmarks of academic self-regulation as including: time management, practice, mastery of learning methods, goal-directedness, and a robust sense of self-efficacy. The construct of academic self-regulation has gained increasing attention in the last two decades, resulting in studies in a variety of settings with individuals representing different age and achievement groups, and disability status (see, for example, Brinckerhoff et al., 2002; Schunk & Zimmerman, 1994, 1998), as well as several longitudinal studies (e.g., Vermetten et al., 1999).

Self-regulated learning is an important component for college students, as postsecondary settings place greater emphasis on students' self-directedness and independence. The term *self-regulated learning* describes "independent, academically effective forms of learning that involve metacognition, intrinsic motivation, and strategic action" (Perry, 2002, p. 1). In contrast to K–12 students, most college students have control over their own time management as well as over how they structure their studying and learning activities (Pintrich, 1995). Models of self-regulated learning provide a useful description of what effective learners do in college courses (Pressley & McGormick, 1995). Educational researchers have devoted considerable attention to instructional approaches that promote students' development of academic self-regulation (Butler, 1998; Schunk & Zimmerman, 1998). Given that focus on content remediation is not effective for students with LD (Deshler, Ellis, & Lenz, 1996), and even counterproductive for high-ability students with LD (Baldwin, 1999; Reis et al., 2000), the current focus on fostering students' regulation of their own learning and motivation becomes particularly important (Butler, 1998; Policastro, 1993; Schunk & Zimmerman, 1998).

SELF-REGULATED LEARNING STRATEGIES AND ACADEMIC ACHIEVEMENT

A major component of academic self-regulation is self-regulated learning (SRL) strategies, defined by Zimmerman (1989) as "actions and processes directed at acquiring information or skills that involve agency, purpose, and instrumentality perceptions by the learners" (p. 329). Zimmerman and Martinez-Pons (1986, 1988) identified 14 types of SRL strategies in high school students, including such methods as organizing and transforming information, self-consequating, seeking information, and rehearsing and using memory aids. Students' use of these strategies was highly correlated with their achievement and with teachers' ratings of their self-regulation in a class setting. In fact, students' reports of their use of these SRL strategies predicted their achievement track in school with 93% accuracy, and 13 of the 14 strategies discriminated significantly between students from the upper achievement track and students from lower tracks. The SRL strategies described by Zimmerman (1989) encompass three classes of strategies that all students use to improve self-regulation of their (a) personal functioning; (b) academic behavioral performance; and (c) learning environment (Bandura, 1986; Zimmerman, 1989).

An Interplay among Self-Regulation, Metacognition, and Executive Functions

Researchers have found significant differences in the use of study skills and learning strategies among low-achieving students, high-achieving students, and students with LD, which, in turn, provides a strong link to their academic achievement (Pintrich et al., 1994; Schunk & Zimmerman, 1994, 1998). Sternberg and Davidson (1986) and Schiff et al. (1981), among others, have examined the apparent deficiency of students with LD in the process of learning. Extensive studies conducted at the University of Kansas by Deshler et al. (1996) corroborated other researchers' findings that students with LD are either "strategy deficient" or "actively inefficient," or, in other words, unable to spontaneously transfer the strategies they learned from previous contexts to new contexts (Wang & Pallinsar, 1989; Wong & Jones, 1992). As an example, the Strategic Intervention Model (SIM) developed at the University of Kansas (Ellis, 1990) is predicated on the idea that, if students become empowered with strategic approaches to learning, then, in addition to learning skills, they will also learn why and when to apply these skills and monitor their implementation, as part of an important process referred to as executive functioning (Bursuck & Jayanthi, 1993; Stuss & Benson, 1986).

Research has suggested that the use of metacognition can help talented students process information more efficiently; and academic self-regulation can help them to learn more effectively (Hannah & Shore, 1995; Shore & Dover, 1987; Sternberg, 1981). Several case studies of gifted students with LD poignantly illustrated the frustration between understanding complex information and having a disability in the regular information-processing mode (Baum et al., 1991, 1996; Whitmore & Maker, 1978). As Hannah and Shore (1995) aptly noted, "their giftedness suggests metacognitive strength, their learning disabilities suggest metacognitive weakness" (p. 96).

Academic Self-Regulation: Differing Views

Some differences in views on academic self-regulation exist among researchers. According to Zimmerman and Paulsen (1995), some investigators treat self-regulation as an *idiosyncratic* set of skills that each student must develop personally as he or she progresses through school. In particular, Crux (1991) argues that each student with learning disabilities needs to develop a personalized set of compensation strategies whose functionality depends on the utility of a particular strategy in certain contexts and circumstances. Other researchers assume that a common or *standard* set of self-regulatory skills exists and is used by a general population of students (Pintrich & Garcia, 1991; Zimmerman & Martinez-Pons, 1986, 1988). Recent research (Schunk & Zimmerman, 1994, 1998) has shown that a common set of self-regulatory skills does exist, that these skills are highly predictive of students' academic success, and that these skills can be taught. Strategies described by Zimmerman (1989) are *standard* SRL strategies that arguably all academically successful students use. Reis et al. (2000), however, described a set of *specific* compensation strategies that included some similar and some different strategies to those identified by Zimmerman (1989). Reis et al. (2000) defined *compensation strategies* to include "study strategies, cognitive or learning strategies, compensatory supports, environmental accommodations, opportunities for counseling, and the development of an individual plan incorporating a focus on metacognition and executive functions" (p. 124). In another recent study, Ruban (Ruban, 2000; Ruban et al., in press), found empirical evidence supporting the previous research by Reis et al. (2000) suggesting that a specific set of strategies is used primarily by students with LD, and that these compensatory strategies differ from the larger set of standard SRL strategies used by a general population of students.

MOTIVATION IN USING SELF-REGULATED LEARNING STRATEGIES AS A FUNCTION OF THEIR UTILITY

In addition to monitoring and controlling cognitive and metacognitive strategies, self-regulated learners also actively manage other important aspects of their classroom learning (Wolters, 1998). In particular, according to the social cognitive theory of academic self-regulation, students regulate the motivational, affective, and social determinants of their intellectual functioning as well as the cognitive aspects (Corno, 1989; Corno & Kanfer, 1993; Deci & Ryan, 1985; Sansone et al., 1992). In fact, Bandura (1997) contends that the cognitive aspects of self-regulated learning cannot be viewed separately from the motivational aspects. For example, a student may have adaptive cognitive and metacognitive skills, but such skills will exert little influence on academic performance if he or she fails to use them or fails to find personal utility in them. Personal utility refers to students' personal and informal assessment of the usefulness of a particular learning strategy or method in their own academic work. Simply put, if students do not find ways to internalize a particular learning strategy and apply it consistently in their courses, they will not use it (Garner, 1990; Nolen & Flaladyna, 1990). As a consequence, motivation, characterized as a student's willingness or desire to be engaged and commit effort to completing a task, is an important component of classroom learning that students may choose to self-regulate (Deci & Ryan, 1985; Sansone et al., 1992; Wolters, 1998).

Research On Academic Self-Regulation and the Use of Compensation Strategies by High-Ability Students with Learning Disabilities

Accumulated research findings have afforded a rich base for understanding the nature of human exceptionality, including giftedness and learning disabilities. Importantly, a study of dual exceptionalities (e.g., gifted students with LD, and/or Attention Deficit Hyperactivity Disorder) has made significant strides in the last decade. Researchers studying academic self-regulation have conducted studies in both K–12 and postsecondary settings. It appears that designing studies that make use of the accumulated knowledge gained by the cross-fertilization of different though related fields can provide rich insights into the study of such complex phenomena as giftedness, learning disabilities, dual exceptionalities, and academic self-regulation.

The description of two empirical studies that follows has served to fill this gap. The first study (Reis et al., 1995, 2000) is unique in that it identified compensation strategies used by successful high-ability students with LD in a college environment. The second study (Ruban, 2000; Ruban et al., in press) explored the question of whether university students with and without learning disabilities (including high-ability students with LD) use similar or different SRL strategies to succeed in a challenging university environment; whether the pattern of the use of these strategies differs among different populations of students (i.e., normal-, low-, and high-achieving students, and students with LD); and whether the differences in these patterns of strategy use are at least partially a function of students' essential goals and motivations.

Study 1:
Investigating the Use of Compensation Strategies by High-Ability University Students with Learning Disabilities

Reis et al. (2000) used qualitative methods to investigate compensation strategies used by talented students with LD in elementary and secondary school learning disabilities programs, finding that multiple compensation strategies were employed by all of the participants in this study to succeed in challenging university settings. Each participant used some of the individual strategies within each of the major categories of compensation strategies to be successful in a challenging university setting. All participants attributed their success in scholastic environments to their ability to employ these strategies. Study and time management strategies included but were not limited to: methods of learning to study, note taking, identifying key points when reading and preparing for tests, library skills, and the use of daily, weekly, and monthly calendars. Compensation strategies included the use of computers, word processors, books on tape, and self-advocacy. Executive functions included planning techniques such as time management, metacognition, setting work priorities, and self directed speech to help in difficult academic situations. Most of the participants in the study had previously learned only limited compensation strategies without the benefit of a formal, structured LD program in their elementary or secondary careers. One participant explained:

> I learned to compensate for some of my learning problems but for others, I was still working it out. I knew I had learning disabilities. I knew that was why I couldn't do things the same way other people did them, but I didn't necessarily know how to work it out [the other problems].

Some of the compensation strategies were quite simple. For example, it was difficult, if not impossible, for many of the participants to listen and take notes at the same time, because taking notes required so much effort, due to reading, writing and spelling difficulties. These students often learned to photocopy someone else's notes and compare them with their notes to determine whether they had missed anything important during lectures.

Another common compensation strategy was taking a reduced load of courses. Students who used this strategy usually took four, or occasionally three classes a semester, as compared to five classes, considered a full course load at their university. This strategy provided the flexibility to invest additional time and effort in their studying to compensate for disabilities. Most of the students acknowledged that their use of compensation strategies was due to their participation in the University Program for College Students with Learning Disabilities (UPLD). It was because of this program that they became aware of and learned to ask for accommodations such as the use of extended time for examinations, or taking an exam using a computer. Many requested extra help from professors who were aware of students' learning problems because the students had disclosed their difficulties when requesting accommodations. One participant explained:

> I work with my professors. I even go to one of my professors with my notebook, and she takes the time to sit with me and read through my notebook. She sees that I miss certain things, and she discusses the notes that I have missed. Another professor goes through major concepts and ideas with me, and I have learned to use visual cues to help my memory.

Most of the participants acknowledged that their use of various types of equipment such as computers, tape recorders, or books on tape was due to their participation in the UPLD. Most also used various learning strategies described in the SQ3R strategy including: preview reading, structured reading (i.e., reviewing what they will focus on by using boldfaced topic headings), reading abstracts or chapter summaries that provide a "blueprint" of key information, and planning considerable amounts of time for reading. The participants in this study also indicated that they used outlining and notecards as well as mnemonic techniques. While many of the students mentioned multiple learning and compensation strategies, each had developed an individual set of strategies that enabled him/her to succeed. For some participants, this system included various study strategies, such as organizing their time to find the large blocks needed to complete their reading, and analyzing their own difficulties to be able to overcome them. One explained his system:

> Well, I've become better at planning. To improve my grades at school, I request untimed test time for the testing accommodations to enable me the time to read the questions thoroughly and ask for help if I cannot read a word. Planning and organizing have taught me to carry a calendar around and I go through all my syllabi and plan out when the exams are and what reading has to be done. I don't always get it all done. Right now I'm behind in a couple classes. But, I know what I need to do and I have to do it in little pieces... Chunking is the term that they use. It keeps me from getting overwhelmed, if I have a list of eight chapters that I need to do by next Saturday, that's overwhelming for me. I have to break it up, I have to start with chapter one on Sunday and continue through the week adding a chapter each day. If the chapters are really long, I do sections of chapters at different times of the day. Self-awareness is a big thing for me as I have to know how long I need to do something. When I started college I couldn't plan out how long I needed to read a chapter. How long I needed to work on something. Now I have learned how much time it takes me to do my work and I have a much better idea of how to plan.

Most participants also indicated that they could not be employed during the academic year because of the amount of time necessary for them to complete their academic work. One participant, who worked at a job related to his passion and avocation, bicycling, took only two courses a semester, but most worked only in the summer.

Several of the participants also mentioned what could be labeled an "underground network," that included a system of checking with other students about professors from whom they should take classes. These students tried to find professors who were regarded as fair, would make the necessary accommodations for students with LD, and whose lectures were keyed to the assigned text. The option of selecting these professors was possible because participants attended a large university and had many choices while at a smaller college, fewer choices would exist. One student indicated that selection of professors was a major "success" strategy for him. "I learned to cope by getting the right teachers, those who let me compensate for my learning disability."

Three themes emerged relating to compensation and learning strategies used by successful high-ability university students with LD. First, each participant used a unique system developed in consideration of the nature of the disability, his/her personal styles and preferences, and a set of appropriate compensation strategies. Second, these successful students devoted an extraordinary amount of time, effort, and energy to their studies, as summarized by one participant who described his preparation for a chemistry exam:

> For the last chemistry exam, for example, my notes run very close to the book. I went through the book. I took notes on nearly everything in the book that was considered important. All the major theories of people!! On the six chapters, I took 12 pages of notes, and then I went through that, and what I did is, I studied that, and then I rewrote everything that I didn't feel like I had the first time. I would just do that until I knew everything backwards and forwards, and then I went through the notes in the book, and anything I hadn't studied already in the book and the notes. I just wrote down what to study, but I spend days of doing that amount of studying. It wasn't just taking the notes. I didn't count that as just studying. I would finish reading the chapters about a week before the exam, and spend a couple of days taking notes on the exam, for the exam from the book. I'd say I probably put in 30 hours or more studying for the exam. I mean that... I'd put in the days before the exam perhaps, 3 to 5 hours a day for at least 4 to 5 days in a row.

The third theme was the degree of comfort the participants gained using the various learned compensation strategies. A continuum existed relating to the adjustment these students experienced around the use of compensation strategies for their learning problems. Some participants believed they were "cheating" or not really working if they used reasonable accommodations such as extended time for tests and the use of a word processor for exams. Several had been constantly told in elementary and secondary school that if she would only work and study harder, she could overcome her learning problems. Accordingly, in the university setting, one young woman continued to believe that asking for help was analogous to admitting she hadn't worked hard enough.

> If I got an A, I wanted to get it under the same circumstances as everybody else. Because I felt like maybe I was cheating in my work if I had an advantage that they [other students] didn't. After a while, though, I realized that I am at a slight disadvantage, anyway, so it [using extra time in exams] just balances out. Now that doesn't bother me at all anymore, and like I said, with the extra time in exams, sometimes I use it. I am always prepared to use (this

accommodation), like I will get there early, or I will have the option to stay late.

Approximately half of the students used services provided by the UPLD and various learned compensation strategies easily and without guilt, while still others analyzed and reflected about why they needed help and why it may be difficult to request assistance. Another participant in the study explains:

I think that the hardest thing is to... know when I need more help, and when I can do it on my own. I am an individual, and I don't like someone else doing things for me, or even doing things with me, and it was very hard to get to the point to say, "I need help learning to memorize things." I want to be able to do it on my own, and I was constantly being told that I was smart enough to do it on my own, and it was frustrating to realize that I have to do extra to get to [the] same point that other people can get to just by reading it.

While many of the students mentioned multiple learning and compensation strategies, it is clear that each student selected the particular strategies that worked best for him/her. Each participant developed an individual system, defined by Stuss and Benton (1986) as executive functions, sometimes intuitively, and sometimes collaboratively with the help of a learning specialist from the UPLD, which enabled him/her to succeed using a combination of compensation and learning strategies.

Self-Perceived Strengths

Another strategy for success developed by almost all of the participants was the acquisition of excellent work habits in response to difficulties. Dedication was needed to succeed in a challenging university system, and many students emphasized their strong belief in their own potential and a willingness to go to great lengths to realize that potential. The majority believed that their capacity for hard work was their greatest asset. Each of these students learned how to work hard because of his/her learning disability, and the determination and motivation of each of these students was quite clear in their interviews and in the corresponding interviews with their parents.

The work ethic described by the participants transferred into their employment; each had one or a number of summer jobs to defray college costs. The motivation that enabled them to work hard usually focused on obtaining a university degree. In fact, many of the participants in this study became *more* committed to graduating because of their learning disability.

Several of the participants had to change their majors in order to succeed in a challenging university setting. For those who must spend hours reading what students who do not have learning disabilities can read in minutes, the pursuit of a liberal arts degree remains challenging, even when the most sophisticated compensation strategies are used. Some of the students in this study majored in liberal arts, and used many compensation and learning strategies. However, other students learned to select majors in areas that enabled them to tap into their strengths and succeed without the hours of reading required in the liberal arts curriculum. Some of the majors selected by this group include mathematics, engineering, sciences, physical therapy, and music.

Counseling

Half of the participants were affected by what happened to them as elementary and secondary students as a result of the discrepancy created by their high abilities and their learning disabilities. Complex emotions continue to affect many of them, and half of the sample sought counseling to reconcile some of the problems and mixed messages that they believed had been caused by their educational backgrounds. Two considered suicide and one actually planned her death:

This is a good one. What I did as a senior was, I watched all these kids apply at schools. They were my best friends applying to schools and everything else you know, and they were 1st, 2nd, 3rd, and 4th in class, and I said, 'what the hell am I going to do?' My father has this nice job. My uncle is a professor at Cornell, and I am this real shameful thing in the family, I mean, it was really awful and I knew, there wasn't anything that I could do. I couldn't take notes. There were so many things that I couldn't do, so I decided that suicide was the answer, and I planned to do it before graduation. I carried it right out, I mean, I gave all my stuff away. I did all the things that kids do when they are planning to kill themselves. And I decided I'd make peace with everyone. I had a teacher pull me in, and she said, 'are you thinking about suicide?' And it was so abrupt and straightforward. I didn't know what to do except say, yes.

Appropriate interventions were made for this young woman, who eventually gained compensation strategies that enabled her to become extremely successful in both college and graduate school. However, she required counseling during much of that period of her life. In all probability, similar counseling opportunities will be necessary for other high-ability students with LD.

Discussion of the Findings in Study 1

These studies indicate that some high-ability students with LD succeed in a challenging, rigorous university setting with the help of various compensation strategies. Too often, however, the learning disability programs in which students participated in elementary and secondary school focused on remediation of content-related deficits or the opportunity to do homework or catch up on work missed in class instead of instruction in the compensation strategies they needed. Their subsequent participation in a university program for students with LD provided their first organized opportunity for training in compensation and learning strategies, and they all believed that this postsecondary program was essential to their success.

Participants in the study were able to resolve the conflict between their abilities and their disabilities. Some learned the compensation strategies needed directly to address their learning disability and become successful in an area that may have initially appeared difficult, if not impossible. Some participants were careful to select an academic direction in which they had strengths *and* in which their success was not dependent upon the acquisition of compensation strategies or the mastery of academic content directly affected by their learning disability. These options are not available to an elementary or secondary student who has either no choices or extremely limited academic choices in school. The majority of participants combined the two options mentioned above as they attempted to both compensate for their learning disability and also select a major area of concentration that fostered the use of their strengths to enhance their academic performance. Baum's (1984) observations about the importance of focusing on a talent while developing compensatory strategies are certainly affirmed by these successful adults with learning disabilities, as was Sternberg's notion of successful intelligence (Sternberg, 1995, 1997), which calls for a focus on strengths and compensation for deficits. Renzulli's theories (1977; Renzulli & Reis, 1985, Renzulli & Reis, 1997) about the importance of focusing on interests, learning styles, and curriculum strength areas were also found to be accurate for the population studied.

The creation of a personal plan for academic success varied among participants, but always included these elements: the use of carefully selected and individually necessary compensation strategies, and the integration of certain executive functions that guided the students' decisions and the directions they either followed or ignored. All successful participants shared the ability to focus on developing their talents instead of focusing on their deficits. Educators must reexamine the approaches used at the elementary and secondary levels to address the special education needs of high-ability students with LD. Remediation programs will not help this population. Instruction in compensatory strategies and self-advocacy must be incorporated in a program that fosters self-regulation and self-reliance, a critical factor for success in future academic and life endeavors.

Study 2:
Comparing the Use of Self-Regulated Learning Strategies and Compensation Strategies Among University Students With and Without Learning Disabilities

Ruban (Ruban, 2000; Ruban et al., in press) used survey research methods to examine patterns in the use of SRL strategies and compensation strategies among university students with and without learning disabilities. The sample of respondents (N=470) was composed of four groups of undergraduate students from a large research university in the Northeast: normal-achieving students (N=89), low-achieving students (N=102), high-achieving students (N=227), and students with LD (N=53). A convenience sample of undergraduates who were enrolled in an introductory learning class represented the normal-achieving group; students who, at the time of the administration of the survey, were on academic probation for failing to meet the university's minimum scholastic requirements represented low-achieving students; a random sample of university Honors Scholars comprised the high-achieving group; and students with LD were sampled from the same comprehensive support program for students with LD from which participants in Study 1 were sampled (UPLD, or University Program for College Students with Learning Disabilities).

A new instrument called the *Learning Strategies and Study Skills Survey* (LSSS, Ruban & Reis, 1999) was developed for this study. The LSSS survey was designed to explore the relationship between the use of SRL strategies/compensation strategies and academic achievement of different groups university students, using Zimmerman's (1989) work on self-regulated learning, Schmeck, Ribich, and Ramanaiah's (1977) study of individual learning preferences, and Reis et al.'s (1995, 2000) work on compensation strategies used by academically successful students with LD. The LSSS survey was designed to assess college students' self-reported study behaviors in generic learning situations, and confirmatory factor analysis provided sufficient support for the construct validity of the survey, ^{2} (642)=1080.63, TLI=.90, CFI=.91; RMSEA=0.038. The instrument included six factors. The first three factors represented standard SRL strategies (Conceptual Skills; Study Routines; and Routine Memorization), while the last three factors represented compensation strategies (Reading & Writing Metacognitive Strategies; Compensatory Supports; and Help Seeking).

Participants were also asked to respond to two open-ended questions related to two areas. First, they were asked to consider any special ways of studying or creative approaches that they found useful in their academic work (such as figuring out how to study difficult material more efficiently, or finding a good way to memorize important information). The second question examined students' motivations for using these SRL strategies or study skills by asking the students to explain the reasons why self-regulatory methods help them to succeed academically.

A combination of quantitative and qualitative methods was used to add breadth and scope to the findings (Creswell, 1994). Quantitative data techniques included confirmatory factor analysis (CFA, Kline, 1998) to examine the psychometric properties of the LSSS survey, and discriminant function analysis to examine group differences among normal-, low-, high-achieving students and students with LD regarding the use of SRL strategies and compensation strategies (i.e., mean scale scores on the LSSS survey) (Tabachnick & Fidell, 2001). Qualitative data analyses were conducted for both open-ended questions using the coding paradigm suggested by Strauss and Corbin (1990), which included open coding, axial coding, and selective coding. Inter-rater agreement for coding both questions was fairly high (88% and 80%, respectively). Highlights of the major findings from this study are presented below.

Group Differences Using a Quantitative Approach

The discriminant function analysis used to examine group differences with respect to the use of self-regulatory and compensatory methods among the students with and without LD resulted in three significant discriminant functions, with a combined $\chi^2 (18) = 271.822$, $p <$ .001. The three functions accounted for 38%, 4%, and 2% of the between-group variability, respectively. The first function separated low achievers and students with LD from normal and high achievers. The second function discriminated low achievers from normal achievers and the learning disabilities group. The third function separated normal achievers from students with LD. The loading matrix of correlations between predictors and discriminant functions suggested that the best predictors for distinguishing between normal/high achievers and low achievers/LD students were conceptual skills and compensatory supports. Low achievers differed from normal achievers and students with LD on help seeking (with low achievers seeking less help and students with LD seeking most help), and study routines (with LD students studying the most of all groups). The high-achieving group reported the highest mean on conceptual skills, and the lowest mean on study routines. It is likely that these students may be more likely to use more differentiated and complex strategies than other students, or that they may have internalized strategies to the extent that they are no longer consciously aware that they actually use them. As one high achiever described, "I don't even realize that I am using study skills or learning strategies—I feel that it comes naturally—so maybe it was taught at such a young age that it is automatic now." Finally, students with LD differed from normal achievers on routine memorization, with LD students using memorization the least. The two most important (i.e., reported as being used most frequently) strategies for normal-, low-, and high-achieving students were conceptual skills and memorization (i.e., standard SRL strategies). In contrast, the most important strategies for students with LD were help seeking (i.e., a compensation strategy) and study routines (a standard SRL strategy). Interestingly, routine memorization was least important for these students. Students with LD reported using many learning strategies (both standard and compensatory) in order to compensate for their learning difficulties and to succeed academically in a challenging university environment.

Patterns of Use of Self-Regulation Strategies and Compensation Strategies Among Students with and Without Disabilities

Themes were also identified as students' responses to the open-ended question across the four groups were classified into salient themes and compared to the 14 categories of standard SRL strategies originally developed by Zimmerman and Martinez-Pons (1986, 1988). A total of 305 students provided responses to the first open-ended question. In the present study, as the result of the open, axial, and selective coding, as well as through the discussion between the researchers with respect to the relationship between and among the codes, it became apparent that some of the categories that emerged from the analysis were similar to, and some were more differentiated than the original 14 categories proposed by Zimmerman. In addition, several new categories emerged. Based on the results of Strauss and Corbin's (1990) coding scheme, the following major categories of SRL strategies and compensation strategies emerged: self-evaluating; managing time and redistributing work load; organizing and transforming material; keeping records and monitoring; structuring study environment; memorizing, rehearsing and retaining material in routine and creative ways; reviewing records and clustering material; utilizing support networks; using compensation strategies; and non-strategic behaviors. Each of these major categories included specific self-regulation strategies and compensation strategies.

When frequencies and percentages of strategy use for each group were tabulated, interesting patterns of group differences emerged among the four groups of students. Using the total number of students using a particular strategy, the most frequently used strategies were ranked for each group in terms of the strategy's importance. Even though there was some overlap in the pattern of strategy use, there were marked differences among the groups. For instance, the five top strategies used by low achievers were using flashcards, reviewing notes, planning time, seeking social assistance, and reviewing text. For normal achievers, using mnemonics and visual cues and memorizing material routinely was rated as most important, followed by condensing notes, and highlighting and color-coding. High achievers reported high use of condensing of notes and mnemonics combined with visual cues, and outlining material and writing summaries. Students with LD were the only group who reported regular use of compensation strategies to help them with their academic work. Using flashcards, seeking social assistance and highlighting and color-coding were rated as most frequently used strategies.

Careful examination of the students' responses across the four groups revealed that there was wide variability in their comments. For instance, some students merely listed strategy or strategies they use; others elaborated in great detail in what contexts they use these strategies, or under what circumstance, thus making a reflective link to the utility function of these strategies. In addition, some students described strategies that appeared to be at a higher level of complexity than other strategies. For instance, whereas one of the low achievers wrote, "I just keep reading it till I get it," several students, including high achievers and students with LD, provided greater elaboration indicative of the strategy's level of complexity. For instance, a high-achieving student with LD explained his use of mnemonics and visual cues, "I often use an erase board to help me visualize what is being asked or to help me learn how things work together as a system or mechanism (works primarily with my science courses)." Several high-achieving students described strategies for meaningful learning and constructing meaning, as illustrated in the following comment, "I try to make connections and see how everything works together to make sense either within the course or between past and present knowledge." Notably, several students expressed metacognitive awareness about the usefulness of learning strategies in their academic work, as illustrated in the following two comments: "I don't use study skills, and therefore do poorly in my classes (a low-achieving student); "Learning strategies—I live by them" (a student with LD).

Many students with LD provided interesting insights into the nature of the academic self-regulation of their study behaviors. These students often sought social assistance, for example, asking professors for lecture notes, using office hours (one student wrote emphatically, "It's very important for students with LD to use office hours. I'd say, 'Abuse' office hours!"), asking teaching assistants for help, utilizing resources of the comprehensive college support program for students with LD, etc. These students also often created their own individualized methods for making flashcards (such as color coding important terms, or using different color cards for different concepts, etc.). Some students with LD found it helpful to draw pictures in their notes and on the back of their flashcards to help associate concepts with words and meanings, or to help learn and memorize information (e.g., "For classes that are very visual, like Art History, I take notes in class, draw little pictures on the side what the art looked like. Later, I make lots of different flashcards with photocopied pictures on one side and information about it on the other."). One student reported sitting in front of the class and taking only a few notes as an environmental/personal structuring strategy, in order to help him better concentrate on the material presented in class (e.g., "I sit on front of class and try to understand everything my professors say or write on the board rather than just copying it down in my notes. I take a few notes on the lecture, only important things I haven't seen before.").

Group Differences in the Motivation for Using Strategies

In addition, students were invited to respond to another open-ended question that asked students to describe what motivated them to use learning strategies and study skills, and how the use of these self-regulatory methods helps them in their academic work. A total of 176 students across the four groups provided responses to this question. As with the first open-ended question, students' responses were coded into salient themes using Strauss and Corbin's (1990) coding scheme, and the "top five" reasons for using SRL strategies and study skills were identified for each group, which provided interesting insights into the nature of students' self-reported motivation for using academic self-regulation. The pattern of the rankings of strategies varied by the group and reflected different degrees of emphasis that students in these groups placed on the use of these strategies, as low-, normal-, high-achievers and students with LD perceived varying degrees of utility or usefulness of strategies, depending on their motivations for using these strategies.

Low achievers who were struggling to improve their grades emphasized the use of time management, organizing their study environment, using strategies for test preparation and increasing their academic self-efficacy, and motivation to improve their academic standing to avoid dropping out because of academic non-performance. In contrast to this "academic survival" model, students in the other three groups reported qualitatively different reasons for using SRL strategies and study skills. For instance, the most important reason for high achievers' use of self-regulation was to facilitate the process of understanding information and relating concepts to each other. However, an important differentiation occurred. Whereas many high and normal achievers and students with LD linked the use of the learning strategies with linking concepts in a meaningful and coherent way to organize their personal schemata and deep understanding (not routine memorization) of the material, low achievers associated the reason for using learning strategies and study skills with facilitating basic information and memorization of information for exams.

Additionally, the pattern of the rankings presented revealing results. Some similarity was found in the pattern of rankings for some strategies among normal achievers, high achievers and students with LD, but there were also marked differences. For instance, understanding information/bringing concepts together was ranked as the highest priority by high achievers, but it received a lower ranking by students with LD, who first needed to make sure that they could manage their time effectively and organize material and concepts. Interestingly, students with LD found it was very important to learn how to become more efficient and develop learned creativity to adapt and succeed in a postsecondary setting. In addition, students with LD were the only group who reported that using self-regulatory study methods helped them compensate for and manage their LD.

Discussion of the Findings in Study 2

Several themes emerged from the data in this study, and they raise some interesting questions. First, group differences emerged in the use of academic self-regulation among different student populations, corroborating what previous research has suggested (Borkowski & Thorpe, 1994; Krouse & Krouse, 1981; Vogel & Adelman, 1993; Zimmerman & Martinez-Pons, 1990). However, moving beyond group differences for the sake of group differences, this study considered students' motivation for using self-regulation, and suggests a strong link between self-reported study behaviors and reasons for using self-regulatory methods among different student populations. Low-achieving students have different goals and motives (to survive academically) than high-achieving students (to enhance their deep understandings, and further focus their learning goals). Students with LD use self-regulation to compensate for their learning disability, identify strengths and weaknesses, and to succeed academically. These students use self-regulatory techniques that would be of highest use to them under given circumstances, and what clearly emerges through this research is that although some generalizations can be made about the way in which different populations of students self-regulate their study behaviors and motivations, a great deal of individual variation exists within each population.

In this study, students with LD represented a unique population of students in terms of regulating their own learning. Because students with LD are a heterogeneous group, they showed similarities and differences in academic self-regulation as compared to low, normal, and high achievers. This study provided support for the hypothesis that students with LD use both standard SRL strategies and compensation strategies, depending on a complex interplay of factors, such as the type of their LD, severity of LD, and the co-morbity of LD with giftedness, and the utility of particular strategies and methods in certain academic contexts.

Perhaps one of the most provocative ideas to emerge in this research is that academic self-regulation by students with LD and/or with dual exceptionalities (e.g., with both giftedness and learning disabilities, or with learning disabilities and ADHD) has its own idiosyncrasies. It appears that individuals with LD have to undertake an additional step in regulating their own learning behaviors and motivation. First, because they have processing deficits or difficulties, they have to find out what their strengths and weaknesses are, and utilize SRL strategies and compensatory strategies. Then, an equally important purpose for students with LD becomes how to learn effectively on their own and become self-directed learners. Despite the fact that many students with LD in this study exhibited high ability, they had to work much harder than other students to succeed academically in a challenging university environment, because the coexistence of learning disability and giftedness created additional challenges.

Implications of this Research for Practice

A growing number of researchers believe that the study of students with LD who also demonstrate high ability provides useful insights into the nature of giftedness (Baum et al., 1991; Baum & Olenchak, 2002; Hannah & Shore, 1995; Reis et al., 2000). They argue that the combination of exceptionalities is interesting because both giftedness and learning disabilities have been previously studied in isolation from each other, and also because gifted students with LD have received increasing attention as a special population (Baldwin, 1999; Baldwin & Viale, 1999; Hannah & Shore, 1995; Olenchak, 1994, 1995). As a consequence, studying students with dual exceptionalities appears to provide particularly provocative and deep insights into the nature of human exceptionality and the additional challenges associated with comorbity of giftedness with leaning disabilities. In particular, research conducted in the fields of giftedness, learning disabilities, and academic self-regulation, respectively, may help researchers and educators to better understand the complex tapestry of factors that come into play when studying the characteristics, needs, identification, assessment and service delivery issues related to this unique population. Even though research on students with dual exceptionalities in secondary settings has gained momentum (Baldwin, 1999; Baum & Olenchak, 2002; Baum et al., 1991; Hannah & Shore, 1995), research on academically talented college students with LD is still in its infancy (Reis et al., 2002; Ruban, 2000; Ruban et al., in press).

As research findings in different fields serve to enrich each other, so does research conducted at the secondary level inform research conducted at the postsecondary level, and vice versa. Therefore, exemplars of effective intervention models focusing on strategic and meaningful learning and effective transitioning strategies for students with LD at the secondary level (Deshler et al., 1996; Ellis, 1990) should inform postsecondary practice about how to help students with exceptionalities succeed academically and learn how to become self-directed learners. On the other hand, research conducted in postsecondary settings, which has helped students with LD and/or dual exceptionalities become academically successful, may provide an effective model for considering service delivery systems that can be found in the education of secondary students with LD (Brinckerhoff et al., 2002; Shaw et al., 1991). The continuity of services, the opportunities, and support that students with LD and/or dual exceptionalities receive in high school becomes particularly important when they transition into postsecondary settings, given that such students face additional obstacles in the independent and self-directed environment of the postsecondary arena (Brinckerhoff et al., 2002; Dalke, 1993; Reis et al., 2000).

Brinckerhoff et al. (2002) noted that in the postsecondary education of students with LD, there are emerging signs of the ever-increasing visibility of this previously "invisible" category (p. ix). Researchers in this area acknowledge the fact that many of these individuals are also academically talented and have developed an extensive repertoire of finely tuned compensation strategies that can further confound the diagnosis of LD or ADHD, making it even more difficult to demonstrate need for accommodations. As evidence of this increasing visibility, the researchers cited postsecondary enrollment statistics, components of federal legislation, the increased number of the specialized summer pre-college preparation programs, coverage by media, and college policies and procedures.

In particular, students with LD continue to represent the fastest-growing category of disability reported by first-time, full-time college freshmen (Henderson, 1999). Henderson (1999) reported that in 1998, 41% of all such freshmen identified themselves as having a learning disability, whereas 10 years earlier, only 15% of these applicants had made such self-disclosure. Perhaps as further evidence of attempts at "leveling the playing field," the College Board recently announced that it will no longer flag the SAT score reports of students who were granted extra time because of disabilities (Hoover, 2002). Sid Wolinksy, director of litigation of Disability Rights Advocates, referred to the flag as "a scarlet letter" that stigmatized individuals with disabilities who didn't want to be identified as disabled (Hoover, 2002). Such high-stakes challenges may have implications for college admissions and for individuals with exceptionalities who apply to colleges. According to Brinckerhoff et al. (2002), these positive changes have become possible to attain because of the legal underpinnings of the Americans with Disabilities Act (ADA, 1990), the reauthorization of the Individuals with Disabilities Education Act (IDEA, 1997), and, in Canada, the Canadian Charter of Rights and Freedoms. As a consequence, in Brinckerhoff et al.'s interpretation, these laws have worked to enhance the integration and participation of individuals with disabilities in all aspects of society, including both postsecondary education and the arena of competitive employment. This positive trend has been evidenced in the number of colleges and universities offering comprehensive LD support programs or LD services to students with exceptionalities, particularly students with LD (Lewis & Farris, 1999). Whereas a decade ago, some postsecondary institutions were just beginning to offer such services and programs, currently over 1,200 campuses in the United States and Canada offer such services (Mangrum & Strichart, 1997).

Despite the many challenges faced by individuals with LD and gifted individuals with LD, many of them are enrolling in colleges and universities better prepared academically, with higher aspirations and senses of self-efficacy rooted in their successful academic records, and augmented by the support provided by teachers, LD and gifted-and-talented personnel, and parents (Baum & Olenchak, 2002; Brinckerhoff et al., 2002). Research provides convincing evidence that comprehensive and effective LD support programs and talent development programs designed to identify and nurture gifts, abilities, and talents can reverse the negative pattern of underachievement, low levels of motivation and task dedication, and inaccurate self-perceptions and perceptions of others with dual exceptionalities (Baum et al., 1991). In particular, Baum and Olenchak (2002) provide a convincing argument that meeting the needs of twice-exceptional children must include "focused attention to the gift, inclusion in a supportive environment, allowance for compensation strategies, and counseling sessions to cope with social, emotional, and behavioral issues" (p. 89). It appears that the confluence of the accumulated research findings in the fields of learning disabilities, giftedness, and academic self-regulation at the K–12 and postsecondary levels have converged to provide a powerful framework with implications for designing effective interventions programs for students with LD and dual exceptionalities. Grounded in such synthesis of research, Tables 1 and 2 describe different types of empirically based strategies shown to be effective in ensuring academic success and fostering talent development in individuals with LD and dual exceptionalities, in the secondary and postsecondary arenas. Research and practice have underscored the importance of using a variety of strategies at different levels, such as academic, legal, and career-related strategies; self-regulation and compensation strategies; social–emotional strategies; and talent development strategies. To achieve the goals of successful transition, talent development, and the fulfillment of personal potential, collaboration among different stakeholders needs to occur on several levels, such as teachers, LD personnel, gifted-and-talented specialists, professionals, parents, teachers, and, last but not least, students themselves as key agents in developing their potentials and shaping their lives.

TABLE 1. Compensatory and Non-Compensatory Strategies for Making a Successful Transition from High School to College

Strategies and Goals	Reference
Academic, Legal, and Career-Related Strategies	
Develop a clear understanding of what learning disabilities (LD) are and are not • Provide a general overview of LD (LD teachers) • Discuss common terminology (LD teacher)	Brinckerhoff et al. (2002); Cowen (1993); Field & Hoffman (1996)
Learn about one's own legal rights • Learn about changes in legal rights under Section 504; ADA; and IDEA (LD teachers) • Learn about accommodations provided by law (LD teachers)	Brinckerhoff et al. (1993); Heyward (1998); Latham & Latham (1998); Vogel (1997)
Select courses to prepare a student academically for college; and to get ready for and take the SAT/ ACT • Encourage the student to take college preparatory courses; consider quality (counselors) • Be wary of modified or simplified courses (parents) • Try to complete a wide array of courses and avoid course waivers if possible (parents) • Use a multiyear educational plan (counselors) • Involve parents as part of the educational team (teachers; LD specialists; counselors)	Barr et al. (1998); Cowen (1993); McGuire et al. (1991); Koehler & Kravets (1998); Reis et al. (1995); Whitmore (1980)

TABLE 1. Compensatory and Non-Compensatory Strategies for Making a Successful Transition from High School to College (Cont'd)

Explore career & postsecondary options	Biller (1985); Brinckerhoff et al. (2002); Cowen, 1993; DuChossois & Stein, 1992; McGuire & Shaw (1987); Patton & Dunn (1998); Wehman (1992)
• Explore ways to incorporate strengths and weaknesses into a career plan	
• Participate in a career exploration program	
• Explore careers through extracurricular activities, hobbies, and work experiences	
• Explore colleges that do not require the SAT or ACT (counselors; parents)	
• Use college resource guides/directories/web sites, including specialized LD sources	
• Create a list of 6–10 schools, including: (a) "sure bet," (b) "reasonable reach"; (c) "far shot."	
Explore college options with comprehensive LD programs versus LD services	
• Consider each college's distance from home	

elf-Regulation and Compensation Strategies

Begin developing a repertoire of personalized compensation strategies	Bryant et al. (2002); Bursuck & Jayanthi (1993); Butler (1998); Crux (1991); Deshler et al. (1996); Reis et al. (2000); Shaw et al. (1991)
• Help a student begin developing generalizable study skills	
• Help a student begin developing a personalized set of compensation strategies to promote academic success (LD specialist; parents)	
• Steer clear of traditional remediation resource room models	
• Promote strategic learning and problem solving	
• Explore the benefits of assistive technology	

TABLE 1. Compensatory and Non-Compensatory Strategies for Making a Successful Transition from High School to College (Cont'd)

Develop a general understanding of the nature of one's own disability • What the nature of one's own LD is (LD teachers; parents) • Understand one's own profile of strengths and weaknesses (parents) • Understand connection between one's own LD and academic performance (teachers)	Aune (1991); Brinckerhoff (1994); Cowen (1993); Dalke & Howard (1994); Wilson (1994)
Foster self-determination • Help a student develop self-advocacy skills • Help a student to set goals and then implement the plan (parents; teachers; counselors) • Teach a student assertive communication, understanding oneself as a learner (LD specialists; teachers; counselors; parents) • Encourage the student to reach for postsecondary education (parents; teachers)	Brinckerhoff et al. (2002); Eaton (1996); Price (1988); Tessler (1997); Wilson (1994)
Develop greater independence • Consider taking a summer job to establish work ethic (parents) • Refine academic skills and career options (teachers; counselors; parents) • Help a student understand his/her psycho-educational report (school psychologist) • Become aware of accommodations available for taking standardized tests (counselors)	Anderson (1993); Aune & Ness (1991); Cowen (1993); Eaton & Coull (1998); Vogel & Reder (1998)

182

TABLE 1. Compensatory and Non-Compensatory Strategies for Making a Successful Transition from High School to College (Cont'd)

Talent Development and Enrichment Strategies

• Take AP or Honors classes if appropriate (teachers; parents)	Baldwin (1999); Baum & Olenchak (2002);); Baum & Owen (1988); Baum et al. (1991); Purcell & Renzulli (1998); Reis et al. (1995, 2000); Renzulli & Reis (1997); Silverman (1989); Vogel & Reder (1998)
• Participate in extracurricular activities to broaden a student's horizons (parents; teachers)	
• Participate in summer mentorship programs (parents)	
• Encourage development of independent projects (G/T teachers)	
• Encourage involvement in extracurricular clubs, team sports, theatrical performances	
• Evaluate one's own career interests through extracurricular activities, hobbies & work experiences (parents; G/T teachers)	
• Explore interests through interest & career inventories (teachers; parents)	
• Create and maintain Personal Transition Talent Portfolio (G/T teacher; LD teacher; parents)	
• Participate in an enrichment program based on students strengths and interests	

TABLE 2. Compensatory and Non-Compensatory Strategies for Promoting Student Academic Success in College

Strategies and Goals	Reference
Self-Regulation and Compensation Strategies	Pintrich (1995); Wolters (1998); Zimmerman & Martinez-Pons (1986, 1988; Schunk & Zimmerman (1994
Focus on further development of generalizable learning strategies and study skills	
• Self-evaluation; organizing material; transforming material (e.g., use flashcards); goal-setting and planning; seeking information; keeping records & monitoring; structuring environment; using self-consequating (i.e., self-rewards); rehearsing & memorizing; reviewing records	
Focus on development and internalization of a wide array of personalized compensation strategies of high practical utility	Baum (1984); Bursuck & Jayanthi (1993); Deshler et al. (1996); Hodge & Preston-Sabin (1997); McGuire et al. (1991); Schumaker & Deshler (1984); Reis et al. (2000); Shaw et al. (1991); Vaughan (1989); Vogel & Adelman (1993)

TABLE 2. Compensatory and Non-Compensatory Strategies for Promoting Student Academic Success in College (Cont'd)

- Environmental and social support and study skills: learn how to get around campus; where to go for the services; when it is appropriate to ask for assistance; ask professors for lecture notes; ask teaching assistants for help; use office hours to clarify assignments; ask others which professors are more understanding and more accommodating of LDs)

- Study strategies: learn library skills; develop personalized strategies for taking exams; learn ways to manage course materials (e.g., use color coded binders)

- Cognitive, memory & study strategies: time management; chunking material & time; monitoring assignments; using weekly & monthly organizers; using mnemonics; rehearsal; flashcards

- Note taking and written expression strategies: note taking; condensing notes; clustering material for exams; using graphical organizers in notes and with the help of computer programs; highlighting in notes; color coding notes & flashcards

  • Performance strategies for written expression, reading, comprehension, and mathematical processing: concept maps to organize material & see connections among concepts; SQ3R method (survey, question, read, recite, review); repeated readings if necessary; write one's own essays to ensure deepunderstanding of material; teach material to peers

185

TABLE 2. Compensatory and Non-Compensatory Strategies for Promoting Student Academic Success in College (Cont'd)

Continue exploring the benefits and utility functions of assistive technology	Bryant et al. (2002); Elkind, Black, & Murray (1996); Higgins & Raskind (1995); McNaughton et al (1993); Raskind & Higgins (1998); Vogel & Reder (1998)

- Seek instructors who use instructional adaptations (e.g., alternative responding modes & modified instructional materials) (student; help of peers)
- Reading & comprehension: speech synthesis programs; optical character recognition programs; variable speech tape recorders (depending on the nature & severity of LD) (student)
- Written language: word processing; word prediction software; spell checking; speech or voice recognition; outlining and concept mapping software programs s (student, LD support personnel)
- Mathematics: talking calculators; word problems (student, disability services)
- Personal organization & study skills: personal data managers (software or hand-held units such as Palm Pilot or iPAQ); free-form databases (i.e., computerized Post-It systems); electronic reference materials; web-based access; taking tests on a laptop (student, parents)

TABLE 2. Compensatory and Non-Compensatory Strategies for Promoting Student Academic Success in College (Cont'd)

Foster student's motivation • Enhance a student's regulation of his/her own motivation (parents; student) • Learn to use strategies designed to maintain effort for achieving goals: environmental (e.g., block out distractions); attention (focus attention); emotion (improve physical or emotional readiness to learn) (student; LD professionals) • Make flexible use of information processing, extrinsic, intrinsic strategies, or volitional strategies depending on the context/ situation (student) • Associate use of personalized compensation strategies with academic success and personal adjustment (parents, student) • Become aware that self-regulation helps promote success not only in academic but also in professional settings (parents, student) Explore interests in greater depth to help foster motivation (student, parents)	Corno (1989); Corno & Kanfer (1993); Deci & Ryan (1985); Kuhl (1984, 1992); Sansone et al . (1992); Pintrich & Schrauben (1992); Schunk & Zimmerman (1994); Wolters (1998)
Foster student's self-determination & advocacy skills • Disclose LD to access services and ensure access to accommodations (student) SEVERAL REPEATS) • Discuss one's own LD with an instructor during office hours (student) • Discuss the nature of the course requirements during office hours (student) • Request instructor in advance to accommodations for the course (student) • Make use of the course materials posted by the instructor online (student) Take note that distance learning courses may be particularly difficult for students with LD (student; parents; LD specialist)	American Council on Education (2000); Brinckerhoff et al. (2002); Crux (1991); Hodge & Preston-Sabin (1997); McGuire et al. (1991); McGuire & Madaus (1999); Phipps & Merisotis (1999).

TABLE 2. Compensatory and Non-Compensatory Strategies for Promoting Student Academic Success in College (Cont'd)

Accessing Accommodations Mandated by Law: Academic and Non-Academic Issues	
Strategies for learning in the college classroom (also: See Compensation Strategies) Request a note taker if applicable (student) • Request carbonless note paper for someone else to take notes • Tape record lectures, particularly if material is hard; request transcription services • Use laptop in class for taking notes, particularly a small laptop such as Alpha Smart • Request seating in front if instructor assigns seating in a lecture hall	Brinckerhoff et al. (2002); Crux (1991); Dalke (1993); Heyward (1998); Lewis & Farris (1999); McGuire et al. (1991); Reis et al. (2000)
Strategies for ensuring testing considerations • Upon approval of the college LD support program, request testing accommodations, in terms of: extended time on test; alternative testing location; format of the test; content of the test; mode of presentation (visual or auditory) • Discuss an alternative mode of demonstrating course mastery if applicable, such as doing a course project instead of the multiple-choice exam, or doing an oral presentation, etc.	Lewis & Farris (1998); Yost et al. (1994); Dalke (1993); King & Jarrow (1990); Patton & Polloway (1996); McGuire (1998)

TABLE 2. Compensatory and Non-Compensatory Strategies for Promoting Student Academic Success in College (Cont'd)

Strategies for learning outside the classroom.

- Make use of computer labs and ask qualified personnel for help, if needed, in terms of: word processing; completion of class assignments; accessing & using Internet resources
- Utilize assistive technology to enhance learning in computer labs and/ or the Disability Services Office (student)
- Access books on tape and e-texts via the college's resources or the Recording for the Blind & Dyslexic office, if applicable (student; LD specialist or support personnel)
- Utilize a full range of services offered by a comprehensive college LD support program
- Request a private dorm room to minimize distractions (student; parents)
- Access the help of tutors via the college's resources

Consideration of the college's programmatic requirements
- Request reduced course load and course substitution(s), if applicable (college's policy)
- Request priority registration (college's policy)
- Explore accommodations in the area of financial aid (college's policy)
- Request course substitution(s), if applicable
- Request accommodations in a field or clinical setting or internship in advance

Adler (1989); Bryant et al. (2002); Day & Edwards (1996); Jarrow (1997); Heyward (1998); McGuire & Madaus (1999); Raskind & Higgins (1998); Reis et al. (2000)

Brinckerhoff et al. (2002); Ganschow, Sparks, & Javorsky (1998);Wells & Hanebrink (1998)

189

TABLE 2. Compensatory and Non-Compensatory Strategies for Promoting Student Academic Success in College (Cont'd)

Social & Emotional Strategies

- Avoid unhealthy pressure for exclusivity of the top grades (parents)
- Encourage the student to stay resilient and persistent in the face of difficulties (parents)
- Nurture the student's talents and interests (parents; teachers)
- Foster the student's self-concept and self-esteem (parents; teachers)
- Help the student associate benefits of using compensation strategies with academic success and personal adjustment (parents; LD professionals/specialists)
- Reframe a learning disability in a positive sense (parents; LD specialists)

Foster the development of the student's personal characteristics (determination, resilience; integrity, work ethic, and social skills) (parents; LD specialists)

Talent Development Strategies

- Continue exploring and nurturing talents and abilities (parents)
- Work with a mentor on a project in an area of interest (student; professors)
- Help resolve conflicts among abilities and disabilities (parents; LD specialist)
- Select a major considering profile of strengths and weaknesses (student)
- Explore and nurture talents in other places (student; parents)
- Create a personal plan for academic success (student; LD specialist; parents)
- Work to resolve a conflict between abilities and disabilities (student; parents)

Baldwin (1999); Gerber et al. (1992); Gerber & Reiff (1991); Hebért & Olenchak (2000); Neihart, Reis, Robinson & Moon (2001); Reis et al. (2000); Reis et al. (1995); Silverman (1989); Tannenbaum & Baldwin (1983); Whitmore (1980)

Baum & Olenchak (2002); Baum et al. (1991); Hannah & Shore (1995); Hebért & Olenchak (2000); Olenchak (1994); Renzulli & Reis (1997); Reis et al. (2000); Silverman (1989)

Conclusions

Reflecting on almost two decades of research, Renzulli and Reis (1991) concluded that giftedness occurs in certain people, at certain times, and under certain circumstances, as does academic self-regulation, as certain students may choose to use certain self-regulatory methods depending on the context and the self-perceived reasons for using these methods. As with giftedness, making generalizations and creating lists of "typical traits" of gifted students or gifted students with LD is not informative, and may actually be damaging if these lists result in acceptable recognized traits, rather than an understanding of the multiple ways that talents and gifts may emerge. After decades of studying giftedness as traits, as something innate to the individual, something an individual either "has" or "doesn't have," a growing number of researchers have advocated for the broadened definition of giftedness, which presupposes greater emphasis on giftedness as a manifestation of gifted behavior, not as an aptitude (Gardner, 1993, 1999; Renzulli, 1978; 1991; Renzulli & Reis, 1997; Sternberg, 1995, 1997). A similar trend has gained momentum in the field of academic self-regulation. According to Perry (2002), the present trend has moved away from studying self-regulation as an aptitude, which traditionally resides in the internal characteristics that remain stable across situations and can be aggregated and generalized for certain groups. In contrast, current research efforts reflect a growing interest among researchers "in finding way to study this phenomenon in real contexts and in real time, in events rather than aptitudes" (Perry, 2002, p. 1). While making generalizations and noting patterns may provide some insights into the complex nature of a phenomenon such as giftedness or academic self-regulation, it should be noted that between-group generalizations should not mask the richness of the individual variation within groups, whether we are studying high-achieving or low-achieving students, or students with dual exceptionalities.

NOTES

1. Research for this report was supported under the Javits Act Program (Grant No. R206R00001) as administered by the Office of Educational Research and Improvement, U.S. Department of Education. Grantees undertaking such projects are encouraged to express freely their professional judgment. This report, therefore, does not necessarily represent positions or policies of the Government, and no official endorsement should be inferred.

REFERENCES

Adler, R. (1989). Library orientation: Intervention strategies for students with learning disabilities. *Journal of Postsecondary Education and Disability, 7*(2), 45–52.

American College Testing Program. (1989). *Preliminary technical manual of mental disorders* (3rd ed.). Washington, DC: Author.

American Council on Education. (2000). *Student issues.* [Online]. Available: www.acenet.edu/washington/distance_ed/2000/03march/distance_ed.html#top

Americans With Disabilities Act of 1990, 42 U.S.C. § 12101 *et seq.*

Anderson, P. L. (1993). Issues in assessment and diagnosis. In L. C. Brinckerhoff, S. F. Shaw, & J. M. McGuire (Eds.), *Promoting postsecondary education for students with learning disabilities* (pp. 89–136). Austin, TX: PRO-ED.

Aune, E. (1991). A transition model for post-secondary bound students with learning disabilities. *Learning Disabilities Research and Practice, 6,* 177–187.

Aune, E., & Ness, J. (1991). *Tools for transition: Preparing students with learning disabilities for postsecondary education.* Circle Pines, MN: American Guidance Service.

Baldwin. L. (1999). USA perspective. In A. Y. Baldwin & W. Vialle (Eds.), *The many faces of giftedness: Lifting the masks* (pp. 103–134). Albany, NY: Wadsworth.

Baldwin, A. Y., & Vialle, W. (1999) (Eds.), *The many faces of giftedness: Lifting the masks.* Albany, NY: Wadsworth.

Bandura, A. (1986*). Social foundations of thought and action: A social cognitive theory.* Englewood Cliffs, NJ: Prentice Hall.

Bandura, A. (1997). *Self-efficacy: The exercise of control.* New York: Freeman.

Barr, V., Hartman, R., & Spillane, S. (1998). Getting ready for college: Advising high school students with learning disabilities. *The Postsecondary LD Report.*

Barton, J. M., & Starnes, W. T. (1989). Identifying distinguishing characteristics of gifted and talented/learning disabled students. *Roeper Review, 12,* 23–29.

Baum, S. (1984). Meeting the needs of the learning disabled gifted students. *Roeper Review, 7,* 16–19.

Baum, S. (1988). An enrichment program for gifted learning-disabled students. *Gifted Child Quarterly, 32,* 226–230.

Baum, S. M., & Olenchak, F. R. (2002). The alphabet children: GT, ADHD, and more. *Exceptionality, 10*(2), 77–91.

Baum, S. M., & Owen, S. V. (1988). High ability/learning disabled students: How are they different? *Gifted Child Quarterly, 32*(3), 321–326.

Baum, S. M., Owen, S. V., & Dixon, J. (1991). *To be gifted and learning disabled: From definitions to practical intervention strategies.* Mansfield Center, CT: Creative Learning Press.

Baum, S. M., Owen, S. V., & Oreck, B. (1996). Talent beyond words: Identification of potential talent in dance and music in elementary students. *Gifted Child Quarterly, 40,* 93–102.

Baum, S. M., Renzulli, J. S., & Hebert, T. P. (1994). Reversing underachievement: Stories of *success. Educational Leadership, 52,* 48–53.

Borkowski, J. G., & Thorpe, P. K. (1994). Self-regulation and motivation: A life-span perspective. In D. H. Schunk & B. J. Zimmerman (Eds.), *Self-regulation of learning and performance: Issues and educational implications* (pp. 45–74). Hillsdale, NJ: Erlbaum.

Biller, E. (1985). *Understanding and guiding the career development of adolescents and young adults with learning disabilities.* Springfield, IL: Thomas.

Bouffard-Bouchard, T., Parent, S., & Larivee, S. (1993). Self-regulation on a concept-formation task among average and gifted students. *Journal of Experimental Child Psychology, 56,* 115–134.

Bragstad, B. J., & Stumpf, S. M. (1987). *A guidebook for teaching: Study skills and motivation* (2nd ed.). Newton, MA: Allyn & Bacon.

Bryant, B. R., Bryant, D. P., & Rieth, H. J. (2002). The use of assistive technology in postsecondary education. In L. C. Brinckerhoff, J. M. McGuire, & S. F. Shaw (Eds.),

Postsecondary Education and transition for students with learning disabilities (2nd ed.) (pp. 389–430). Austin, TX: PRO-ED.

Brinckerhoff, L. C. (1994). Developing effective self-advocacy skills in college-bound students with learning disabilities. *Intervention in School and Clinic, 29,* 229–237.

Brinckerhoff, L. C., McGuire, J. M., & Shaw, S. F. (Eds.) (2002). *Postsecondary education and transition for students with learning disabilities* (2nd ed.). Austin, TX: PRO-ED.

Brinckerhoff, L. C., Shaw, S. F., & McGuire, J. M. (Eds.). (1993). *Promoting postsecondary education for students with learning disabilities: A handbook for practitioners.* Austin, TX: PRO-ED.

Bursuck, W. D., & Jayanthi, M. (1993). Strategy instruction: Programming for independent study skills usage. In S. A. Vogel & P. B. Adelman (Eds.), *Success for college students with learning disabilities* (pp. 177–205). New York: Springer-Verlag.

Butler, D. L. (1998). A strategic content learning approach to promoting self-regulated learning by students with learning disabilities. In D. H. Schunk & B. J. Zimmerman (Eds.), *Self-regulated learning: From teaching to self-reflective practice* (pp. 160–183). New York: Guilford Press.

Corno, L. (1989). Self-regulated learning: A volitional analysis. In B. J. Zimmerman & D. H Schunk (Eds.), *Self-regulated learning and academic achievement: Theory, research, and practice* (pp. 111–141). New York: Sringer-Verlag.

Corno, L., & Kanfer, R. (1993). The role of volition in learning and performance. In L. Darling-Hammond (Ed.), *Review of research in education* (vol. 19, pp. 301–341). Washington, DC: American Educational Research Association.

Cowen, S. (1993). Transition planning for LD college-bound students. In S. A. Vogel & P. B. Adelman (Eds.), *Success for college students with learning disabilities* (pp. 39–56). New York: Springer-Verlag.

Creswell, J. W. (1994). *Research design: Qualitative and quantitative approaches.* Thousand Oaks, CA: Sage.

Crux, S. C. (1991). *Learning strategies for adults: Compensations for learning disabilities.* Middletown, OH: Wall & Emerson.

Dalke, C. (1993). Programming for independent study skills usage. In S. S. Vogel and P. B. Adelman (Eds.), *Success for college students with learning disabilities* (pp. 57–80). New York: Springer-Verlag.

Dalke, C., & Howard, D. (1994). *Life works: A transition program for high school students.* East Moline, IL: LinguiSystems.

Daniels, P. R. (1983). *Teaching the learning-disabled/gifted child.* Rockville, MD: Aspen.

Daniels, P. R. (1986). Educator urges schools to identify plan for gifted/learning disabled. *Hilltop Spectrum, 4*(2), 1–6.

Day, S. L., & Edwards, B. J. (1996). Assistive technology for postsecondary students with learning disabilities. *Journal of Learning Disabilities, 29,* 486–493.

Deci, E. L., & Ryan, R. M. (1985). *Intrinsic motivation and self-determinism in human motivation.* New York: Plenum Press.

Deshler, D. D., Ellis, E. S., & Lenz, B. K. (1996). *Teaching adolescents with learning disabilities: Strategies and methods* (2nd ed.). Denver, CO: Love.

DuChossois, G., & Stein, E. (1992). *Choosing the right college: A step-by-step system to aid the students with learning disabilities in selecting the suitable college for them.* New York: New York University.

Eaton, H. (1996). *How students with learning disabilities can make the transition form high school to college.* Santa Barbara, CA: Excel Publishing.

Eaton, H., & Coull, L. (1998). *Transitions to postsecondary learning: Self-advocacy handbook.* Vancouver, BC: Eaton Coull Learning Group.

Elkind, J., Black, M. S., & Murray, C. (1996). Computer based compensation of adult reading disabilities. *Annals of Dyslexia, 46,* 159–186.

Ellis, E. S. (1990). What's so strategic about teaching teachers to teach strategies? *Teacher Education and Special Education, 13,* 56–62.

Field, S., & Hoffman, A. (1996). Increasing the ability of educators to support youth and self-determination. In L. E. Powers, G. H. S Singer, & J. Sowers (Eds.), *Promoting self-competence in children and youth with disabilities: On the road to autonomy* (pp. 171–187). Baltimore: Brookes.

Fox, L. H., Brody, L., & Tobin, D. (1983). *Learning-disabled/gifted children: Identification and programming.* Baltimore: University Park Press.

Ganschow, L., Sparks, R., & Javorsky, J. (1998). Foreign language learning difficulties: An historical perspective. *Journal of Learning Disabilities, 31*(3), 248–258.

Gardner, H. (1983). *Frames of mind: The theory of multiple intelligences.* New York: Basic Books.

Gardner, H. (1993). *Multiple intelligences: The theory in practice.* New York: Basic Books.

Gardner, H. (1999). *Intelligence reframed: Multiple intelligences for the 21st century.* New York: Basic Books.

Garner, R. (1990). When children and adults do not use learning strategies. *Review of Educational Research, 60,* 517–530.

Gerber, P. J., Ginsberg, R., & Reiff, H. B. (1992). Identifying alterable patterns in employment success for highly successful adults with learning disabilities. *Journal of Learning Disabilities, 25,* 475–487.

Gerber, P. J., & Reiff, H. B. (1991). *Speaking for themselves: Ethnographic interviews with adults with learning disabilities.* Ann Arbor, MI: University of Michigan Press.

Hannah, C. L., & Shore, B. M. (1995). Metacognition and high intellectual ability: insights from the study of learning-disabled gifted students. *Gifted Child Quarterly, 39*(2), 95–109.

Hebért, T. P., & Olenchak, F. R. (2000). Mentors for gifted underachieving males: Developing potential and realizing promise. *Gifted Child Quarterly, 44,* 170–181.

Henderson, C. (1999). *College freshmen with disabilities.* Washington, DC: American Council on Education, HEATH Resource Center.

Heyward, S. (1998). *Disability and higher education: Guidance for Section 504 and ADA compliance.* Horsham, PA: LRP Publications.

Higgins, E. L., & Raskind, M. H. (1995). An investigation of the compensatory effectiveness of speech recognition on the written composition performance of postsecondary students with learning disabilities. *Learning Disability Quarterly, 18,* 159–174.

Hodge, B. M., & Preston-Sabin, J. (1997) (Eds.). *Accommodations—or just good teaching? Strategies for teaching college students with disabilities.* Westport, CT: Praeger.

Hoover, E. (2002, July 26). Removing the "scarlet letter." *The Chronicle of Higher Education,* p. A41–42.

Individuals with Disabilities Education Act Amendments of 1997, 20 U.S.C. §1400 et seq.

Jacobson, V. (1984). *The gifted learning disabled.* Calumer, IN: Purdue University. (ERIC Document Reproduction Service No. ED 254 981)

Jarrow, J. E. (1997). *Higher education and the LDA: Issues and perspectives.* Columbus, OH: Disability Access Information and Support.

King, W., & Jarrow, J. (1990). *Testing accommodations for students with disabilities.* Columbus, OH: AHEAD.

Kline, R. B. (1998). *Principles and practice of structural equation modeling.* New York: Guilford.

Krouse, J. H., & Krouse, H. J. (1981). Toward a multimodal theory of academic achievement. *Educational Psychologist, 16,* 151–164.

Koehler, M., & Kravets, M. (1998). *Counseling secondary students with learning disabilities.* Paramas, NJ: Prentice Hall.

Kuhl. J. (1984). Volitional aspects of achievement motivation and learned helplessness: Toward a comprehensive theory of action control. In B. Maher & W. Maher

(Eds.), *Progress in experimental personality research* (vol. 13, pp. 99–171). New York: Academic Press.

Kuhl, J. (1992). A theory of self-regulation: Action versus state orientation, self-discrimination, and some applications. *Applied Psychology: An International Review, 41,* 97–129.

Latham, P. S., & Latham, P. H. (1998). Legal issues regarding AD/HD at the postsecondary level: Implications for service providers. In P. Quinn & A. McGormick (Eds.), *Re-thinking AD/HD: A guide to fostering success in students with AD/HD at the college level* (pp. 102–107). Bethesda, MD: Advantage Books.

Lewis, L., & Farris, E. (1999). *An institutional perspective on students with disabilities in postsecondary education* (NCES 1999–046). Washington, DC: U. S. Department of Education, Office of Educational Research and Improvement.

Maker, C. J. (1978). *The self-perceptions of successful handicapped scientists.* (Grant No. G00–7701[905]). Washington, DC: U.S. Department of Health, Education, and Welfare, Office of Education, Bureau of the Education for the Handicapped.

Mangrum, C. T., & Strichart, S. (1997). *Peterson's colleges with programs for students with learning disabilities or attention-deficit disorders.* Princeton, NJ: Peterson's.

McGuire, J. M. (1998). Educational accommodations: A university administrator's view. In M. Gordon & S. Keiser (Eds.), *Accommodations in higher education under the Americans With Disabilities Act* (ADA) (pp. 20–45). New York: Guilford Press.

McGuire, J. M., Hall, D., & Litt, A. V. (1991). A field-based study of the direct service needs of college students with learning disabilities. *Journal of College Student Development, 32,* 101–108.

McGuire, J. M., & Madaus, J. W. (1999). *The University of Connecticut Program for College Students with Learning Disabilities (UPLD): 1988–1999.* Storrs, CT: Postsecondary Education Disability Unit, Neag School of Education.

McGuire, J. M., & Shaw, S. F. (1987). A decision-making process for the college-bound student. Matching learner, institution, and support program. *Learning Disability Quarterly, 10*(2), 106–111.

McNaughton, D., Hughes, C., & Clark, K. (1993). *An investigation of the effect of five writing conditions on the spelling performance of college students with disabilities.* Paper presented at the 30th international conference of the Learning Disability Association of America, San Francisco.

Neihardt, M., Reis, S. M., Robinson, N., & Moon, S. M. (Eds.). (2001). *The social and emotional development of gifted children. What do we know?* Waco, TX: Prufrock Press.

Nolen, S. B., & Flaladyna, T. M. (1990). Personal and environmental influences on students' beliefs about effective study strategies. *Contemporary Educational Psychology, 15,* 116–130.

Olenchak, F. R. (1994). Talent development: Accommodating the social and emotional needs of secondary gifted/learning-disabled students. *Journal of Secondary Gifted Education, 5,* 40–52.

Olenchak, F. R. (1995). Effects of enrichment on gifted/learning-disabled students. *Journal for the Education of the Gifted, 18,* 385–399.

Patton, J., & Dunn, C. (1998). *Transition from school to young adulthood.* Austin, TX: PRO-ED.

Patton, J. R., & Polloway, E. A. (1996) (Eds.). *Learning disabilities: The challenges of adulthood.* Austin, TX: PRO-ED.

Perry, N. E. (2002). Introduction: Using qualitative methods to enrich understanding of self-regulated learning. *Educational Psychologist, 37*(1), 1–4.

Phipps, R., & Merisotis, S. J. (1999). *What's the difference? A review of contemporary research on the effectiveness of distance learning in higher education.* Washington, DC: Institute for Higher Education Policy. Available on-line: www.ihep.com/difference.pdf

Pintrich, P. R. (1995). Understanding self-regulated learning. In R. J. Menges & M. D. Svinicki (Eds.), *New directions for teaching and learning* (vol. 63, pp. 3–12). San Francisco, CA: Jossey-Bass.

Pintrich, P. R., Anderman, E. M., & Klobukar, C. (1994). Intraindividual differences in motivation and cognition in students with and without learning disabilities. *Journal of Learning Disabilities, 27,* 360–370.

Pintrich, P. R., & De Groot, E. (1990). Motivational and self-regulated components of classroom academic performance. *Journal of Educational Psychology, 82,* 33–40.

Pintrich, P. R., & Garcia, T. (1991). Students' goal orientation and self-regulation in the college classroom. *Advances in Motivation And Achievement, 7,* 371–402.

Pintrich, P. R., Anderman, E. M., & Klobukar, C. (1994). Intraindividual differences in motivation and cognition in students with and without learning disabilities. *Journal of Learning Disabilities, 27,* 360–370.

Pintrich, P. R., & Schrauben, B. (1992). Students' motivational beliefs and their cognitive engagement in classroom tasks. In D. Schunk & J. Meece (Eds.), *Student perceptions in the classroom: Causes and consequences* (pp. 149–183). Hillsdale, NJ: Erlbaum.

Policastro, M. M. (1993). Assessing and developing metacognitive attributes in college students with learning disabilities. In S. A. Vogel & P. B. Adelman (Eds.), *Success for college students with learning disabilities* (pp. 151–176). New York: Springer-Verlag.

Pressley, M., & McGormick, C. B. (1995). *Advanced educational psychology for educators, researchers, and policymakers.* New York: Harper Collins.

Price, L. (1988). Support groups work! *Journal of Counseling and Human Services Professions, 2,* 35–46.

Purcell, J. H., & Renzulli, J. S. (1998). *Total talent portfolio: A systematic plan to identify and nurture gifts and talents.* Mansfield, CT: Creative Learning Press.

Raskind, M., & Higgins, E. (1998). Assistive technology for postsecondary students with learning disabilities: An overview. *Journal of Learning Disabilities, 31*(1), 27–40.

Reis, S. M., Neu, T. W., & McGuire, J. M. (1995). *Talents in two places: Case studies of high ability students with learning disabilities who have achieved.* Research monograph No 95114, Storrs, CT: The National Research Center on the Gifted and Talented.

Reis, S. M., McGuire, J. M., & Neu, T. W. (2000). Compensation strategies used by high ability students with learning disabilities. *Gifted Child Quarterly, 44*(2), 123–134.

Renzulli, J. S. (1977). *The Enrichment Triad Model: A guide for developing defensible programs for the gifted and talented.* Mansfield Center, CT: Creative Learning Press.

Renzulli, J. S. (1978). What makes giftedness? *Phi Delta Kappan, 60*(3), 180–184, 261.

Renzulli, J. S. (1986). The three-ring conception of giftedness: A developmental model for creative productivity. In R. J. Sternberg & J. E. Davidson (Eds.), *Conceptions of Giftedness* (pp. 53–92). New York: Cambridge University Press.

Renzulli, J. S., & Reis, S. M. (1991). The reform movement and the quiet crisis in gifted education. *Gifted Child Quarterly, 35*(1), 26–35.

Renzulli, J. S., & Reis, S. M. (1997). *The Schoolwide Enrichment Model: A how-to guide to educational excellence.* Mansfield, CT: Creative Learning Press.

Rosner, S. L., & Seymour, J. (1983). The gifted child with a learning disability: Clinical evidence. In L. H. Fox, L. Brody & D. Tobin (Eds.), *Learning-disabled/gifted children: Identification and programming* (p. 77–97). Baltimore, MD: University Park.

Ruban, L. M. (2000). Patterns of self-regulated learning and academic achievement among university students with and without learning disabilities (Doctoral Dissertation, University of Connecticut, 2000). *Dissertation Abstracts International* (UMI No. TX 5-179-576)

Ruban, L. M., McCoach, D. B., McGuire, J. M., & Reis, S. M. (in press). The differential impact of self-regulatory methods on academic achievement among university students with and without learning disabilities. *Journal of Learning Disabilities.*

Ruban, L. M., & Reis, S. M. (1999). *Learning Strategies and Study Skills survey.* Unpublished instrument, University of Connecticut, Storrs.

Sansone, C., Weir, C., Harpster, L., & Morgan, C. (1992). Once a boring task always a boring task? Interest as a self-regulatory mechanism. *Journal of Personality and Social Psychology, 63,* 379–390.

Schiff, M., Kaufman, A. S., & Kaufman, N. L. (1981). Scatter analysis of WISC-R profiles for learning disabled children with superior intelligence. *Journal of Learning Disabilities, 14*(7), 400–404.

Schmeck, R., Ribich, F., Ramanaiha, N. (1977). Development of a self-report inventory for assessing individual differences in learning process. *Applied Psychological Measurement, 1,* 413–431.

Schumaker, J. B., Deshler, D. D. (1984). Setting demand variables: A major factor in program planning for the LD adolescent. *Topics in language disorders, 4*(2), 22–40.

Schunk, D. H., & Zimmerman, B. J. (Eds.). (1994). *Self-regulation of learning and performance: Issues and educational implications* (pp. 75–99). Hillsdale, NJ: Erlbaum.

Schunk, D. H., & Zimmerman, B. J. (Eds.). (1998). *Self-regulated learning: From teaching to self-reflective practice.* New York: Guilford.

Silverman, L. K. (1989). Invisible gifts, invisible handicaps. *Roper Review, 12*(1), 37–42.

Shaw, S. F., Brinckerhoff, L. C., Kistler, J. K., & McGuire, J. M. (1991). Preparing students with learning disabilities for postsecondary education: Issues and future needs. *Learning Disabilities: A Multidisciplinary Journal, 2,* 21–26.

Shore, B. M., & Dover, A. C. (1987). Metacognition, intelligence and giftedness. *Gifted Child Quarterly, 31*(1), 37–39.

Sternberg, R. J. (1981). A componential theory of intellectual giftedness. *Gifted Child Quarterly, 25*(2), 86–93.

Sternberg, R. J. (1995). *A triarchic approach to giftedness. Roeper Review, 20,* 204–210.

Sternberg, R. J. (1997). What does it mean to be smart? *Educational Leadership, 54,* 20–24.

Sternberg, R. J., & Davidson, J. E. (Eds.). (1986). *Conceptions of giftedness.* New York: Cambridge University Press.

Strauss, A. L., & Corbin, J. (1990). *Basics of qualitative research.* Newbury Park, CA: Sage Publications.

Stuss, D. T., & Benson, D. F. (1986). *The frontal lobes.* New York: Raven Press.

Suter, D. P., & Wolf, J. S. (1987). Issues in the identification and programming of the gifted/learning disabled child. *Journal for the Education of the Gifted 10,* 227–237.

Tabachnick, B. G., Fidell, L. S. (2001). *Using multivariate statistics* (4th ed.). Boston: Allyn & Bacon.

Tannebaum, A. J., & Baldwin, L. J. (1983). Giftedness and learning disability: A paradoxical combination. In L. H. Fox, L. Brody, & D. Tobin (Eds.), *Learning disabled/gifted children* (pp. 11–36). Baltimore: University Park Press.

Tessler, L. (1997, September/October). How college students with learning disabilities can advocate for themselves. *LDA Newsbriefs.*

Vermetten, Y. J., Vermunt, J. D., & Lodewijks, H. G. (1999). A longitudinal perspective on learning strategies in higher education: Different viewpoints towards development. *British Journal of Educational Psychology, 69,* 221–242.

Vogel, S. (1997). *College students with leaning disabilities: A handbook.* (Available from ADA bookstore, 4156 Library Road, Pittsburg, PA, 15234, 412/341–1515)

Vogel, S. A., & Adelman, P. B. (1993) (Eds.). *Success for college students with learning disabilities.* New York: Springer-Verlag.

Vogel, S. A., & Reder, S. (1998). *Learning disabilities, literacy, and adult education.* Baltimore: Brookes.

Wang, M. C., & Palinsar, A. S. (1989). Teaching students to assume an active role in their learning. In M. C. Reynolds (Ed.), *Knowledge base for the beginning teacher* (pp. 71–84). Elmsford, NY: Pergamon.

Wehman, P. (1992). *Life beyond the classroom: Transition strategies for young people with disabilities.* Baltimore: Brookes.

Wells, S., & Hanebrink, S. (1998). Auxiliary aids, academic adjustments, and reasonable accommodations. In S. Scott, S. Wells, & S. Hanebrink (Eds.), *Educating college students with disabilities: What academic and fieldwork educators need to know* (pp. 37–49). Bethesda, MD: American Occupational Therapy Association.

Whitmore, J. (1980). *Giftedness, conflict, and underachievement.* Boston, MA: Allyn & Bacon.

Whitmore, J. R., & Maker, J. (1985). *Intellectual giftedness in disabled persons.* Rockville, MD: Aspen Publications.

Wilson, G. L. (1994). Self-advocacy skills. In C. A. Michaels (Ed.), *Transition strategies for persons with learning disabilities* (pp. 153–184). San Diego, CA: Singular.

Wolters, C. A. (1998). Self-regulated learning and college students' regulation of their motivation. *Journal of Educational Psychology, 90*(2), 224–235.

Wong, B. Y., & Jones, W. (1992). Increasing metacomprehension in learning disabled and normally achieving students through self-questioning training. *Learning Disability Quarterly, 5,* 228–238.

Yost, D., Shaw, S., Cullen, J., & Bigai, S. (1994). Practices and attitudes of postsecondary LD service providers in North America. *Journal of Learning Disabilities, 27,* 631–640.

Zimmerman, B. J. (1989). A social cognitive view of self-regulated academic learning. *Journal of Educational Psychology, 81,* 329–339.

Zimmerman, B. J. (1990). Self-regulated academic learning and achievement: The emergence of a social cognitive perspective. *Educational Psychology Review, 2,* 173–201.

Zimmerman, B. J. (1998a). Academic studying and the development of personal skill: A self-regulatory perspective. *Educational Psychologist, 33*(2/3), 73–86.

Zimmerman, B. J. (1998b). Developing self-fulfilling cycles of academic regulation: An analysis of exemplary instructional models. In D. H. Schunk & B. J. Zimmerman (Eds.), *Developing self-regulated learners: From teaching to self-reflective practice* (pp. 1–19). New York: Guilford Press.

Zimmerman, B. J., & Martinez-Pons, M. (1986). Development of a structured interview for assessing student use of self-regulated learning strategies. *American Educational Research Journal, 23,* 614–628.

Zimmerman, B. J., & Martinez-Pons, M. (1988). Construct validation of a strategy model of student self-regulated learning. *Journal of Educational Psychology, 80*(3), 284–290.

Zimmerman, B. J., & Martinez-Pons, M. (1990). Student differences in self-regulated learning: Relating grade, sex, and giftedness to self-efficacy and strategy use. *Journal of Educational Psychology, 82,* 51–59.

Zimmerman, B. J., & Paulsen, A. S. (1995). Self-monitoring during collegiate studying: An invaluable tool for academic self-regulation. In P. R. Pintrich (Ed.), *Understanding self-regulated learning* (pp. 13–28). San Francisco, CA: Jossey-Bass.

Zimmerman, B. J., & Schunk, D. H. (Eds.). (1989). *Self-regulated learning and academic achievement: Theory, research, and practice.* New York: Springer-Verlag.

Chapter 9

SUMMONING UP THE SPIRITS FROM THE VAST DEEP: LD AND GIFTEDNESS IN HISTORIC PERSONS[1]

P.G. Aaron
Indiana State University

R. Malatesha Joshi
Emily S. Ocker
Texas A&M University

Abstract

In this chapter, we present evidence gleaned from a variety of sources to show that some talented individuals from the historic past had learning disabilities (LD). The coexistence of talent and LD ceases to be a paradox if the ability to decode printed words and spell them is considered to be a skill that is independent of higher-level cognitive functions such as linguistic comprehension. We call this proposition the Component model of the reading process. After presenting the rationale of the Component model, we examine relevant information available on six famous historic persons—two inventors, two artists, and two literary figures—for evidence of LD. The practical implications of this investigation are that teachers should be careful not to generalize and evaluate intellectual abilities of individuals on the basis of their performances on skill-based tasks such as word recognition, spelling, and grammar.

INTRODUCTION

Two questions are generally raised when it is claimed that some gifted historic individuals had learning disabilities (LD, hereafter). One is how an individual can be gifted and at the same time have LD; the second question is how we can assert that individuals who are no longer living, a situation that precludes firsthand evaluation, had LD. Before presenting evidence for concluding that some famous individuals had LD, we will address these two questions briefly.

QUESTION 1:
How Can Giftedness and LD Co-Exist?

Even though several definitions of LD are available, they all have one thing in common: All definitions of LD are built on the basis of the unexpected nature of the condition, a paradoxical phenomenon when the general intellectual ability of the individual who has LD is taken into consideration. In fact, many years ago, LD was referred to as "unexpected reading failure" (Symmes & Rapoport, 1972).

The unexpected nature of LD becomes understandable when the component nature of the reading process is taken into account. In recent years, the concept of "components" has been studied in detail and is found to be useful in understanding the development and functioning of cognitive systems (Newell & Simon, 1972; Sternberg, 1977). According to Sternberg (1984), "A component is an *elementary* information process that operates upon internal representations of objects or symbols" (p. 164). A defining characteristic of a component is that, being elementary, it is independent of other cognitive processes. The independent nature of the component also means that a component within a cognitive system can fail to develop normally while other components within the same cognitive system could progress unhindered. As Sternberg (1984) notes, retardation appears to derive largely from the inadequate functioning of componential subsystems. The independent nature of cognitive components is well illustrated by studies of idiot savants who can display extraordinary skill in music, computation, or art but are extremely deficient in general intelligence (O'Connor, N. & Hermelin, B. (1987, 1989).

The component model was applied to reading by Gough & Tunmer, (1986) and was used successfully in diagnosis of reading disabilities and their remediation by Aaron & Joshi (1992) and Aaron & Kotva, (1999). According to Gough and Tunmer (1986), reading comprehension (RC) is the product of linguistic comprehension (LC) and decoding (DC). Linguistic comprehension can be evaluated by tests of listening comprehension whereas decoding skill could be assessed by tests of word attack. The componential nature of the reading process can be expressed in the form of the formula, $RC = LC \times DC$.
It follows then that if listening comprehension is 0, then reading comprehension is also 0; conversely, if decoding skill is 0, then reading comprehension is also 0.

Evidence for the componential nature of the reading process comes from neuropsychology, developmental psychology, experimental psychology, and genetic studies. As far back as 1891, Dejerine, a French physician, reported the case of an elderly stroke patient who had lost his reading ability even though his listening comprehension and other cognitive abilities were intact. Psychological data supporting the bi-componential nature of reading comes from studies initiated by Marshall and Newcombe (1966, 1973) who described two different forms of reading failure in literate adults who lost their ability to read isolated words correctly. The investigators labeled the two forms of reading disorders as "deep dyslexia" and "surface dyslexia." Individuals with deep dyslexia committed paralexic errors by reading words such as *father* and *shut* as *dad* and *close* whereas individuals with surface dyslexia read the word *sale* as *sally* and *listen* as *liston*. When asked what these words meant, surface dyslexics would say that *sale* is the name of a girl and *listen* is the name of the boxer. These two types of neurological impairment, therefore, show that decoding and comprehension can be affected independently.

Developmental studies also show that comprehension and decoding can be affected independent of each other. Frith and Snowling (1983) have shown that children with dyslexia comprehend much better than they can read aloud, and some autistic children with hyperlexic symptoms can decode print with considerable skill but comprehend very poorly what they have read.

In an experimental investigation, Jackson and McClelland (1979) studied undergraduate students and found that comprehension ability and reaction time in a letter-matching task accounted for nearly all of the variance seen in reading ability. Similar results were obtained and by Palmer, McCleod, Hunt, and Davidson (1985).

Genetic studies also support the notion that comprehension and pronunciation skills are independent. DeFries, Fulker, and La Buda (1987) found significant heritability for recognition, spelling, and WISC-R digit span but not for reading comprehension.

Available evidence, therefore, strongly suggests that reading is a multi-componential process with decoding and comprehension being the two major components. As noted earlier, since components are independent of each other, word recognition skill and comprehension skill can follow independent courses of development. As a result, it is not surprising that there are individuals who are above average in intelligence or even gifted but have poor decoding and word recognition skills because the skills component has failed to develop normally whereas the comprehension component has progressed superbly.

A majority of children identified as having LD have reading difficulties. The core deficit of RD appears to be in the phonological processing domain of language (Stanovich, 1988). While all beginning readers invest a good deal of attention in decoding the printed word, skilled readers decode words rapidly and almost effortlessly. Most of the attention of the skilled reader, therefore, can be directed towards comprehending the written text. This transition from beginning reader to skilled reader is described as progress from "controlled" to "automatic" processing of information. It must also be noted that when attention is focused almost entirely on decoding, fewer processing resources are available for comprehension. When the decoding requirement is eliminated, comprehension becomes the main focus of attention. This is the reason why an individual with LD can listen and comprehend much better than read and understand text. In fact, many of the gifted individuals discussed in this chapter were articulate and creative with language. This dissociation between a skills component and the comprehension component also explains how historical figures could have achieved remarkable success in areas that involve language even if they had LD.

The first question relating to LD and giftedness—how these two could go together—can therefore be explained within the framework of the Component model, particularly when LD is seen as a result of a less than optimally functioning skills component and giftedness as the result of a flourishing compensatory higher-level cognitive component.

QUESTION 2:
How Can LD Be Diagnosed in Deceased Individuals?

The second question raises the issue of how we can diagnose LD in deceased individuals when this task is difficult even in living individuals (Adelman & Adelman, 1987). Understandably, any judgment made about historic persons has to be inferential based upon the individual's past performance and any other evidence they have left behind. The best evidence that is indicative of LD is any record of academic difficulties the person experienced in school. Any evidence to the contrary, of course, will decidedly rule out the possibility that the historic person had LD. Such is the case of Albert Einstein, whose mother wrote to his uncle, more than once, that young Albert once again stood on top of his class (Thomas, 2000).

Admittedly, difficulties at school can be caused by extraneous factors such as poor motivation, inadequate opportunities for learning, or sensory impairment. The possibility of any of these factors being the source of learning problems must be dealt with and eliminated. Although evidence presented in this chapter cannot claim to be comprehensive, what is presented here, for the most part, is based on examination of the original material pertaining to the historic individuals.

THE RATIONALE FOR THE COMPONENT MODEL-BASED INVESTIGATION OF LD.

Inferences made about LD in the historically gifted individuals rely on four sources of information.
I. Biographical information
    1. School records
    2. Self-reports
    3. Descriptive accounts by biographers
II. Cognitive characteristics

1. Written spelling errors
2. Errors of morphology and syntax in written language
3. Deficits in sequential processing of information
4. Superior ability in simultaneous processing of information

III. Neuropsychological characteristics
   1. Evidence of atypical cerebral organization
   2. Handedness

IV. Biological characteristics
   1. Genetic predisposition to reading disability
   2. Immune system disorders.

I. Biographical Information

Biographical information includes information from records, self-reports, and descriptions provided by biographers.

1. School records: These provide relatively objective data and, therefore, present reliable information about the person's academic performance. In combination with information regarding environmental factors, school records can be of tremendous help in the diagnosis of LD.

2. Self-reports: Unsolicited self-disclosures regarding one's reading and learning difficulties are sometimes recorded by individuals in their personal diaries. Occasionally, their correspondences also contain reference to learning problems.

3. Descriptive accounts by biographers: Information provided by biographers adds to the total picture of cognitive competencies of historical individuals. However, caution should be exercised in using this source of information as unequivocal evidence of learning disability because biographers have been known to embellish their portrayal of the personalities they write about.

II. Cognitive Characteristics

Researchers who try to track down the cause of difficulties in learning to read by children in general and dyslexics in particular are in agreement that phonological deficit is at the heart of the reading problem (Siegel, 1992; Stanovich, 1988). The phonological core deficit often manifests itself in the form of difficulties in converting graphemes into phonemes (decoding) as well as difficulties in converting phonemes into graphemes (spelling). Decoding problems also slow down the processing speed of the reader.

1. Written spelling errors: Spelling and reading could be considered as two sides of the same coin since both require a mastery of the grapheme–phoneme relationship. It is not surprising, therefore, that poor readers are also poor spellers (Bryant & Bradley, 1980; Cook, 1981). Joshi & Aaron (1991) have presented data to show that the processes that underlie reading by

decoding and spelling are likely to be the same. Poor spelling is, therefore, a marker for LD.

2. Errors of morphology and syntax in written language: Omissions or substitutions of suffixes and prefixes of words are representative of morphological errors. Since these grammatical elements lack content and have to be processed by phonological mechanisms, rather than semantic mechanisms, such errors can be viewed as yet another manifestation of phonological deficit. There is experimental evidence to show that in reading, grammatical morphemes and lexical morphemes are processed independently by separate mechanisms (Gibson & Guinett, 1971). On the basis of observations made on patients with Broca's aphasia, Kean (1977) has argued that the agrammatical errors committed by these patients are the result of their difficulties in processing phonological features. Gardner, Denes, & Zurif (1975) have also shown that while Broca's aphasics can read substantive picturable words relatively well, they commit many errors while reading nonpicturable linguistic elements such as function words, which probably have to be handled by phonological mechanisms.

3. Deficits in sequential processing of information: A number of studies show that poor readers, in general, experience difficulties in processing information that is sequentially presented (Denckla & Rudel, 1976; Kirby & Robinson, 1987). Tasks that require sequential processing include decoding, spelling, carrying out arithmetic operations, remembering dates, and recalling verbal information that is presented over time. Syntactical integrity of a sentence also involves the accurate ordering of words in the sentence. Neuropsychological studies show that patients with Broca's aphasia also experience difficulty in processing information that is sequentially presented (Benson, 1977).

4. Superior ability in simultaneous processing of information: It has been frequently observed that in dyslexic subjects, poor sequential skills are compensated for by above-average simultaneous information-processing skills (Aaron, 1978; Das, Kirby, & Jarman, 1979; Kirby & Robinson, 1987). Many researchers have reported that children with reading disability have intact or even superior spatial–holistic processing skills (Benton, 1984; Fisher & Frankfutter, 1977). On the basis of her experimental studies, (Witelson, 1977) concluded that in tasks that require the use of both simultaneous and successive processing, dyslexics tend to use spatial–holistic strategies more than normally achieving children do.

This may be the reason why many dyslexic children continue to reverse words in their writing because when they read and write, they tend to process words as picture gestalts. Since pictures are usually processed without regard to directionality, dyslexic children tend to reverse words in a random fashion. Dyslexic children are also reported to have superior orthographic skills as compared to their phonological skills (Siegel, Share, & Geva, 1999). An association between superior visual–artistic skills and a tendency to reverse words in writing is not unexpected.

III. Neuropsychological Characteristics

1. Evidence of atypical cerebral organization: Bradshaw and Nettleton (1981), who have reviewed the extensive research in the area of hemispheric specialization, note that the left hemisphere tends to process information sequentially over time, whereas the right hemisphere tends to process information holistically, and simultaneously. It has been reported that an excessive dependency on one strategy at the expense of the other leads to processing deficits such as dyslexia (Kershner, 1977; Witelson, 1977). An association between poor lateralization of cerebral functions and reading disability has been suggested by Bryden (1982), who has reviewed a number of related studies. In historical figures, the presence of atypical cerebral organization could be inferred through examining the sequel of cerebro–vascular accidents. In the general population, stroke in Broca's area produces aphasic symptoms in addition to spasticity of the right hand. If language is diffusely organized, such a language deficit may not be associated with spasticity of the right hand.

2. Handedness: The relationship between left-handedness and cerebral lateralization is quite complex. Nevertheless, it appears that "left handers are less likely to demonstrate clear-cut cerebral organization than right handers" (Bryden, 1982, p. 173). A significant relationship between left-handedness and reading difficulties has been reported by many investigators (Annett, 1981; Geschwind & Behan, 1982). These claims, however, have not gained universal acceptance.

IV. Biological Characteristics

1. Genetic predisposition to reading disability: The genetic etiology of reading disability has been well established through projects such as the Colorado Reading Project (DeFries & Alarcon, 1996) and the Colorado Learning Disabilities Research (DeFries et al, 1997). Even though a familial tendency toward disabilities has been observed by early investigators such as Hinshelwood and Orton, the exact mechanisms are not yet clearly understood. In the present context, the presence of learning difficulties in immediate members of the family can add to the evidence of presence of LD in historic figures.

2. Immune system disorders: After surveying nearly 1,500 individuals, Geschwind and Behan (1982) and Geschwind (1983) have reported a positive familial clustering of learning disabilities, immune system disorders, and left-handedness. These investigators attributed this association to excessive testosterone, which may have a retarding effect on the maturation of the left cerebral hemisphere and may have a similar effect on the thymus, an important component of the immune system.

CASE STUDIES OF HISTORICAL PERSONS

Leonardo da Vinci

Leonardo da Vinci was born out of wedlock on April 15, 1452, in the small village of Vinci, which lies in the Tuscan valley of Italy, about 20 miles north of Florence. Information regarding da Vinci's birth is contained in a tax return statement submitted by his grandfather, the notary Ser Antonio da Vinci and is preserved along with state documents in Florence (Payne, 1978). According to the document, da Vinci was baptized by a local priest in a ceremony attended by nine family friends. A tax return filed by da Vinci's father, Ser Piero, includes young da Vinci's name as a member of the household. It is, therefore, reasonable to assume that da Vinci was accepted and raised by his father's family. When he was about 12 years old, da Vinci was sent to work as an apprentice under Verrochio, a talented sculptor, goldsmith, and painter.

Da Vinci came from a family of generations of notaries. In Renaissance Italy, notaries functioned much like lawyers and acted as legal advisers to ecclesiastical institutions and wealthy citizens. In contrast, artists of that period, unless they had risen to fame, were considered mere craftsmen. Given these facts, the question why da Vinci, raised by a family of notaries, was sent to become a craftsman is significant.

I. Biographical Information

1. School records: We have little information about da Vinci's early education.

2. Self-reports: Starting from about the age of 37, da Vinci recorded most of his thoughts by writing them down on loose sheets of paper. In his will, he bequeathed all his diaries and papers to Francesco Melzi, who was his disciple and companion for more than 10 years. Hidden among this jumble of information could be found self-critical remarks such as "I being not a man of letters," "having a lack of literary training," etc. (Reti, 1974, p. 293). Marioni (1974), who has translated two manuscripts (Codex Madrid I & II), quotes similar self-deprecatory remarks.

3. Descriptive accounts by biographers: The fact that da Vinci was an illegitimate child is sometimes advanced to explain the fact that he did not pursue formal education. Although illegitimacy carried a stain of some sort in Italian Renaissance society, power, position, and money could be used to secure special dispensation and, thus, soften the stigma (Martines, 1968).

According to Payne (1978), da Vinci had difficulty in learning languages; it was not that he could not apply himself to the task, for at one time he made a serious attempt to learn Latin (p. 238). A lack of aptitude for learning languages (LD?) and a rigid curriculum, which was loaded with language learning, emerges as a potential reason why da Vinci was sent to become a craftsman.

II. Cognitive Characteristics

1. <u>Written spelling errors</u>: Unlike English orthography, Italian orthography is shallow and, therefore, minimizes the opportunities for making spelling errors. Errors in writing, however, could occur due to incorrect parsing, segmentation, and blending. For example, *la radio* could be incorrectly parsed as "l aradio" or blended as "laradio." Errors could also occur due to consonant omission, substitution, or doubling. Sartori (1987) has compared da Vinci's spelling errors with those committed by a dyslexic Italian boy. The following are examples of da Vinci's misspellings with the correct spelling shown in parenthesis: *cicommette* (*chi commette*); *muta tion* (*mutation*); *lumj nosa* (*lumijnosa*); *aritro vare* (*a rit rovare*); *ino ccidente* (*in occidente*); *quelqij* (*quelgi*); *sciatta* (*schiatta*); *totard* (*toccare*), etc.

Alternate hypotheses could be advanced to account for the idiosyncrasies of da Vinci's writing and they deserve to be examined. One such possibility is that during the Renaissance, firm rules of spelling were not laid down and as such, Italian spelling was inconsistent. Sartori (1987) compared the spontaneous writings of Michelangelo Buonarroti and those of Francesco Melzi with those of da Vinci. Both Michelangelo and Melzi were da Vinci's contemporaries and came from the same Tuscan region. Sartori could not find any single error in the writings of Michelangelo or Melzi similar to that of da Vinci. Furthermore, a comparison of da Vinci's original manuscript and copies made by Melzi shows that Melzi corrected all of da Vinci's spelling and punctuation errors (Marioni, 1974, p. 63).

2. <u>Morphological errors in written language</u>: Some of da Vinci's narratives are reduced to mere strings of words that were freed from rhetorical encumbrances and are devoid of grammatical connections (Marinoni, 1974). According to Richter (1939), da Vinci gave little attention to punctuation, and did not use accents or apostrophes at all.

3. <u>Deficits in sequential processing of information</u>: Da Vinci had some difficulty in processing sequences of words, remembering days and dates, and carrying out arithmetic operations (for samples of his arithmetic errors, see Aaron, Phillips & Larsen, 1988). He recorded Caterina's (possibly his mother) arrival by writing "On the 16th day of July Caterina came on the 16th day of July 1493" (MacCurdy, 1958, p. 1156). His diary entry of his father's death reads:

> On the ninth day of July 1504, on Wednesday at seven o'clock, died, at the Palace of Podesta, Ser Piero da Vinci, notary, my father, at seven o'clock; he was eighty years old, he left ten sons and two daughters (MacCurdy, 1958, p. 1159).

In addition to the repetition of the phrase "seven o'clock," there are other errors too. The day of death was Tuesday and not Wednesday; his father's age was 77 and not 80. Payne (1978) states that Ser Piero had three daughters.

4. Superior ability in simultaneous processing of information: Da Vinci relied a great deal on drawings and sketches to communicate his ideas; his diaries and notebooks are filled with rebuses, sketches, and drawings. For him, drawings and sketches constituted the primary medium of expression and communication.

Da Vinci's painting of the Virgin and Child with St. Anne provides further evidence of his superior spatial visualization. This theme posed a problem for artists who have previously unsuccessfully attempted to merge the three figures. Da Vinci solved it through a gestalt-like fusion. A similar fusion of figures is also seen in the painting *The Last Supper*. Da Vinci's manuscripts from 1496 through 1499 devote more space to geometry than to any other subject. His illustrations and designs are extraordinary for their depth and accuracy.

III. Neuropsychological Characteristics

1. Evidence of atypical cerebral organization: During the last year of his life, when he was the resident artist at the court of the French king Francis I at Amboise, da Vinci suffered a stroke. Evidence of this illness comes from a record made by Antonio de'Beatis, a secretary of the Cardinal of Argon, who visited da Vinci on October 10, 1517. The secretary's observation that da Vinci's right arm was paralyzed indicates that the impairment was localized in the left cerebral hemisphere. The Cardinal's secretary had conversations with da Vinci, but still did not make reference to any speech impediments.

In right-handed individuals, such a stroke can lead to aphasic symptoms. Furthermore, six months after the secretary's visit, da Vinci went to the chambers of the royal notary at Amboise and made his last will. An intricate document with 18 separate clauses, it contains private information, indicating that he was able to communicate complex information successfully to the panel of notaries.

2. Handedness: Da Vinci wrote, drew, and painted with his left hand (Marinoni, 1974; Vasari, 1959). Since he also used his right hand for writing (Marionini, 1974), he should be considered ambidextrous.

IV. Biological Characterstics

Little information is available about da Vinci regarding genetic disposition or immune system functioning.

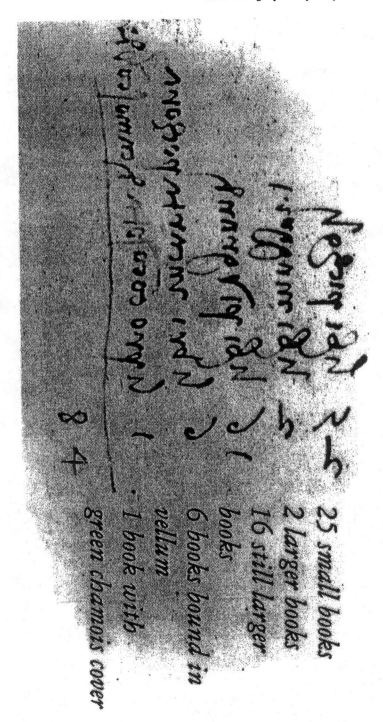

Figure 1. Leonardo's arithmetic calculation. Courtesy Da Vinci's museum, Da Vinci.

Thomas Alva Edison

Thomas Alva Edison was born on February 11, 1847. A few years earlier, his parents had migrated from Canada. His father, Samuel Edison, operated a lumber mill on the banks of a canal in Milan, Ohio. Edison's mother, Nancy, was the daughter of the Reverend John Elliott, and according to Josephson (1959), she had taught in a two-room school in Vienna, Ontario. With the coming of railroads, Milan lost much of its canal business and the Edison family was obliged to move again. According to Josephson, the family moved during the spring of 1854, when Edison was seven years old, and settled in Port Huron, Michigan. It is not known whether the Edisons owned or rented their house in Port Huron, but it was a substantial two-story, six-bedroom house (Conot, 1979) with columned balconies and four fireplaces, set amidst a grove of pine trees on a 10-acre tract. This information is significant because in the present context, it is important to know whether the limited schooling Edison received was because of financial difficulties or Edison's own difficulties in acquiring an education.

In the fall of 1855, when he was eight years old, young Edison was enrolled in the one-room school of Reverend Engle (Josephson, 1959). If this date is accurate, there was a one-year gap between the family's move to Port Huron and Edison entering school. Since biographers have attached little importance to this unaccounted year, it is difficult to ascertain the reason for Edison's late entry into school. According to Wachhorst (1981), nearly 5% of the nearly 2,100 anecdotes about Edison's boyhood refer to the story that his teacher called him "addled." Although it is unlikely that this single episode was responsible for the termination of young Edison's education, it appears certain that Edison's first encounter with academia was neither pleasant nor long-lasting.

After Edison left school, his mother apparently took up the responsibility of tutoring him (Josephson, 1959). Even though most biographers have reported that Edison had no more than three months of formal education, according to Connot (1979), he not only went to three schools at Fort Gratiot and Port Huron, but also attended classes at Cooper Union.

By the time he was nine years old, Edison must have been exposed to sufficient reading instruction because he inscribed on the cover page of Parker's Natural and Experimental Philosophy, which he later donated to the Ford Museum in Greenfield Village, "Parkers (sic) philosophy was the first book in science that I had when (sic) a boy 9year's old I picked out (sic) as it was the first one I could understand".

Parker's book has 470 pages in fine print and has chapters on topics such as mechanics, hydraulics, acoustics, optics, astronomy, electricity, and magnetism. In addition, it has a chapter on electromagnetic telegraphy. One can raise the question "How can a nine-year-old boy read such a big book, let alone a boy with reading disabilities?"

There are two possible answers to this question. One is that Edison exaggerated his ability to read and understand; the inelegant autographic inscription he wrote on the cover page of the book indicates such a possibility. The second potential answer is that Parker's book is profusely illustrated, so that the reader does not have to depend much on reading to understand the contents. Being "visually talented," Edison might have relied more on diagrams and illustrations than on the written text to figure out the contents of the book.

Between the ages of 12 and 15, when Edison was a vendor on the railroad, he had a layover of about four hours in Detroit, which he spent in the Detroit public library. Later on he stated, "I started with the first book on the bottom shelf and went through the lot, one by one. I didn't read a few books, I read the library." (Runes, 1948, p. 48). Edison probably meant the Young Men's Society, whose library was later organized into the Detroit Free Library. There is evidence that Edison obtained membership in this library at a cost of two dollars. In his introduction to the works of Thomas Paine, Edison wrote:

> My father had a set of Tom Paine's books on the shelf at home. I must have opened the covers about the time I was 13. And I can still remember the flash of enlightenment which shone from his pages. It was a revelation, indeed to encounter his views on political and religious matters (Runes, 1948, p. 154).

Given these observations, Edison's early life can be summarized by stating that even though he had only a limited amount of formal education, he was exposed to reading more than an ordinary child of his age would have been.

I. Biographical Information

1. School records: School records regarding Edison's academic performance are unavailable.

2. Self-reports: Edison's descriptions of his own performance at school come from the biographical notes he dictated to Meadowcroft (Dyer, Martin, & Meadowcrost, 1929) and from newspaper articles written by reporters who had interviewed Edison. He reportedly said,

> I remember I used never to be able to get along at school. I was always at the foot of the class. I used to feel that the teachers did not sympathize with me and that my father thought I was stupid (p. 20).

3. Descriptive accounts by biographers: Edison's biographers have used phrases such as "wayward" and "different from other boys" (Josephson, 1959, p. 25) to describe him as a boy. The most frequently used epithet is "addled," allegedly used by his first teacher.

II. Cognitive Characteristics

1. Written spelling errors: In July 1885, Edison spent about a week in the beachside house of his friend and associate Ezra Gilliland in Woodside, Massachusetts. Being on vacation and having plenty of time on hand, he decided to put his thoughts down in a diary. By this time, Edison was 38 years old and had become known for his improvement of the telephone and the establishment of the Pearl Street electricity station. By the time he wrote the diary, he had read numerous articles and books on applied science. For these reasons, the diary, although short, is of great value for studying Edison's written language.

In 1948, Rune published a version of the diary, with the errors removed. Errors of spelling and syntax described in the following section are from Edison's original diary, which is preserved in the Edison National Historic site, West Orange, New Jersey. The correct spelling and the date of the diary entry are shown in parentheses: *tarter* (tartar); *Macauley* (Macaulay, July 12); *inexhaustable* (inexhaustible), *receeding* (receding), *dasies* (daisies), *Daisie's* (Daisy's), *anethized* (anaesthetized, July 14); *articutating* (articulating); *progedy* (prodigy); *beleivear* (believer), *marvellous* (marvelous, July 18); *shreik* (shriek, July 21); *insecrtiverous* (insectivorous), *disect* (dissect); *innocuated* (inoculated); *tenticles* (tentacles, July 22).

The following spelling errors were found after a random search of a few letters deposited in the Edison Institute, Greenfield Village, Dearborn, Michigan: *peice* (piece, Oct. 30, 1870); *beleiver* (believer, April 7, 1871); *reccommendation* (recommendation, Feb. 23, 1878), *adjument* (adjustment), *mouthpeice* (mouthpiece, March 1878); *interferance* (interference, Oct. 13, 1917). In view of the fact that Edison had read Parker's 470-page book at the age of nine, and an entire library soon thereafter, these errors cannot be attributed to limited reading experience.

Numerous spelling errors can be seen in the *Weekly Herald*, the newspaper Edison published on board a train when he was 15 years old. According to Professor Reese Jenkins, director of the Edison Papers Project at Rutgers University, the evidence of the Weekly Herald, however, is fraught with problems (personal communication). Nevertheless, Edison, age 15 when he published the two-page news bulletin, had been exposed to books as well as to reading. Furthermore, the spelling errors found in the *Weekly Herald* are "phonetic" and are similar to the ones found in his diary, written almost two decades later, which suggests that the spelling errors persisted over the years in spite of additional reading experience. The misspelled words also indicate that Edison's vocabulary was larger than that of an average 15-year old boy. Thus, there is a marked discrepancy between the range of his vocabulary and his spelling skills. The errors seen in one page of the news bulletin are: *intellengence* (intelligence), *obligeing* (obliging); *profiesser* (professor), *seams* (seems), *leaveing* (leaving), *supprise* (surprise), *stateing* (stating), *villians* (villains), *posession* (possession), *quantitys* (quantities); *delayid* (delayed); *oppisition* (opposition); *propietor* (proprietor); *accommadation* (accommodation).

2. Errors of morphology and syntax in written language: Josephson (1959, p.22), in support of his statement that Edison never learned how to spell and that up to the time of his adulthood his grammar and syntax were appalling, quotes the following letter written by Edison to his mother when he was about 19 years old.

> Started the store several weeks I have growed considerably. I dont look much like a Boy now—Hows all the folks did you receive a Box of Books from Memphis that he promised to send them—languages.
> *Your son AL*

Edison's diary, written when he was 38 years old, also contains errors of syntax. The grammatical elements omitted are shown in parentheses.

> I didn't hear (a) word he said. Put my spongy mind at work on life (of) Goethe. Boston ought to be buoyed and charts furnished (for) strangers. This removed the articulat(ing) upholstery. Hell will get (up) a reputation as a summer resort. It would stagger the mind of Raphael (in) a dream to imagine a being comparable to the Maid. Last night (the) room was close(d). Mrs. Roberts caught cold in her arm (and her) cough is better. I would strik(e) them. I am getting caloric(ally) stupid.

3. Deficits in processing sequential information: One diary entry, dated July 18, 1885, implies that Edison was not skilled in recalling information in the order in which it was presented. He wrote:

> Went out yechting, all the ladies in attendance... Ladies played (a) game called memory scheme. No 1 calls out (the) name of (a) prominent author, No.2 repeats this name and adds another and so on. Soon one has to remember a dozen names, all of which must be repeated in the order given. Miss Daisy had the best and I the poorest memory.

If mathematics could be viewed as a form of analytical language, Edison could not be considered as being particularly strong in it. Arithmetic errors could be seen in Edison's laboratory worksheets (Conot, 1979, p.73). He worked around the use of mathematics by adopting the trial-and-error method. He reportedly remarked, "I do not depend on figures at all. I try an experiment and reason out the result, somehow by methods which I could not explain (Conot, 1979, p. 32).

He also wrote that he tried to read Newton's *Principia Mathematica* and(delete marker)came to the conclusion that Newton could have dispensed his knowledge in a much wider field had he known less about figures. It gave me a distaste for mathematics from which I never recovered (Runes, 1948, p. 45).

Later on, however, while working on the electricity distribution system, he was obliged to hire Francis Upton, a mathematical physicist from Princeton because "it is just as well to have one mathematical fellow around, in case we have to calculate something out" (Josephson, 1959, p. 136).

4. Superior ability in simultaneous processing of information: According to Jenkins (Byrnes, 1978), Edison was basically nonmathematical; he thought in a visual and tactile way with the aid of little drawings, sketches, and models. In fact, Edison's sketches have a striking resemblance to those of Leonardo da Vinci. Josephson quotes one of Edison's sons as saying that he (Edison) had really very little power of abstraction and had to be able, above all, to visualize things (1959, p. 123). Thus, there seems to be a consensus among these writers that Edison's cognitive style was visual–spatial and gestalt in nature.

Edison's simultaneous–gestalt style of solving problems is evident nowhere more than in his development of the incandescent light bulb into a commercially lucrative enterprise. Edison did not invent the prototype of the light bulb; Joseph Swan of England had an incandescent lamp in operation when Edison began to tackle the problem. Sigfried Marcus of Vienna had already filed a patent for an incandescent lamp. These prototype incandescent lamps, however, required thick carbon rods in order to withstand intense heat. In order to light up a block, this system would have needed copper cables of gigantic proportions. Edison was creative in solving several problems all at once, thus making the incandescent lamp a commercial success. He saw that because voltage, resistance, and amperage were inversely related, he could reduce the amount of current required by increasing the resistance of the filament in the bulb with the use of thin carbon filament. Edison also simultaneously adopted the parallel circuit instead of a serial circuit. Edison could see the forest whereas his competitors were lost in the woods because they could see only trees.

III. Neuropsychological Characteristics

Other than the fact that Edison was right handed, we have very little information in this regard.

IV. Biological Characteristics

1. Genetic predisposition to reading disability: The information that would allow any meaningful pedigree analysis is meager. According to Edison's biographers, his father, Sam Edison, was a political radical who supported a movement for representative government for Canada. This is in accord with Edison's statement that his father possessed books such as the one by Thomas Paine. In light of this, the following brief message written by Sam Edison to his son Alva is significant: "This Packedg contains all mast entr Discription of Dockaments know to the civilesed world" (Conot, 1979, p. 79).

Edison had four sons and two daughters. It is difficult to determine whether the poor academic performance of three of Edison's four sons was the result of any form of learning disability or not.

Adelman and Adelman (1987) cite Edison's poor hearing as a possible reason by for his learning difficulties. It is known that Edison could receive telegraphic messages even under the noisiest conditions. There is no evidence that he was even partially deaf. Edison himself wrote: "The things that I have needed to hear, I have heard" (Runes, 1948, p.48).

2. Immune system disorders: Several biographers note that in Edison's family there was a history of bronchial problems. It is uncertain, however, if such health condition was immunological in nature.

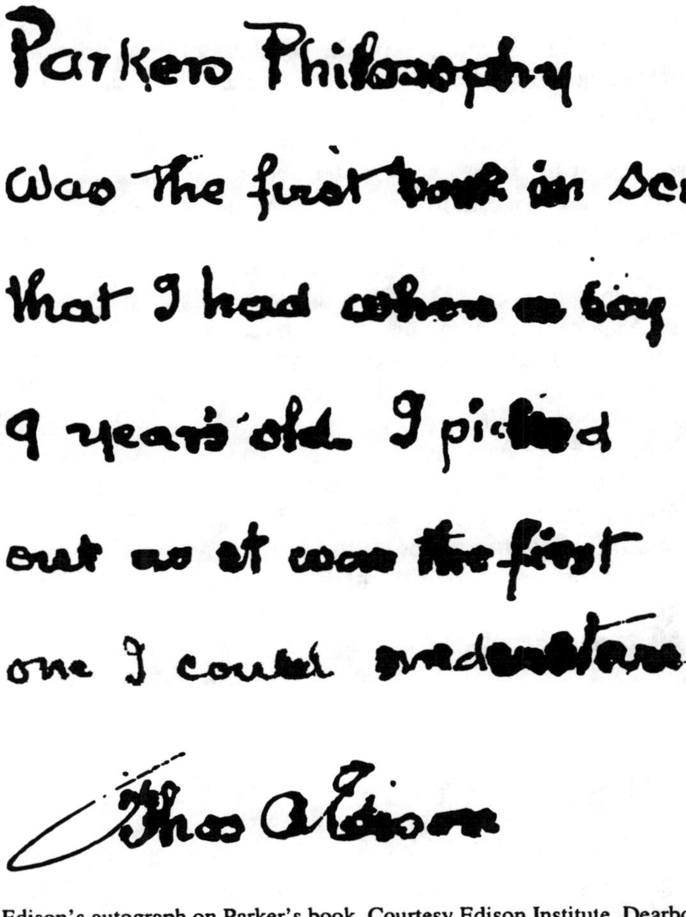

Figure 2. Edison's autograph on Parker's book. Courtesy Edison Institute, Dearborn, Michigan.

Auguste Rodin[2]

It is sometimes said that Rodin is the greatest sculptor since Michelangelo. Although some of his sculptures such as *The Thinker* and *The Kiss* have gained universal acclaim, others such as *Balzac* and *The Burghers of Calais* have aroused a good deal of controversy and criticism. Art historians often compare Rodin to Claude Monet, the impressionist painter, in that Rodin is the pioneer who introduced impressionism into the field of sculpture. According to Descharnes and Chabrun (1967), whose book on Rodin is based on substantial research, he is the last of the great classical sculptors and the first of the great modern sculptors.

Rodin's parents were of humble origin; his father was a clerk in a police precinct in Paris and his mother was a housewife. At the age of eight, Rodin started attending a school run by the Brothers of the Christian Doctrine. Three years later, he was sent to a boarding school in Beauvais, where his uncle, Hippolyte Rodin, was the headmaster. The decision to send young Rodin to a boarding school 100 miles away from home may not be unrelated to his performance at his first school. After about two years, at the age of 14, Rodin returned to Paris and entered the *Petite Ecole*, where he started to learn drawing, painting, and sculpting. To summarize, Rodin received six or seven years of education, which was more than most ordinary children in those days. When Rodin was about 22, Maria, his older sister with whom he was very close, died. Depressed over this loss, Rodin entered the novitiate in the Order of the Fathers of the Very Holy Sacrament, but returned to sculpting and painting a year later. It can, therefore, be surmised that Rodin had opportunities to read and write.

When he was 24 years old, Rodin met Rose Beuret, who, a year later, bore him a son. Even though Rodin's liaison with Rose remained unbound by marriage almost his entire life, the two were eventually married a few months before his death. Other important people in Rodin's life were Camille Claudel, his student and associate in more than one sense; Judith Cladell, a faithful companion, particularly during Rodin's last days, and the best informed of his biographers; and Marcelle Tirel, the most patient and longest lasting of his secretaries, who also wrote an informal but intimate account of the sculptor.

I. Biographical Information

1. School records: We have no records about Rodin's performance at the schools he attended. Champignuelle (1967), in his book on Rodin, provides a description of Rodin's school days:

> He attended the Ecoles Chretiennes in the Rue du Val-de-Grace but had great difficulty in learning to read and write despite the Brothers' noted achievements in the field of primary education. At the age of

nine, he was packed off to his paternal uncle Alexandre who ran a boys' boarding school at Beauvais...As for his studies, he seemed to be genuinely retarded. His dictation was riddled with crass spelling mistakes. He never succeeded in learning Latin like others, and his mathematics were non-existent. He drove his teachers to despair... When he was thirteen, his uncle decided that there was nothing more to be done with him and sent him back to Paris (pp 11–12).

2. Self-reports: In his edited book on Rodin, Elsen (1965) included a monologue by Rodin that was originally published by Dujardin-Beaumetz in 1913 under the title *Entretiens avec Rodin*. Dujardin-Beaumetz was the undersecretary of state for fine arts in France and the report was based on notes made by him during his many interviews with Rodin. About his education, Rodin said:

When I was about fourteen, I boarded at Beauvais, at my uncle's. The students there studied Latin. I don't know why, but I didn't like Latin. I've often regretted (it). (p. 145).

The Musée Rodin in Paris has published four volumes of *Correspondance de Rodin*, which contains the following statement in a letter by Rodin to Helene Wahl dated October 1895:

You know that I am not a scholar and that writing and speaking turn me to confusion. My natural means of expression are clay and pencil" (Vo. 1, p. 7).

3. Descriptive accounts by biographers: According to Elsen, who has written extensively on Rodin as an artist, Rodin did have problems with grammar and punctuation, and contended himself with writing mostly short notes, well over 100,000. Rodin, however, was an avid reader, even when desperately poor (personal communication, 1988).

From 1906 until Rodin's death in 1917, Marcelle Tirel was his secretary and a companion. In *The Last Years of Rodin* (1925), Tirel gives some intimate accounts of the talents and foibles of Rodin. The book shows a deep respect for Rodin and is set in a tone of adulation. Statements regarding Rodin's literacy skills, therefore, can be taken to be reliable. According to Tirel, Rodin had doubts about his own literary ability and at times would say, "I shall never be able to write well." He would write *areoplane* for "aeroplane," cariathide for "cariatide." When told that "cariatide" does not have the letter "h" in it, he was most astonished but remarked "those are trifles for a man like myself" (pp. 99, 103). He would remark, "Why should people want to make of a sculptor of genius what he could never be, a man of letters?" (p. 112).

II. Cognitive Characteristics

1. <u>Written spelling errors</u>: By about 1900, Rodin became affluent enough to hire secretaries. As a result, he himself wrote few letters after this date. After commenting on Rodin's writings, Tirel wrote:

> I have before me an unpublished fragment of those *Thoughts*, scrawled in pencil on the back of a letter from a model; the letters are badly formed, the words stumble and trip, the sentences are incomplete" (p. 115).

The sample writing Tirel wrote about is reproduced here:

> Ces nuages frisés blancs, cette crême fouettée. Ils sont dans le perspective anonyme quand ils passent au-dessus de vastes arbres...entre les arbres on voit comme des terres de géographies immenses sur les cieux découpé. La majesté des arbres réunis en bouquet ose se composer au ciel.... Ily a pour les bêtes la joie d' aimer la beaute. Nous, on nous forme au malheur ... les gens intelligents ne savant plus ce que les bêtes savent ... nos mauvaises éducations entretènues avec soin nous cachent la lumiere... Toute une vie de suicides, dont on sourira ... les nations neurastheniques. Bourrée—Pendant qu' elle danse elle est inondé de liminère ... ma lumiere; les pulsations de mon coeur qui bat aussi la mesure.

The fact that Rodin's writing did not improve over the years is evident from the following letter he wrote to Helene de Nostitz in 1908.

> noble et cher amie:
> J'ai recu votre belle lettre la comparaison de ceux qui travaillent et tour a coup appercoivent la nature la vallée admirable est bien vrai...et comme par tradition le Chef d'oeuvre de la femme et l'enfant a cte souvent compris non pas trop dutemps des Grecs, ou l'enfant etait l'amour, et Venus; mais du temps des Egyptiens ou la femme et l'enfant est de toutes les deesses et dieux, la plus grande. Reprise par la tradition chrétienne elle reposait cette gloire, des Raphaels madones si sévères a l'epoque Espagnole des 12 siècle (Vol. 2, p. 12).

2. <u>Morphological and syntactic errors in written language</u>: These have been presented in the previous sections.

III & IV. Neuropsychological and Biological Characteristics

We do not have any reliable data that can be useful in drawing any valid conclusions in this regard.

1. Deficits in sequential processing of information: Rodin was not good at remembering dates and events. Often, he would make appointments with models only to forget until they showed up. Nor was he good at remembering the sequence and dates and places of his exhibitions. His poor memory for dates is revealed by an anecdote recorded by Tirel. One day he hurriedly got dressed to attend the funeral of his old friend Dr. Bigot. When he reached the gravesite, he recognized nobody and no one knew who he was. When he returned home and reread the telegram, he realized that the funeral service was seven days before and he was late by one week.

2. Superior ability in simultaneous processing of information: Superior accomplishments in painting and sculpturing require extraordinary visual–spatial skills. By this measure, we can conclude that Rodin had superior visual–simultaneous information-processing skills.

Charles Marion Russell

In the introduction to *Good Medicine* (Russell, 1929), which contains a collection of Charles Russell's letters adorned with watercolor illustrations, Will Rogers wrote, "He was a philosopher. He was a great humorist... If he had devoted the same time to writing that he had to his brush, he would have left a tremendous impression in that line" (pp. 13–15). Along with well-knows artists Karl Bodmer and George Catlin, Russell is also considered to be a great chronicler of the history of the West, not with the pen, but with the brush. Russell, unlike Western artists such as Frederick Remington, seldom portrayed Indians and the U.S. cavalry as antagonists. The Indian maids he painted were tender, independent, and self-assured; they were portrayed not as serfs but as fulfilling roles of domestic and social responsibility (G.Renner, 1984). Russell was also a great storyteller and as Frederick Renner (1984) put it, he has a "gorgeous darting wit which tickled but never stung" (p. 31). He wrote in the same style as he told his tales. His book *Trails Plowed Under* (1927) is notable for its great humor and earthly wit. Appropriately, the people of Montana call their territory Russell Country.

Charles Russell was born in St. Louis in 1864 into a family prominent in business and public affairs. His father had attended Yale University and was later involved in the Russell Mining and Manufacturing Company, a family-owned business. Russell Sr. was also on the board of the Oak Hill School, which young Charlie attended as a child. Russell's mother also came from an illustrious family and was an artist herself. Before entering school, Russell, along with his brothers and sisters, appears to have been tutored at home.

Russell started attending Oak Hill School during the 1870/1871 school year and continued there until 1879, when he was sent to the Burlington Military Academy in New Jersey. Why? Based on the information he got from some of Russell's relatives, Woodcock (1982) wrote that at Oak Hill School, young Russell had the habit of skipping school; when he did attend, he would fill his lunch box with beeswax and spend a good deal of his time modeling figures for his classmates. (This habit seems to have persisted throughout his lifetime. When one of the authors of this chapter (Aaron) interviewed one of Russell's early acquaintances in Montana, the acquaintance related that when she told Russell that she was engaged to be married, he stuck his hand into his pocket, pulled out some clay and fashioned a mini sculpture of a horse and a rabbit and gave it to her as a wedding gift. She still had it on her mantelpiece.)

The decision to send Russell to the military academy might have been a desperate effort by his parents to salvage his education by placing him in a structured environment where academics were stressed. The academy, however, also failed to prod him into taking his studies seriously. After one term in the academy, his parents presented Russell with a trip to the West, perhaps in the hope that the harsh realities of the West would bring him back to the placid atmosphere of the school. They were mistaken. At that point, Russell was almost 16 years and had had about nine years of formal education.

I. Biographical Information

1. School records: No school records were available. According to Woodcock (personal communication), all school records were damaged in the tornado of 1927 and were discarded. The Burlington Military Academy no longer exists.

2. Self-reports: Charles Russell made occasional remarks about his own writing skills and was quite candid about his lack of skill in this area. It should, however, be noted that by writing skill, Russell refers to spelling and syntax and not the creative aspect of his writing. While on vacation, he was in the habit of writing small postcards to his friends with humorous notes accompanied with watercolor paintings. These are preserved in the Montana Historical Museum. Examples of his writings include a note he wrote to Senator Paris Gibson: "As I am verry poor writer I will make a kind of Injun letter mostly pictures" (Russell, 1929, p. 20). To W.M. Armstrong, he wrote in 1922, " I m better than a green hand with talk but with a pen Im plenty lame so Im limping in with my thanks" (Russell, 1919 p. 111). To "Mr. Hart" he wrote, " I am average on talk but hand me this tools, pen and ink, an Im deaf and dum" (Russell, 1929, p. 30). In one of his illustrated letters to a former schoolmate he wrote "Dear Charley,... I guess you remember old Smith our teacher and the lickinges he gave us it has been maney years ago but he is till fresh in my memory" (Montana State Historical Society, Russell Papers).

3. Descriptive accounts by biographers: The unimpressive school accomplishment of Charles Russell is well documented not only by his biographers but also by his wife Nancy. As she put it,

School had no charm for Russell, and he spent a considerable amount of time on Guard duty for inattention while at Burlington Military Academy. His teachers gave him up because he could not be made to read books. Again, he was made to walk guard for hours because book study was not in his mind. (Nancy Russell, in Russell. 1929, p. 18).

II. Cognitive Characteristics

1. Written spelling errors: One need not search too far to locate errors of spelling and syntax in Russell's writings. Practically every other word is misspelled, phonetically. This is in spite of Russell being a voracious reader who built up an extensive library during his life (Ginger Renner, personal communication). His letters (Russell, 1929) contain statements such as, "Im sending you a book which I hope you enjoy" (p. 77); "thank yu for the book you sent me I ingoyed the book verry much" (p. 77). " I enjoyed your book *Let her buck* very much" (p. 102). Sometimes it is claimed that Russell meant to be theatrical and followed an oral style and misspelled words deliberately in order to inject a sense of humor. These errors, creative and funny as they may be, are too numerous to be considered deliberate and humorous. In fact, they hinder easy reading and distract the reader from enjoying the wit and humor of Russell's artful writing. Furthermore, Russell also misspelled peoples' names, a slip that may not be considered amusing even by close friends. In one of his letters, he wrote "To Harry Carry Bill Hart Douglass Farbanks Afreal Hart Bill Rodgers or aney other moovey man " (Montana Historical Society). When he wrote a letter to Senator Paris Gibson, he addressed the letter to "Senitor Paris Gibson" (Russell, 1929, p. 70). He spelled the name of the town *Havre* variously as "Haver", "Havrre", and "Havre."

2. Errors of morphology and syntax in written language: Russell's writings simply ignore punctuation and other syntactical constraints even though they do not affect the meaning. Even when he expressed an awareness of his own misspellings, he did not care for syntax. For instance, in a letter to Ed Neitzling he wrote, "the old rumitism I dont know wheter that the way to spell it or not but it is still with me" (Russell, 1929, p. 90). To friend Joe, he wrote, " Youd have don better with a hay knife it would give more teck neque maby that aint spelt right but you savvy" (Russell, 1929, p. 126).

III & IV. Neuropsychological and Biological Characteristics

We do not have any information in these areas to make any meaningful statements. His writings and paintings, however, indicate that Russell was more visual than verbal and he tended to process written words as ideograms. In fact, he described written work as "word pictures" and remarked that there are two kinds of men, those who paint with their brush and those who paint with their pen. Russell's superb use of metaphors lends credence to this statement. For him, the historical past of the West was "days before the wires," and "trails ploughed under"; milk was "cow juice"; New York was "the big camp"; "New Yorkers were "cliff dwellers"; writing was "paper talk"; and "life is a trail and a birthday is a place where one stops and looks back."

Figure 3. Russell's letter to a friend. Courtesy Russell Museum, Helena, Montana

Hans Christian Andersen[3]

Even though in English-speaking countries Andersen is known for his fairy tales and children's stories, he has also published five major novels. According to Bredsdorff (1975), his most authoritative biographer, Andersen was accepted in the past as a writer of great literary distinction both in Britain and America. His first biography was written not by a Danish writer but by Nisbet Bain, an Englishman.

Hans Christian Andersen was born in Odense, Denmark, on April 2, 1805. His father was a cobbler with very little education, although Andersen writes that his father could read. Andersen's mother, a washerwoman, was equally uneducated. Even as a young boy, Andersen was possessed with a vision of one day becoming a *digter*, a playwright.

Because Odense was a small, provincial town, it was necessary for Andersen to seek his fortunes as an actor and playwright elsewhere, and he left for Copenhagen at the age of 14. In Copenhagen he could get only minor roles in the theater, and at the end of the third year even that became impossible. During that time, Andersen submitted a play to the Royal Theater, which was also rejected. The members of the board of directors, however, were sympathetic. Impressed by his youthful ambitions but dismayed by the number of mistakes in spelling and grammar in the manuscript, they recommended that he attend grammar school and acquire the elements of education. The board asked Jonas Collin, one of the members, to make the necessary financial arrangements. Collin eventually became Andersen's benefactor and mentor.

At the age of 17, Andersen joined the grammar school at Slagelse, a small town near Copenhagen, and was admitted into the seventh grade. According to Bredsdorff (1975), all other boys in his class looked at him with astonishment because they were only 11 years old and Andersen towered above them. The headmaster of the school was Dr. Simon Meisling, a name that came to haunt Andersen all his life. Even though at the end of the first year he managed to pass from the seventh to the eighth grade, he was detained during the subsequent year. After five years of struggle, Andersen left the grammar school without a diploma, partly because of his difficulties in learning Latin and Greek and partly as a result of interpersonal difficulties with Dr. Meisling. He returned to Copenhagen and with the help of private tutors, finally passed the "Examen Artium" which qualified him to enter the university, even though he never took advantage of it.

I. Biographical Information

1. School records: As noted earlier, in spite of his diligence, Andersen barely passed from seventh to eighth grade and had to repeat the eighth grade. Available records show that his most difficult subjects were Latin and Greek, with math presenting no difficulty at all.

2. Self-reports: While at the grammar school in Slagelse, Andersen kept a diary, and some of the entries reveal the agony he went through while at school. The following excerpts are taken from Bredsdorff's (1975) biography of Andersen:

> Sept. 19, 1825—"Unfortunate person—did badly in Latin. You won't get into the fourth, will have to leave school (p.57); Dec.5, 1825— Yes, he (Dr. Meisling) treats me kindly, O God, if only I could show some progress but I am scared of the exam. I'm balancing somewhere between the two bottom marks. (p. 57).

Andersen's letters to his friends also reveal his difficulties at school. In one of his letters to a friend he wrote, "I wish my father had burnt every book I ever got hold of and had forced me to make shoes, then I would never have become mad" (Bredsdorff, 1975, p. 64). In a letter to Edvard Collin, his benefactor's son and a friend, he wrote "Something restless and hasty in my soul which makes it twice as difficult for me to get to grips with languages" (Bredsdorff (1975, p. 61).

3. Descriptive accounts by biographers: According to Keigwin (1976), a literary critic, Andersen's writings are sprinkled with every kind of conversational Copenhagen slang, thrown in with a free use of particles, all with much grammatical license. Molbech, another literary critic, asked, "When will such a prolific writer, already quite well-known in his native country, learn to write his mother tongue correctly?" (Bredsdorff (1975, p. 347).

Some comments made by Charles Dickens, with whom Andersen spent five weeks, in 1857 are pertinent here. Andersen had visited Dickens 10 years earlier and had come to consider him a close friend. Even before Andersen arrived in his house in 1857, Dickens wrote to a friend, Miss Burdett-Coutts: "Hans Christian Andersen may perhaps be with us, but you won't mind him—especially as he speaks no language but his own Danish, and is suspected of not even knowing that" (Bredsdorff 1975, p. 214). During Andersen's visit, Dickens again wrote, "We are suffering a good deal from Andersen. ...I have arrived at the conviction that he cannot speak Danish (Bredsdorff 1975, p. 214). Edvard Collin, who read many of Andersen's manuscripts before they went to press, wrote in his book, "He was diligent, he read much; ...he learned many things, but he never learned to learn properly" (Bredsdorff 1975, p. 69). Bredsdorff himself writes, "Andersen never learnt to spell properly and if he had lived in our time he would probably have been dubbed dyslectic" (p. 19). Ten years later, Bredsdorff was still "completely convinced that Andersen suffered from dyslexia" (personal communication, May 1985).

II. Cognitive Characteristics

1. Written spelling errors: Andersen's manuscripts contain numerous spelling errors. Rosendal (1975), after rejecting potential explanations such as Andersen's Funen dialect and lack of timely education, concludes "he must have been a constitutional dyslexic" (p. 160). A formal letter written by Andersen in 1824, when he was 19 years old, to Mr. Hempel, an editor, has the following six spelling errors in one page. The correct spellings are in parenthesis. *Desippel* (*Discipel*); *Gulberg* (Guldberg's); *Indtaekten* (*Indtaegten*); *tilfald* (*tilfaldt*); *sadt* (*sat*); *Olenhlaeger* (Oehlenschlaeger). Occassionally, Andersen misspelled even his benefactor's name Collin as *Colin*.

2. Errors of morphology and syntax in written language: Rosendal (1975) notes that Andersen experienced difficulties expressing himself in writing, which is presumably a reason he adopted an *oral style*, which was a special contribution to Danish literature. Literary critic Molbech frequently commented on Andersen's nasty grammatical errors and orthographic carelessness. The following sample of errors is taken from Andersen's diary, dated 1825 and 1826 (Andersenhus, Odense, Ms. No.40): *deklameret* (*declamerede*); *repeteret* (*repeterede*); *brang* (*bragte*); *for mig Taenker jeg* (*for jeg Taenker mig*); *anbefale* (*anbefalede*); *kom* (*komme*); *og talte vi om* (*vi om talte*).

3. Deficits in processing sequential information: The syntactical errors resulting from the misordering of words in the above phrases are examples of sequential errors.

4. Superior ability in simultaneous processing of information: Anderson made numerous pencil and pen sketches of scenarios during his frequent trips away from Denmark. In spite of not having had any formal training in art, the sketches are artistically pleasing and have a quality of elegant simplicity. Indeed, Van Gogh was aware of Andersen's drawings and wrote to his brother Theo: "Don't you find Andersen's fairy tales very fine? It is certain that Andersen also draws illustrations" (Heltoft, 1969, p.5). The many sketches of quality that have survived warranted their publicaion in the form of a book titled *Hans Christian Andersen as an Artist* by Kjeld Heltoft in 1969.

Another creative outcome of Andersen's superior simultaneous ability is seen in the hundreds of paper cuttings he has left behind. According to one eyewitness, as he was talking, Andersen would fold a large sheet of paper several times, run big scissors through the paper, make several effortless cuts, and then unfold the paper. Suddenly, the plain paper was transformed into a stencil filled with little figures of elves, gnomes, fairies, and animals reminiscent of the ones seen in his fairy tales. In order to create such complex figures, Andersen must have been able to visualize the finished product even before he started to produce it.

III & IV. Neuropsychological and Biological Characteristics

No direct neuropsychological evidence is available to enable us to make meaningful inferences regarding Andersen's cerebral organization. However, Andersen can be considered a visual person. His tales are able to evoke visual images instantly and effortlessly. Andersen's tales are full of metaphors and allegories. It is said that Andersen wrote more self-portraits than Rembrandt painted. He was the swan mistaken for an ugly duckling by the world; he was the little boy who found that the emperor had no clothes; and he was the beautiful top whereas Riborg Voigt, who did not consent to marry him, was the worn-out ball.

Andersen died without marrying. We also do not have any reliable information about his relatives to draw inferences about genetic predisposition.

Figure 4. Andersen's self portrait with the Collins family. Courtesy Andersen Haus, Odense, Denmark

Figure 5. Andersen's paper cutting. Courtesy Andersen Haus, Odense, Denmark.

Agatha Miller Christie

Agatha Miller Christie was born in England in 1890 to Frederick and Clarissa Miller. She received very little formal education but was tutored at home. In addition, Christie reports never having to do lessons for school and not having a governess, but she does recall spending quite a lot of time reading books in the family's library (p. 88). She was briefly tutored in reading and writing as a young child by her older sister and by a series of French tutors from whom she received French lessons. Thus, she learned to read quite early in life, despite her mother's belief that children should not be allowed to read until the age of eight (Christie, 1977, p. 13). However, she had problems in learning to write and spell English as well as French. At the age of 16, she attended a finishing school in Paris where she studied performing arts, piano, and singing for a short time.

Greatly encouraged by her mother in her pursuits, her interest in writing poems and short stories began in her youth. An avid reader of Sherlock Holmes novels, she began her literary career by writing mystery novels such as *The Murder of Roger Ackroyd* and *And Then There Were None*. She was also the author of plays, *Witness for Prosecution* being one of them. By the time of her death in 1976, she had published over 70 detective novels and short stories. It is not just the quantity of her output but also the quality of her writing that prompted three authors to publish her biography (Feinman, 1975; Murdoch, 1976; Morgan, 1984).

I. Biographical Information

1. School records: Since she was home-schooled for the most part of her early life, school records of her academic achievement do not exist.

2. Self-reports: In her autobiography, Agatha Christie (1977) recalls learning to read by the gradual recognition of words and states: "... I had learned to read by the look of words and not by their letters" (p. 14). Once she was able to read, her father suggested that she also learn to write, which she found far more difficult (p. 14). As she writes:

> My faults in French dictation horrified the mistress in charge so much she could hardly believe it. . . .*Vraiment, c'est impossible,* she said, *Vous, qui parlez si bien le français, vous avez vingt-cinq fautes en en dictée, vingt-cinq!...* I was quite an interesting phenomenon by reason of my failure... I spelt it one way or the other purely by chance, hoping I might have hit upon the right one. In some French subjects, literature, recitation, and so on, I was in the top of the class; as regards French grammar and spelling I was practically in the bottom class." (p. 153). Again, "I myself was always recognised, though quite kindly, as the 'slow one' of the family. The reactions of my brother and my sister were unusually quick, I could never keep up. I

was, too, very inarticulate. It was always difficult for me to assemble into words what I wanted to say. 'Agatha's so terribly slow' was always the cry. It was quite true and I knew it and accepted it. It did not worry or distress me. I was resigned to being always the slow one. (p. 153)

3. Descriptive accounts by biographers: After reviewing the evidence for a diagnosis of learning disability, Linda Siegel (1988) is certain that Agatha Christie had a learning disability. One of her biographers, Morgan (1984), makes several remarks about her poor spelling skill. Some of his statements are included in the following sections. According to him, Christie's spelling was such a problem that it forced her to change the title of one of her books. A mystery set in the Caribbean was moved to Nimrud because "Caribbean" was difficult to spell.

II. Cognitive Characteristics

1. Written spelling errors: In her autobiography, Christie notes her difficulties with spelling:

> Every day I had to learn how to spell pages of words. I suppose the exercise did me some good, but I was still an extraordinarily bad speller and have remained so until the present day" (p. 121). When discussing the letters she wrote as a small child to her nurse, Christie (1977) explains, "everyday I wrote to her a short badly written ill-spelled note: writing and spelling were always terribly difficult for me (p. 36).

She also recalls that the first time she wrote a story, both writing and spelling were a "pain" (p. 45). In addition, Christie recalls her difficulty in learning French, in which she was insufficient in both spelling and grammar. She recalls practicing how to spell words, but reports that the exercises did her little good and that she remained an extremely poor speller well into adulthood (p. 118). Further, according to Morgan (1984) "Her spelling was always of the hit and miss sort that characterizes people who remember words by ear rather than by eye" (p. 20). Christie also writes:

> I spoke French colloquially but, of course entirely by ear and the words *été* and *était* sounded exactly the same to me; I spelt it one way or the other purely by chance, hoping I might have hit upon the right one. (p. 153).

2. Errors in syntax and grammar: In her autobiography, Christie (1977) describes her trouble organizing compositions in her youth. She states, "...my compositions were too fanciful. I was severely criticized for not keeping to the subject" (p. 147). She also explains her difficulty in

understanding grammar, particularly the use of prepositions. In addition, she felt her early attempts at writing were unsuccessful and that:

> My letters were without originality. They were practically always the same: 'Darling Nursie, I miss you very much. I hope you are quite well. Tony has a flea. Lots and lots of love and kisses'. Again from Agatha (p. 47).

> And my father said that, as I could read, I had better learn to write. This was not nearly so pleasant. Shaky copybooks full of pot hooks and hangers still turn up in old drawers, or lines of shaky B's and R's, in which I seem to have had great difficulty in distinguishing since I had learned to read by the look of words and not by their letters. (p. 26).

3. <u>Deficits in sequential organization</u>: Arithmetic computation, in contrast to mathematical problem solving, could be considered a skill that involves sequential operations. It is a skill similar to decoding. According to a biographer, (Feinman, 1975), "she never had had a head for figures; she says, and doubts if she will ever be able to unravel the mystery of her two bank accounts; one has a lot of nasty red figures, and her business manager won't allow her to touch the other one" (p. 20). To quote Christie herself:

> I remember how that at an arithmetic exam at Miss Guyer's school I had come out bottom, though I had been top of the class all the week previously. Somehow, when I read the questions at the exam my mind shut up and I was unable to think (p. 154).

4. <u>Superior ability in simultaneous processing of information</u>: In contrast to her weakness in computation, Christie had a flair for solving mathematical and related problems. She notes:

> ...every morning after breakfast I would set up at the dining room window seat, enjoying myself far more with figures than with the recalcitrant letters of the alphabet. Father was proud and pleased with my progress. I was promoted to a little brown book of problems. I loved problems. Though merely sums in disguise, they had an intriguing flavour (p. 26).

According to Feinman (1975), she had a prodigious skill for bridge, chess, crosswords and other intriguing puzzles.

III & IV. Neuropsychological and Biological Characteristics

We were unable to find substantial information regarding cerebral lateralization, handedness or genetic predisposition for reading disability in Agatha Christie's family. However, in her *Autobiography*, Christie briefly mentions the academic pursuits of her siblings. Although her sister was well educated and published articles in various magazines, Christie's brother was dismissed from school as a young adult for being unable to pass his exams.

CONCLUSIONS

The co-occurrence of LD and talent become understandable if the abilities and disabilities of gifted individuals are examined within the framework of the Component model. The disability discussed in the present chapter deals primarily with RD, which is marked by difficulties in decoding, spelling, and frequently grammar but not by deficits in language use and comprehension. If decoding and spelling are taken to be skill-level elementary components whereas inventive, artistic, and literary talents are taken to be higher-level cognitive components, then, by definition, these two sets of components follow independent courses of development. The association between LD and giftedness is, therefore, not a mystery. We have presented six case studies—two inventors, two artists, and two literary figures in support of this hypothesis.

NOTES

1. Parts of the material presented in this chapter have appeared in *Journal of Learning Disabilities*, 1988, 21 (9) and as a chapter in the book *Visual Processing in Reading*, edited by D.M. Willows, R.S. Kruk, and E. Corcos, Hillsdale, NJ.: Lawrence Erlbaum, 1993.
2. Jean-Claude Guillemard, International School Psychology Association, was a collaborator in the study of Rodin.
3. Steen Larsen, Professor, Royal Danish School of Education, Copenhagen, was a collaborator in the study of Andersen.

REFERENCES

Aaron, P. G. (1978). Dyslexia, an imbalance in cerebral information processing strategies. *Perceptual and Motor Skills*, 47, 699–706.

Aaron, P. G., & Joshi, R. M. (1992). *Reading problems: Consultation and remediation*. New York: Guilford.

Aaron, P. G., Phillips, S., & Larsen, S. (1988). Specific reading disability in historically famous persons. *Journal of Learning Disabilities*, 21, 521–584.

Aaron, P. G., & Kotva, H. (1999). Component model-based remedial treatment of reading disabilities. In I. Lundberg, F. E. Tonnessen, & I. Austad (Eds.). *Dyslexia: Advances in theory and practice*. Boston: Kluwer Academic Publishers.

Adelman, K. & Adelman, H. (1987). Rodin, Patton, Edison, Wilson, Einstein: Were they really learning disabled? *Journal of Learning Disabilities, 20*, 210–279.

Annett, M. (1981). The right shift theory of handedness and developmental language problems. *Bulletin of the Orton Society, 31*, 103–121.

Benson, D. F. (1977). The third alexia. *Archives of Neurology, 34*, 327–331.

Benton, A. L. (1984). Dyslexia and spatial thinking. *Annals of Dyslexia, 34*, 69–85.

Bradshaw, J. L, & Nettleton, N. C. (1981). The nature of hemispheric specialization in man. *Behavioral and Brain Sciences, 4*, 51–91.

Bredsdorff, E. (1975). *Hans Christian Andersen*. New York: Charles Scribner.

Bryant, P. E., & Bradley, L. (1980). Why children sometimes write words which they do not read. In U. Frith (Ed.). *Cognitive processes in spelling* (pp. 355–372). New York: Academic Press.

Bryden, M. P. (1982). *Functional asymmetry in the intact brain*. New York: Academic Press.

Champigneulle, B. (1967). Rodin. New York: Harry N. Abrams

Christie, A. (1977). *An autobiography*. London: Collins.

Cladell, J. (1917). *Rodin: The man and his art*. New York: Century

Cook, L. (1981). Misspelling analysis in dyslexia: Observation of developmental strategy shifts. *Bulletin of the Orton Society, 31*, 123–134.

Das, J. P., Kirby, J. R., & Jarman, R. (1979). *Simultaneous and successive cognitive processes*. New York: Academic Press.

DeFries, J. C., Fulker, D., & LaBuda, C. (1987). Evidence for a genetic etiology in reading disability of twins. *Nature, 329*, 537–539.

DeFries, J. C., & Alarcon, M. (1996). Genetics of specific reading disability. *Mental Retardation and Developmental Disabilities Research Reviews, 2*, 39–47.

Defries, J. C., Filipek, P. K., Fulker, D. W., Olson, R. K., Pennington, B. F., Smith S. D., & Wise, B. W. (1997). Colorado Learning Disabilities Research Center. *Learning Disabilities: A Multidisciplinary Journal, 8*, 7–19.

Dejerine, J.C. (1891). Sur un cas de cécité verbale avec agraphie, suivi d'autopsie. *Memoirs Societe Biologie, 3*, 197–201.

Denckla, M.B., & Rudel, R.G. (1976). Rapid automatized naming: Dyslexia differentiated from other learning disabilities. *Neuropsychologia, 14*, 471–479.

Dyer, F.L, Martin, T.C., & Meadowcroft, W.H. (1929). *Edison, his life and inventions*. New York: Harper & Row.

Feinman, J. (1975). *The mysterious world of Agatha Christie*. New York: Award Books.

Fisher, P., & Frankfutter, A. (1977). Normal and disabled readers can locate and identify letters: Where's the perceptual deficit? *Journal of Reading Behavior, 9*, 31–43.

Frith, U., & Snowling, M. (1983). Reading for meaning and reading for sound in autistic and dyslexic children. *British Journal of Developmental Psychology, 1*, 320–342.

Gardner, H., Denes, G., & Zurif, E. (1975). Critical reading at the sentence level in aphasia. Cortex, 11, 60–72.

Geschwind, N. (1983). Biological association of left-handedness. *Annals of Dyslexia, 33*, 29–40.

Geschwind, N. & Behan, P. (1982) Laterality, hormones, and immunity. In N. Geschwind & A.M. Galaburda (Eds.), *Cerebral Dominance: The biological foundations*. Cambridge, MA; Harvard University Press.

Gibson, E. J., & Guinett, L. (1971). Perception of inflexions in brief visual presentation of words. *Journal of Verbal Learning and Verbal Behavior, 10*, 182–189.

Gough, P.B., & Tunmer, W. (1986). Decoding, reading, and reading disability. *Remedial and Special Education, 7*(1), 6–10.

Heltoft, K. (1969). *Hans Christian Andersen as an artist*. Copenhagen: The Royal Danish Ministry of Foreign Affairs.

Jackson, M.D., & McClelland, J. L. (1979). Processing determinants of reading speed. *Journal of Experimental Psychology (General), 108*(2), 151–181.

Josephson, M. (1959). *Edison*. New York: McGraw Hill.

Joshi, R. M. & Aaron, P. G., (2000). The Component Model of reading: Simple view of reading made a little more complex. *Reading Psychology, 21*, 85–97.

Joshi, R. M. & Aaron, P. G. (1991). Developmental reading and spelling disabilities: Are these dissociable?. In R.M. Joshi (Ed.), *Written language disorders* (pp. 1–24). Netherlands: Kluwer Academic Publishers.

Kean, M. L. (1977). The linguistic interpretation of aphasic syndromes: Agrammatism in Broca's aphasia, an example. Cognition, 5, 9–46.

Keigwin, R. (1976). *Hans Christian Andersen: Eighty fairy tales.* New York: Pantheon.

Kershner, J. R. (1977). Cerebral dominance in disabled readers, good readers, and gifted children: Search for a model. *Child Development, 48,* 61–67.

Kirby, R., & Robinson, G. (1987). Simultaneous and successive processing in reading disabled children. *Journal of Learning Disabilities, 20,* 243–252.

MacCurdy, E. (1958). *The notebooks of Leonardo da Vinci.* New York: George Braziller.

Marinoni, A. (1974). Leonardo the writer. In L. Reti (Ed.), *The unknown Leonardo.* New York: McGraw-Hill, (pp. 56–85).

Marshall, J.C., & Newcombe, F. (1966). Syntactic and semantic errors in paralexia. *Neuropsychologia, 4,* 169–176.

Marshall, J.C., & Newcombe, F. (1973).Patterns of paralexia. *Journal of Psycholinguistic Research, 2,* 175–199.

Martines, L. (1968). *Lawyers and statecraft in Renaissance Florence.* Princeton, NJ: Princeton University Press.

Morgan, J. (1984). *Agatha Christie: A biography.* London: Collins.

Murdoch, D. (1976). *The Agatha Christie mystery.* Toronto: Pagarian Press.

Newell, A., & Simon, H.A. (1972). *Human problem solving.* Englewood Cliffs, NJ, Prentice-Hall.

O'Connor, N. & Hermelin, B. (1987). Visual memory and motor programmes: Their use by idiot-savant artists and controls. *British Journal of Psychology, 78;* 307–323.

O'Connor, N. & Hermelin, B (1989), The memory structure of autistic idiot-savant mnemonists. *British Journal of Psychology, 80,* 97–111).

Palmer, J., McCleod, C., Hunt, E., & Davidson, J. (1985). Information processing correlates of reading. *Journal of Memory and Language, 24,* 59–88.

Payne, R. (1978). *Leonardo.* Garden City, NY: Doubleday.

Renner, F. (1984). *Charles M. Russell.* New York: Harry N. Abrams.

Renner, G. (1984). Charlie Russell and the ladies in his life. *Montana, the Magazine of Western Society.* (Montana Historical Society) Autumn, 34–61.

Reti, L. (1974). *The unknown Leonardo.* New York: McGraw-Hill.

Richter, J. P. (1939). *The notebooks of Leonardo da Vinci* (Vol 1). New York: Dover.

Rosendal, A. (1975). The causes of H.C. Andersen's spelling difficulties. *Anderseniana, 3,* 160–184.

Runes, D. D. (1948). *The diary and sundry observations of Thomas Alva Edison.* New York: Philosophical Library.

Russell, C. M. (1927). *Trails plowed under.* Garden City, NY: Doubleday.

Russell, C. M. (1929). *Good medicine.* Garden City, NY: Doubleday.

Santillana, G. D. (1966). Man without letters. In M. Philipson (Ed.), *Leonardo da Vinci: Aspects of the Renaissance genius* (pp. 77–109). New York: George Braziller.

Sartori, G. (1987). Leonardo da Vinci: Omo sanza lettere: A case of surface dyslexia. *Cognitive Neuropsychology, 4,* 1–10.

Siegel, L. S. (1988). Agatha Christie's learning disability. *Canadian Psychology, 29*(2), 213–216.

Siegel, L. S. (1992). Dyslexic vs. poor readers: Is there a difference? *Journal of Learning Disabilities, 25,* 618–629.

Siegel, L. S., Share, D., & Geva, E. (1999). Evidence for superior orthographic skills in dyslexics. *Psychological Science, 6,* 250–254.

Stanovich, K. E. (1988). Explaining the differences between the dyslexic and the garden variety poor reader: The phonological core variable difference model. *Journal of Learning Disabilities, 21,* 590–604.

Sternberg, R. J. (1984). Mechanisms of cognitive development: A componential approach. In R. J. Sternberg, (Ed.), *Mechanisms of cognitive development* (pp. 163–186). New York: W.H. Freeman & Co.

Sternberg, R.J. (1977). Intelligence, information processing, and analogical reasoning: *The componential analysis of human abilities.* Hillsdale, NJ: Erlbaum.

Stites, R.S., Stites, E.M., & Castiglione, P. *The sublimations of Leonardo da Vinci.* Washington, DC: Smithsonian Institution Press.

Symmes, S.J., & Rapoport, L.J. (1972). Unexpected reading failure. *American Journal of Orthopsychiatry, 42,* 82–91.

Thomas, M. (2000). Albert Einstein and LD: An evaluation of the evidence. *Journal of Learning Disabilities, 33*(2), 149–157.

Thompson, L.J., (1969). Language disabilities in men of eminence. *Bulletin of the Orton Society, 14,* 113–120.

Tirel, M. (1925). *The last years of Rodin.* New York: Robert M. McBride.

Vasari, g. (1959). *Lives of the most eminent painters, sculptors, and architects.* New York: Modern Library.

Wachhorst, W. (1981). *Thomas Alva Edison: The American myth.* Cambridge, MA: MIT Press.

Witelson, S. (1977). Developmental dyslexia: Two right hemispheres and none left? *Science, 195,* 309–311.

Woodcock, L. (1982). The St. Louis Heritage of Marion Russell. *Gatgeway Heritage, 2*(4), 2–15.

Chapter 10

INTERVENTIONS WORK BUT WE NEED MORE!

Tina M. Newman
PACE Center, Yale University

INTRODUCTION

Children who are both gifted and who have a learning disability (LD) have unique needs (Bees, 1998; Schubert, 1996; West, 1991) that place them at risk (Robinson, 1999) and that are usually overlooked by the public educational system (Winner, 1999; Brody & Mills, 1997). Although some of these students are provided services for either their gifts or their learning disabilities, very few of these students are eligible for services that both develop their areas of weakness and allow them to explore their areas of strength (Brody & Mills, 1997). This oversight may have significant consequences both indirectly and directly on the students' opportunity to succeed in careers that utilize their areas of strength. Directly, the students will have little or no opportunity to develop their abilities. Indirectly, this lack of services may create a lessened sense of self-efficacy. Although very few programs that simultaneously address the diverse needs of students with gifts and LD have been available to students, the ones that have been developed are reporting great success (e.g., Weinfeld, Barnes-Robinson, Jeweler, Shevitz, 2002). However, these existing programs have been focused primarily on students who demonstrate one distinct profile of the gifted/LD learner—those students whose gifts fall in the domain of analytical ability or high IQ. As this field progresses, we present the case for a broader conception of giftedness to include students who may have gifts in domains such as creative or practical abilities that are often the impetus for success beyond school. We argue that children who demonstrate extraordinary abilities in such domains as leading their peers, or applying what they have learned in practical situations, or finding novel solutions to problems, will be some of our greatest resources for the future and will benefit from the support in developing these abilities. This chapter will begin with a review of the literature on existing intervention programs for students with gifts and learning disabilities and conclude with recommendations for programs that address a broader range of strengths including gifts in the creative and practical domains of ability.

THE IMPORTANCE OF INTERVENTIONS FOR STUDENTS WITH GIFTS AND LEARNING DISABILITIES

Children with special needs that result from such "uneven" profiles of both their high abilities and their learning problems are rarely identified and are often poorly served. Approximately 41% of students with both gifts and LD remain undiagnosed until college (Ferri, Gregg, & Heffoy, 1997) and undoubtedly, there are others who never make it to college. Some of these students have strengths and weaknesses that mask each other and therefore remain undetected in the school system having neither their talents nurtured, nor their weaknesses addressed (Baum, Owen, & Dixon, 1991; Brody & Mills, 1997). Others are placed in programs that only address their weaknesses (Crawford & Snart, 1994; Poplin, 1988), which can result in frustration and alienation from learning (Baum, 1984). Finally, some of these children have such identifiable gifts that they are eligible for gifted programs, but inevitably become frustrated when their LD is not recognized and necessary compensatory scaffolding is not offered, resulting in an inability to perform up to expectations.

Although children may have the motivation to pursue their interests despite discouragement and lack of support at school (Silverman, 1989; Yewchuck, 1992), it is certain they would benefit from support and guidance. Unfortunately, these students rarely qualify for both LD and gifted services (Brody & Mills, 1997) and often end up not identified or placed in school programs only addressing their weaknesses (Poplin, 1988). In a survey of teachers, LaFrance (1994) found that resource teachers felt immense pressure to remediate students' deficits in the short time allotted to them, allowing no time to address the students' areas that were sufficiently developed. However, interventions that only address the students' weakness have been shown to create resentment, frustration, low self-esteem, a decrease in motivation, and even depression in the students (Baum, 1984; Robinson, 1999). In contrast, case studies have shown that students with both LD and gifts, when given the opportunity to explore their gifts, show gains in self-esteem, learning skills, and creativity (Baum, 1988). In addition, these students become more receptive and open to instruction to improve their weaker skills (Baum & Kirschenbaum, 1984). One study following 108 fourth and sixth grade students with both gifts and LD found that when enrichment programs were offered to the students for one year, the students demonstrated significantly more positive attitudes toward school and higher self-concept (Olenchak, 1995). Unfortunately, many teachers consider students with gifts and LD ineligible for gifted programs (Minner, 1990). For example, Tallent-Runnels and Sigler (1995) examined whether gifted students in Texas who had learning disabilities were being identified for gifted programs. They discovered that only 19.7% of all districts surveyed reported selecting gifted students with learning disabilities for gifted programs.

INTERVENTION PROGRAMS IN THE LITERATURE

Given that these students require both gifted services and services for their LD and yet are often excluded from at least one, there have been a number of interventions reported that try to develop services specifically for this population of students. Although focused predominantly on students with high IQ, the case studies and anecdotal reports currently in the literature are offering a promising view of the potential for these programs. Although diverse in nature, these programs are all designed for students with the dual exceptionality of gifts and learning disabilities. Some of these programs are designed to address the specific weaknesses these students possess, for example, programs developed to increase reading decoding ability (Crawford & Snart, 1994). Other programs address areas of weakness but are primarily designed to capitalize on and develop areas of strength through enrichment activities (e.g., Baum, 1988). Finally, a number of programs are designed to develop areas of strength while remediating or compensating for weaknesses (e.g., Weinfeld, et. al., 2002). These programs have taken different approaches toward the goal of serving students with gifts and learning disabilities. Some of these programs are focused exclusively on the emotional well-being of the students and describe counseling interventions that develop students' self-esteem (McEachern & Bornot, 2001), while other programs are geared towards development of the students' academic and cognitive skills through instructional strategies or models (e.g., Weinfeld, et. al., 2002). For the purposes of this chapter we will discuss interventions that capitalize on strengths and remediate for weaknesses through three different service delivery models of school-based interventions that are described in the literature: (1) interventions in the regular classroom (e.g., Weinfeld, et. al., 2002); (2) partial pull-out programs for student with gifts and learning disabilities (e.g., Baum, 1988; Olenchak, 1995); and (3) self-contained programs (e.g., ASSETS School, Hishinuma & Nishimura, 2000).

Interventions in the Regular Classroom

Interventions in the regular classroom allow students to participate fully in the mainstream classroom with their peers. A number of researchers have described interventions for students with gifts and learning disabilities that can be provided by the classroom teachers. These interventions are designed to both recognize and develop areas of strength and also to provide strategies to compensate for and develop areas of weakness.

Strategies that can be infused into the regular curriculum include many of the strategies that have been successful for students with LD and students with gifts.

Table 1. Strategies for Students with Gifts and LD that Can Be Applied in the Regular Classroom

Target Skill	Strategies
Gifted	• Focus on student strengths and interests • Allow self-directed choices • Allow alternative products for the demonstration of knowledge • Differentiate instruction
Thinking Skills	• Teach, model, and practice thinking strategies • Utilize Socratic method to help students formulate questions and think through logic problems • Develop activities to apply abstract concepts to practical problems • Use "Think Alouds" and metacognitive strategies • Have students identify the thinking strategies that work best for them and transfer the strategies to their areas of weakness
Reading	• Focus on comprehension (don't focus on errors that do not impact comprehension) • Use literature, oral discussion, expository reading, and high interest reading material that may be above grade level • Use books on tape and text-to-speech software to support reading • Avoid worksheets, round-robin reading, and below grade level readers
Writing	• Focus on quality of content as opposed to quantity, handwriting, spelling, or punctuation • Use discussion and graphic organizers to develop ideas • Use technology, such as word processing programs, electronic spellers, speech-to-text software, word predictive software and organizational tools • Proofread for one error at a time • Use a highlighter for errors as opposed to red pen
Organization	• Have clear directions, steps, and due dates for assignments, including timelines and checkpoints for long-term projects • Supervise use of visual organizers, other assistive technology, calendars, study guides, homework books and other organizers • Support students in becoming self-sufficient • Post homework to a webpage or have student's e-mail the assignments to an e-mail account at home
Memory	• Present information in a variety of ways • Use assistive technology • Encourage memory techniques, such as mnemonics, visual imagery, outlining, note taking, outlining, and highlighting • Relate new information to previous experience and cue students on important information

Note: The strategies presented above have been summarized from a paper by Weinfeld, Barnes-Robinson, Jeweler, & Shevitz (2002). See these authors for a full discussion of the above strategies.

The goal promoted by these strategies however, is to ensure that students are receiving not just services that focus on their weaknesses (e.g., reading decoding instruction), but also interventions that develop and allow the students to express their areas of strength (Baum, 1988). For example, if the curriculum goal is demonstrating content knowledge, oral reports can be used to replace written reports for students with reading or writing difficulties. Providing opportunities for alternative products is one of many strategies suggested in the literature to help students with gifts and LD. A number of authors including Weinfeld, Barnes-Robinson, Jeweler, and Shevitz (2002) have suggested additional strategies that can be applied by the classroom teacher to allow these students to achieve to their full potential. These strategies have been adapted and summarized in Table 1 above.

The key aspect to consider in the use of these strategies is insuring that a balance is found between attending to strengths and accommodating for weaknesses within a curriculum that is appropriately challenging. Providing gifted and talented curriculum has been found to be the most important component of interventions for these students (Baum, Cooper, Neu, 2001; Weinfeld, et. al., 2002). In addition, opportunities to work on skills affected by the disability and having an individualized plan for education that sets both strength and weakness building goals have been found to be essential is successful classroom interventions (Baum, et. al., 2001; Weinfeld, et. al., 2002). Although delivered by the classroom teacher, this type of educational planning is best achieved through a collaborative effort between classroom teachers and special educators (both gifted and remedial).

Partial Pull-Out Interventions

Partial pull-out programs allow students to participate in the regular classroom while also having time to explore their strengths and develop their areas of weakness in supportive environments with peers who share their learning profile. The importance of this time spent with teachers who are sensitive to their needs and students who share their exceptionalities has been documented by numerous researchers (e.g., Baum, Renzulli, & Hebert, 1995; Bees, 1998; Olenchak, 1995). In particular, many of these pull-out programs have been based on an "enrichment' model of instruction, where students have had opportunities to explore and develop their areas of strengths and interests in an environment that recognizes and compensates for their areas of weakness (e.g., Baum, 1988; Olenchak, 1995).

In one intervention study, Olenchak (1995) followed 108 students with gifts and LD in grades 4 through 6 who were given an IEP that had both the traditional remedial strategies and strength-enhancing strategies. Both remedial and strength-enhancing IEPs were administered by the regular classroom teacher and the gifted-education teacher in collaboration. The strength-enhancing strategies were primarily based on the Schoolwide Enrichment Model (Renzulli & Reis, 1985). In both the regular classroom and in a pull-out program, students had the opportunity to participate in many enrichment activities, including the development of an advanced, in-depth study. After one year of participation in this individualized intervention, students had more positive attitudes towards school and demonstrated gains in self-concept. In addition, the author notes a commitment to long-term creative, productive work as demonstrated by the 74% of students who initiated an advanced, in-depth study completing their project (Olenchak, 1995).

Other authors, implementing a supportive, enrichment model with gifted/LD students have also noted the increase in motivation, self-esteem, and the commitment these students will demonstrate to in-depth, long-term projects that are of interest to them (Baum, 1988). Although based in case studies, evidence suggests that pull-out programs addressing both strengths and weaknesses appear to have a positive impact on students attitudes towards school and their commitment to academic products.

Interventions in a Self-Contained Class

An increasing awareness that students may have both gifts and LD has resulted in an increase in services designed specifically for this population. Of particular interest are the recent reports documenting whole classrooms and even schools that are structured to support the needs of students with this dual exceptionality (e.g., Weinfeld, et. al., 2002).

A recent initiative in Maryland's Montgomery County Public Schools has created a cascade of services for students with a gifted/LD profile (Weinfeld, et. al., 2002). Within these services is the provision of self-contained classes designed specifically for students' with both gifts and LD, who are thought to be best served in this model. Students who demonstrate superior performance on an IQ test, but who are not progressing academically are recommended for Center programs, where they have the opportunity to attend school (1) with other students who have a similar profile and (2) with teachers who recognize their needs (Weinfeld, et. al., 2002). Within this setting, students have the opportunity to work on independent-study projects, use technology such as text to speech software, attend mainstream classes, and use resources suited to their needs such as books with high content-level and low reading-level. The flexible classroom environment, focusing on inquiry-based thinking, and supported by professionals who have expertise in this area has led to a program that is reporting success anecdotally (Weinfeld, et. al., 2002).

In addition to the Maryland program, a number of other programs have been developed either specifically for students with gifts and LD (e.g.,

Project HIGH HOPES, Baum et. al., 2001) or for students who are gifted, LD, or gifted/LD (e.g., ASSETS School; Hishinuma & Nishimura, 2000).

Project HIGH HOPES also used an inquiry-based model of thinking, and authentic problem-solving experiences in a laboratory setting (Baum, et. al., 2001). In a culminating presentation, students demonstrated their integration of basic skills in science (e.g., compare and contrast, evaluate, classify); in communication (e.g., planning, organizing, photography, public speaking, script writing, and video production); in project management (e.g., organizing, sequencing tasks, dividing responsibility, time management); and in collaboration (e.g., working with classmates and mentors). Within this experience, it was reported that students had the opportunity to find their abilities and talents, and were able to use these strengths to compensate for their weaknesses (Baum, et. al., 2001).

Finally, in an evaluation of the effectiveness of ASSETS School, Hishinuma & Nishimura (2000), found that parents reported greater success of components of the school (e.g., curriculum, counseling), than previous schools that their child had attended.

Although primarily anecdotal in nature, there is evidence indicating that self-contained settings for students with gifts and LD can offer an environment that is able to promote strengths and compensate for weaknesses to produce successful students.

BENEFITS OF PROGRAMS DESIGNED TO ADDRESS STRENGTHS AND WEAKNESSES

One of the major benefits of students being enrolled in pull-out, self-contained, or even mainstreamed programs designed to address the students' strengths and weaknesses is an increase in the students' sense of self-worth and self-confidence. A number of these programs describe the increase in self-confidence that transferred to students' work in the mainstream (e.g., Baum et. al., 1995). Resilience is an important issue for students with both gifts and LD. Both the literature on students with gifts and the literature on students with LD describe children who are at greater risk for socio-emotional difficulties such as poor self-concept, and high levels of frustration and anxiety (e.g., Baldwin, 1999). Thus students who possess both gifts and LD are in a position of particular vulnerability for socio-emotional difficulties. If programs designed to address the needs of students with both gifts and learning difficulties increase a student's resilience, self-confidence, and self-efficacy, this result could be a particularly important benefit of such programs.

The programs described above, designed to address the needs of students with concomitant gifts and LD, have found success. However, such programs are designed almost exclusively for students whose gifts are in the analytical/memory domain as determined by a high IQ score or high cognitive ability. There is little research exploring programs designed to address the strengths of students with gifts in other domains. As noted earlier in this volume, gifts can be found in a variety of domains (e.g., vonKarolyi & Winner; Aaron et. al.).

WHAT ABOUT OTHER TYPES OF GIFTS?

As described above, previous intervention research on students with LD and gifts have focused predominantly on students whose gifts are in the area of what is traditionally determined as 'IQ' (e.g., Bees, 1998; Doney, 1995; Holliday, Koller, & Thomas, 1999). These students have been identified as gifted based on a superior score on an IQ test such as the Weschler Scales (WISC-III) or the Stanford-Binet. This type of analytic/memory-based intelligence is important to success in school and life, but is not the only contributing factor.

In contrast to research reviewed above, Sternberg (1997, 1999) has outlined a theory of successful intelligence demonstrating that not only are analytical/memory abilities important to success in life, but that both practical abilities and creative abilities contribute strongly to how successful one becomes. Practical abilities allow us to adapt and apply our knowledge to the world we live in, and creative abilities provide us with the skills to generate new ideas, create, imagine, and design. These traits have been shown to be present in people who have risen to high-level careers or made significant contributions to society. By only identifying giftedness based on superior analytical and memory skills, we may be overlooking a population of gifted individuals who have superior creative or practical abilities and who, with the right support, could contribute significantly to society. In fact, earlier in this book, Aaron et. al. presented evidence to suggest that a number of our most celebrated innovators, such as Thomas Edison and Leonardo DaVinci had specific reading disabilities. We cannot afford to risk losing any of the innovators of the future!

The theory of successful intelligence provides us with a model for identifying students who have gifts not only in the analytical domain, but also in the creative and practical domains of intelligence. We can apply this model to help us identify students with LD who have potential or realized gifts in any of these domains. This identification of creative or practical gifts will guide us in the implementation of a program that will help strengthen the students' areas of weakness and provide them with the support to explore and develop their areas of strength.

THE CASE FOR A BROADENING OF INTERVENTIONS

Prompted by the success of the gifted/LD programs for students whose gifts were in the analytical domain, and recognizing that strengths in other areas could promote success in life, the researchers at the PACE Center are in the process of developing programs to address the creative and practical gifts of children who are experiencing difficulties in their academic subjects. Our goal for these programs is to develop an assessment protocol and enrichment curriculum that allows students to develop their identified strengths in analytical, creative and practical abilities. In addition, while capitalizing on the individual student's strengths, we want to remediate areas of weakness.

For the purposes of our work, giftedness refers to students who (a) are excellent in work they can or do produce, (b) possess this excellence relative to peers, (c) are able to display this excellence through some kind of tangible performance, (d) can repeat this performance multiple times, and (e) excel in a way that is societally valued (the criteria of the pentagonal implicit theory of giftedness—Sternberg & Zhang, 1995—which has been empirically validated both in the United States and China—Zhang & Sternberg, 1998). In addition, students are identified as having a learning difficulty when they experience a specific reading, writing, and/or mathematics deficit as a result of underlying processing deficits, for example, in phonological awareness.

Current Intervention Program

Our current intervention program is based on the theory of successful intelligence (Sternberg, 1997) and is designed to meet the specific needs of gifted children with LD by capitalizing on their strengths and compensating for their weaknesses. The main purpose of this program is to ensure that students who are gifted in the domains of analytical, as well as creative and practical abilities and, in addition, have LD receive the intervention needed to help them reach their full potential.

In implementing an intervention program, Sternberg (1998) has outlined a set of principles that guide teaching for successful intelligence. These principles can be found in Sternberg (1998) and include the following goals of instruction: (1) creating expertise through a well and flexibly organized, easily retrievable, knowledge base; (2) teaching and assessing for analytical, creative, and practical thinking, as well as for memory learning; (3) enabling students to identify and capitalize on their strengths as well as identify, correct, and compensate for weaknesses in both instruction and assessment; (4) utilizing all seven of the metacomponents of the problem-solving cycle, including (a) problem identification, (b) problem definition, (c) formulation of problem-solving strategies, (d) formulation of mental and external representations and organizations of problems and their associated information, (e) allocation of resources, (f) monitoring of problem solving, (g) evaluation of problem solving; (5) utilizing performance components, including (a) encoding of information, (b) inference of relations between chunks of information, (c) mapping of higher order relations among relations, (d) application of information and relations between chunks of information, (e) comparison of alternatives, and (f) response; (6) utilizing knowledge-acquisition components, including (a) selective encoding (distinguishing relevant from irrelevant information), (b) selective comparison (relating old information to new information), and (c) selective combination (putting together disparate pieces of information to reach a conclusion); (7) accounting for individual differences in preferred mental representations, including verbal, quantitative, and figural, as well as modalities for input (visual, auditory, kinesthetic) and output (written, oral, performance-based); (8) optimizing instruction in the zones of (a) relative novelty and (b) automatization for the individual; (9) helping students (a) adapt to the environment (change themselves better to suit the environment), (b) shape the environment (change the environment better to suit them), and (c) select new environments; and (10) providing instruction and assessment that supports integration rather than separation of all of the elements of intelligence.

CONCLUSION

The importance of intervention programs to develop the strengths and weaknesses of students with both gifts and LD has been well documented (Baum, 1984). The frustration of being placed in programs that focus predominantly on weaknesses, or of blending in to an average achievement level, has been shown to alienate these students from school (Baum, 1984; Robinson, 1999). By providing services, especially services that target the students' strengths, researchers have documented the increase in self-esteem and investment in school-work (Baum, et. al., 1995; Olenchak, 1995). However, this previous work has focused predominantly on students whose gifts are in the analytical or high IQ domain. We predict that using the theory of successful intelligence to identify giftedness will include students not previously eligible for gifted services, and providing intervention programs that address the students' varied abilities will improve the students' abilities in both their areas of strengths and weaknesses. In this way, gifted children will be better identified and prepared for making distinguished contributions in later years.

REFERENCES

Baldwin, L. (1999). USA perspective. In A. Y. Baldwin & W. Vialle (Eds.), *The many faces of giftedness: Lifting the masks* (pp. 103–134). Belmont, CA: Wadsworth Publishing Company.

Baum, S. (1984). Meeting the needs of learning disabled gifted students. *Roeper Review, 7,* 16–19.

Baum, S. (1988). An enrichment program for gifted learning disabled students. *Gifted Child Quarterly, 32,* 226–230.

Baum, S. M., Cooper, C. R., & Neu, T. W. (2001). Dual differentiation: An approach for meeting the curricular needs of gifted students with learning disabilities. *Psychology in the Schools, 38,* 477–490.

Baum, S. & Kirschenbaum, R. (1984). Recognizing special talents in learning disabled students. *Teaching Exceptional Children, 54*(4) 92–98.

Baum, S., Owen, S. V., & Dixon, J. (1991). *To be Gifted and Learning Disabled: From Identification to Practical Intervention Strategies.* Mansfield Center, CT: Creative Learning Press.

Baum, S. M., Renzulli, J. S., & Hebert, T. P. (1995). Reversing underachievement: Creative productivity as a systematic intervention. *Gifted Child Quarterly, 39,* 224–235.

Bees, C. (1998). The GOLD program: A program for gifted learning disabled adolescents. *Roeper Review, 21,* 155–161.

Brody L. E. & Mills, C. J. (1997). Gifted children with learning disabilities: A review of the issues. *Journal of Learning Disabilities, 30,* 282–296.

Crawford, S., & Snart, F. (1994). Process-based remediation of decoding in gifted LD students: Three case studies. *Roeper Review, 16,* 247–252.

Doney, C. J. (1995). Creating opportunities, or what is it like to be a Whale? *Journal of Learning Disabilities, 28,* 194–195.

Ferri, B., Gregg, N., & Heffoy, S. (1997). Profiles of college students demonstrating learning disabilities with and without giftedness. *Journal of Learning Disabilities, 30,* 552–559.

Hishinuma, E. S., & Nishimura, S. T. (2000). Parent attitudes on the importance and success of integrated self-contained services for students who are gifted, learning-disabled, and gifted/learning disabled. *Roeper Review, 22,* 241–250.

Holliday, G. A., Koller, J. R., & Thomas, C. D. (1999). Post-high school outcomes of high IQ adults with learning disabilities. *Journal for the Education of the Gifted, 22,* 266–281.

LaFrance, E. B. (1994). An insider's perspective: Teachers observations of creative thinking in exceptional children. *Roeper Review, 16,* 256–259.

Minner, S. (1990). Teacher evaluations of case options of LD gifted children. *Gifted Child Quarterly, 34,* 37–40.

McEachern, A. G., & Bornot, J. (2001). Gifted students with learning disabilities: Implications and strategies for school counselors. *Professional School Counseling, 5,* 34–41.

Olenchak, F. R. (1995). Effects of enrichment on gifted/learning-disabled students. *Journal for the Education of the Gifted, 18,* 385–399.

Poplin, M. S. (1988). Holistic/constructivist principles of the teaching/learning process: Implications for the field of learning disabilities. *Journal of Learning Disabilities, 21,* 401–416.

Renzulli, J. S., & Reis, S. M. (1985). *The schoolwide enrichment model: A comprehensive plan for educational excellence.* Mansfield Center, CT: Creative Learning Press.

Robinson, S. M. (1999). Meeting the needs of students who are gifted and have learning disabilities. *Intervention in School and Clinic, 34,* 195–204.

Schubert, M. (1996). Using participatory action research. *Roeper Review, 18,* 232–233.

Sternberg, R. J. (1997). *Successful intelligence.* New York: Plume.

Sternberg, R. J. (1998). Abilities are forms of developing expertise. *Educational Researcher, 27,* 11–20.

Sternberg, R. J. (1999). The theory of successful intelligence. *Review of General Psychology, 3,* 292–316.

Sternberg, R. J., & Zhang, L.-F. (1995). What do we mean by giftedness?—A pentagonal implicit theory. *Gifted Child Quarterly, 39,* 88–94.

Tallent-Runnels, M. K. & Sigler, E. A. (1995). The status of the selection of gifted students with learning disabilities for gifted programs. *Roeper Review, 17,* 246–248.

West, T. G. (1991). *In the Mind's Eye: Visual Thinkers, Gifted People with Learning Difficulties, Computer Images, and the Ironies of Creativity,* Buffalo, NY: Prometheus Books.

Weinfeld, R., Barnes-Robinson, L., Jeweler, S., & Shevitz, B. (2002). *Academic programs for gifted and talented/learning disabled students. Roeper Review,* 226–233.

Winner, E. (1999). Uncommon talents: Gifted children, prodigies, and savants. *Scientific American Presents,* 32–37.

Yewchuck, C. R. (1992). Educational strategies for gifted learning disabled children. In F. Monks & W. Peters (Eds.), *Talent for the Future* (pp.285–295). AssenMaastricht, The Netherlands: Van Gorcum.

Zhang, L.-F., & Sternberg, R. J. (1998). The pentagonal implicit theory of giftedness revisited: A cross-validation in Hong Kong. *Roeper Review, 21,*149–153.

INDEX

NEUROPSYCHOLOGY AND COGNITION

The purpose of the Neuropsychology and Cognition series is to bring out volumes that promote understanding in topics relating brain and behavior. It is intended for use by both clinicians and research scientists in the fields of neuropsychology, cognitive psychology, psycholinguistics, speech and hearing, as well as eduction. Examples of topics to be covered in this series would relate memory, language acquisition and breakdown, reading, attention, developing and aging brain. By addressing the theoretical, empirical, and applied aspects of brain-behavior relationships, this series will try to present the information in the files of neuropsychology and cognition in a coherent manner.

24. P. Karanth: *Cross-Linguistic Studies of Acquired Reading Disorders:*
     Implications for Reading Models, Disorders, Acquisition, and Training   ISBN 0-306-48319-X
25. T.M. Newman and R.J. Sternberg (eds.): *Students with Both Gifts and*
     Learning Disabilities: Identification, Assessment, and Outcomes   ISBN 0-306-48379-3